THI

Conservative Opposition to Appeasement in the 1930s

THE ANTI-APPEASERS

Conservative Opposition to Appeasement in the 1930s

by NEVILLE THOMPSON

OXFORD
AT THE CLARENDON PRESS
1971

Oxford University Press, Ely House, London W. 1

GLASGOW NEW YORK TORONTO MELBOURNE WELLINGTON
CAPE TOWN SALISBURY IBADAN NAIROBI DAR ES SALAAM LUSAKA ADDIS ABABA
BOMBAY CALCUTTA MADRAS KARACHI LAHORE DACCA
KUALA LUMPUR SINGAPORE HONG KONG TOKYO

PRINTED IN GREAT BRITAIN
AT THE UNIVERSITY PRESS, OXFORD
BY VIVIAN RIDLER
PRINTER TO THE UNIVERSITY

TO GAIL

'If the trumpet give an uncertain sound, who shall prepare himself for battle?'

I CORINTHIANS 14:8

Preface

THIS book originated as a doctoral dissertation written under the supervision of Professor A. J. Mayer of Princeton University. Although our views are not identical I have benefited greatly from his advice and criticism.

The initial research on this subject was made possible by a Philip A. Rollins Fellowship from Princeton University and completed with the aid of two Canada Council grants. I am grateful to the University and the Council for their assistance.

I should like to record my debt to The British Museum, The Public Record Office, The Royal Institute of International Affairs (Chatham House), The Institute for Historical Research, and the following libraries: Princeton University, The Beaverbrook Library, The University of Birmingham, Huron College, The University of Western Ontario, and McMaster University.

Several people who were involved in the events described in this book gave me valuable background information which made the written record of the 1930s more meaningful. For their kindness and hospitality I have to thank Commander Robert T. Bower, Lord Coleraine (formerly Richard Law), Mr. Paul Emrys-Evans, the late Sir Harold Nicolson, Major-General Sir Edward Spears, Mr. Eugen Spier, Lord Strang, and one other person who prefers no acknowledgement. The Rt. Hon. Julian Amery, M.P., generously allowed me to read his father's diary for 1938, 1939, and 1940.

Many friends and colleagues have listened to my views, offered their advice, and encouraged me in my task. It would be impossible to name them all here but I should like to single out for special mention two former colleagues at Huron College, John Henderson and John Rowe, who are entitled to a considerable share of any success this book may enjoy.

Contents

Introduction

SINCE the publication in 1961 of A. J. P. Taylor's controversial book, *The Origins of the Second World War*, British foreign policy in the 1930s has been the subject of much re-examination and considerable reappraisal. The critics of that policy have not been so well served. Until recently there was no satisfactory analysis of the Labour party's foreign policy[1] and there is still no study of the Liberal party's views or Lloyd George's vacillating attitude towards the problems that arose in those years. Yet appeasement, like any foreign policy, can only be properly understood in relation to domestic politics and to the internal condition of the country at the time. This book is designed to illuminate one important but neglected area of the domestic debate on foreign policy.

It is almost a convention of books dealing with the 1930s that there was a group of Conservatives who resolutely opposed appeasement and whose alternative policies can be used as a standard by which to judge the National Government's performance. Martin Gilbert and Richard Gott, for example, were inspired to write their indictment of *The Appeasers* by 'the example of Englishmen who refused to be bullied by Nazi bombasts; who saw German threats for what they were, the brash noises of a successful bully; who determined to stand up to that bully and by firm words to caution him; and who urged England not to compromise with evil but to face the dictators with courage and conviction'.[2] Other writers, adopting a more heroic theme, have singled out Winston Churchill as 'the only voice of sanity in this period'.[3]

Needless to say there is ample evidence to support these views in Churchill's *The Gathering Storm* and in the memoirs of other

[1] John F. Naylor, *Labour's International Policy: The Labour Party in the 1930s* (London, 1969).

[2] Governmental M.P.s who served as examples for Gilbert and Gott were Robert Boothby, Harold Nicolson, Duncan Sandys, Leopold Amery, Duff Cooper, and Anthony Eden. Martin Gilbert and Richard Gott, *The Appeasers* (London, 1963), pp. ix and xi.

[3] Earl of Birkenhead, *Halifax: The Life of Lord Halifax* (London, 1965), p. 340.

Conservatives fortunate enough to be excluded from the National Government. But these retrospective accounts, written by men concerned to justify their past and safeguard their historical reputations, must be approached in a sceptical spirit. Each of them contains considerable, if selective, truth; but they have to be compared to each other and to contemporary sources to yield a complete story.

On closer examination Conservative opposition to appeasement is rather like a mirage: the more it is studied the less substantial it appears; but in this case it never vanishes completely. What remains is a picture of sporadic and discontinuous dissent, of individual critics and small cliques but no cohesive group. Until Anthony Eden's resignation as Foreign Secretary in February 1938 there was no group at all; and even after Eden's retirement to the back benches there was only a loose collection of private M.P.s who shared a common concern about the direction of foreign affairs but who were unable to agree on policy or tactics. This nebulousness makes it difficult to draw a clear-cut distinction between the appeasers and their opponents even in the last part of the decade.[4] Indeed the attempt to draw such a distinction would be misleading, as practically everyone was in favour of appeasement, if not of Germany then of Italy and certainly of Japan, at one time or another. But if the story of Conservative dissent is essentially a negative one it is, like the dog that did not bark in the night, not without interest or significance. At the very least it may serve as a supplement and corrective to other accounts of appeasement and British politics in the 1930s.

This study ends on 10 May 1940, rather than 3 September, 1939, because it was the formation of Churchill's Government, not the outbreak of war, that ended a political era which had opened with the formation of the National Government in 1931. Although Churchill and Eden joined the Cabinet when the war began, political control remained in the hands of those who had

[4] Donald L. Lammers has attempted to quantify the differences between 'the most commonly named supporters of the policy of appeasement' and 'the most commonly named opponents of the policy of appeasement' (a rather different group from the one studied here) in the appendix to his *Explaining Munich: The Search for Motive in British Policy* (Stanford, 1966). The significant differences are that more of the opponents attended public schools than the appeasers (83 per cent against 64 per cent) and more of them had served in the Foreign Office either politically or professionally (67 per cent against 21 per cent).

managed the country's affairs for the best part of a decade. Nor did criticism of the administration cease with the beginning of hostilities. After a short truce following the initial shock of war opposition was renewed on both sides of the House of Commons. Those who had previously challenged the government's handling of foreign affairs now took issue with its conduct of the war. Neville Chamberlain's resignation, forced by a Conservative revolt, finally ended the political feuds and a line of criticism which had originated in the domestic, imperial, and foreign events of the early 1930s.

When the story of Conservative opposition to appeasement is pieced together two basic questions stand out: why were there so few critics and why were they so ineffective? The answer to both questions lies in the difficulty of devising an acceptable alternative to appeasement, party pressure on the sceptics to accept the policy laid down by the party leaders, and the failure of the back benches to produce a leader capable of mobilizing and focusing the discontent about foreign policy. These factors are discussed in the first two chapters. The rest of the book is devoted to an investigation of Conservative dissent during the major international crises of the decade.

Some of the conditions which inhibited criticism were imposed on the dissenters from without; but others came from within, from their own doubts and hesitations about the kind of criticism and tactics to adopt. In their memoirs the critics were eager to dissociate themselves from the failures of the thirties while heaping blame and scorn on the Government and even on the Opposition, which never held more than a third of the seats in the House of Commons. But their dissociation was not as complete as they later represented. None of them made a clear break with the party or advocated consistently the policy they afterwards claimed was so obvious. No doubt there were good reasons for this, but judged by the tests of clearsightedness and consistency which they applied to others these men were also failures, though no more so that other politicians in that tragic decade. And they at least had the consolation of seeing their version of events accepted long enough for them to reach an honourable retirement or the grave.

I. THE CONDITIONS

1. The Parameters of Dissent

THE development of highly organized and structured parties in Britain in the century since the Second Reform Bill of 1867 has made it notoriously difficult for back-bench M.P.s to pursue an independent course on important issues. The party leader, his senior colleagues and advisers, formulate policy which the rank and file are expected to support. If they are unwilling to confine their misgivings to the party caucus they can be coerced into silence by the party whips. When the party is in opposition its members have considerable freedom to attack the government in their several ways; but when the party is in power they are expected to abandon their various critical attitudes and endorse everything the administration proposes by their votes and by their speeches.

This was the situation which the supporters of the National Government faced in the 1930s. Those who had doubts about appeasement are entitled to point to these difficulties and to emphasize that the chief whip in that period, Captain David Margesson, was unusually hostile to any kind of dissent. But it can also be argued that for most of the decade it was easier for back-benchers to challenge the National Government than the administrations which preceded or succeeded it. As the National Government was a three-party coalition, at least in theory, Conservatives could take exception to its policies while claiming to be loyal to the principles of their own party. This was particularly true from 1931 to 1935 when the Prime Minister was Ramsay MacDonald, a Labourite who had been drummed out of his own party, and the Cabinet contained Liberals and National Labour members out of all proportion to the number of seats they held in the House of Commons. When Stanley Baldwin replaced MacDonald in 1935 it became harder for back-benchers to attack a Prime Minister who was at the same time leader of their party; but even then they could find fault with a leader who had joined a coalition with a socialist, and who supported policies which his right-wing supporters detested and the left-wingers thought were too feeble. Moreover, as Baldwin seemed to be constitutionally incapable of making up his mind or taking a firm stand on any issue, jolting him into action could be represented as being in the best interests of the party and the country. This favourable climate for dissent suddenly changed when Neville Chamberlain became Prime Minister in 1937. An energetic, autocrat, and precise man, Chamberlain soon made it clear to his followers that he resented any disagreement with his policies. But Chamberlain's attitude, if not his manner, was not much different from that of most Prime Ministers.

From the very beginning the National Government was a source of controversy within the Conservative party. Stanley Baldwin, who had been instrumental in breaking the Lloyd George coalition in 1922, agreed without much hesitation to join the new combination formed to deal with the financial crisis on 24 August 1931. No doubt he honestly believed that this was in the best interests of the country, but considering the troubles within his own party and the precariousness of his position, MacDonald's offer must have been a godsend. For the time being Baldwin had managed to fend off the press lords who were trying to oust him from the party leadership, but Winston Churchill had been busy for some months marshalling the die-hard imperialists to pull him down for agreeing to more self-government for India. Baldwin might have survived this latest challenge and continued at the head of a weakened party, but the alliance with MacDonald and the Liberal leaders provided him with a convenient way of avoiding the issue altogether while enhancing his reputation as a national figure who was prepared to put his country above party. As only a limited number of places in the new Administration could be assigned to Conservatives it was easy to see that these were given to moderates while the die-hards were left in the wilderness. This naturally provoked great bitterness among right-wing Conservatives, but they soon discovered that they had to suppress their hostility in order to secure re-election in October when the National Government appealed to the country for a 'doctor's mandate' to cure the country's economic ills.

At the general election the Conservatives won 473 seats in a House of 615. The other parties in the coalition won a total of 81: National Liberals (Simonites) 35; Liberals (Samuelites) 33; and National Labour 13. The opposition was in disarray: the Labour party won 46 seats; the Independent Labour party 6; and the Lloyd George Liberals 4. Contemplating this landslide, some Conservatives called for an end to 'this monstrous hybrid coalition'[1] and the creation of a solidly Conservative administration. Neville Chamberlain hoped that 'we may presently develop into a National Party and get rid of that odious title of Conservative, which has kept many from joining us.'[2] This seemed about to happen in September 1932 when the free traders, Philip Snowden and the Samuelite Liberals, withdrew from the coalition over the introduction of protection and imperial preference. Chamberlain believed that those who remained would move towards 'the fused party under a National name which I regard as certain to come'.[3] In practice this was what happened, as the National Liberals and National Labourites became indistinguishable from Conservatives, but the elaborate pretence of a coalition was kept up. After the Liberals had left the Cabinet and MacDonald was questioning whether the National Government should continue its existence (or looking to his colleagues for assurance), Baldwin was emphatic that 'the Prime Minister's own duty was clear; he had taken command of the ship for a definite purpose and must see it through. No member of the Conservative Party thought otherwise. They intended to see the business through and to reach a successful conclusion.'[4] The Conservative leader had no intention of disentangling himself from the 'MacDonald Tar Baby' (Leopold Amery's epithet)[5] or transforming the National Government into an ordinary political party. The amiable arrangement by which he had the power and MacDonald the honour was too comfortable. Either road back to party politics would involve concessions to right-wing Conservatives and might cost him the support of moderate, liberal opinion. So MacDonald was kept on as captain, or figurehead, until his mental powers and eyesight deteriorated so far that he became a liability rather than an asset. The *Spectator*, the voice of liberal Conservatism, commented on his indispensability: 'The Prime Minister's chief strength lies to-day where it has always lain, in the difficulty of finding anyone

[1] A. R. Wise, 3 Dec. 1931. 260 H.C. Deb. 5s., col. 1362.

[2] Quoted in Keith Feiling, *The Life of Neville Chamberlain* (London, 1946), p. 197.

[3] Ibid., p. 216.

[4] Cabinet Minutes, 28 Sept. 1932. Cab. 23/72.

[5] L. S. Amery, *The Unforgiving Years 1929–1940* (London, 1955), p. 67.

to take his place. He saves the Cabinet from being a purely Conservative administration, and he saves the Conservatives from the need for deciding whether they are prepared to serve under Mr. Baldwin or not.'[6]

It was not in Baldwin's interests to clarify this vague but agreeable situation. With his two arch-opponents, Winston Churchill and Lloyd George, firmly excluded from power[7] and enjoying the support of a large number of young, progressive M.P.s, many of them elected for the first time in 1931, Baldwin's position in the Administration and in his own party was safer than it had ever been. His indifference to narrow party interests met with the approval of the new M.P.s who

between them represent a remarkable variety of interests, experience and talents. . . . They intend to emphasize the national character of the Government, being very clear about the basis on which they were elected, and will not readily lend themselves to sectional intrigues. Indeed, they seem more apathetic about Party in the ordinary sense, therein no doubt, reflecting the feeling of the nation that returned them.[8]

'A Young Conservative' wrote:

However much he may be lacking in the more spectacular qualities of leadership it cannot be denied that Mr. Baldwin has always been fully aware (as Mr. Churchill, for example, or Sir Henry Page Croft, have not always been) that he is living in a new and unprecedented world. And it is the unique characteristic of the younger members of his party that virtually they have known no other.[9]

Even the *New Statesman* had to concede that Baldwin was 'the Mr. Asquith of our generation—the decent Liberal leader'.[10]

Much as Baldwin may have appreciated this kind of support, he did little to mobilize the skills of these M.P.s. He often spoke of 'giving youth its chance' and 'the missing generation', but he and his contemporaries kept a firm hand on the important positions. And apparently he did not have a very high regard for those young men he did admit to the Cabinet: in 1935 he confided to Sir Austen Chamberlain that they had been 'a great

[6] Janus, 'A Spectator's Notebook', *Spectator*, 25 Aug. 1933.

[7] See L. S. Amery, *War and Peace 1914–1929* (London, 1953), p. 511 for the view that Baldwin joined the 'unnatural' coalition with MacDonald to keep Churchill and Lloyd George out of the government.

[8] Auspex, 'A Spectator's Notebook', *Spectator*, 2 Jan. 1932.

[9] 'A Post-War House of Commons', *Spectator*, 5 Mar. 1932.

[10] Critic, 'A London Diary', 4 May 1935.

disappointment to him'.[11] Neville Chamberlain, the second-ranking Conservative, was more outspoken, complaining of the 'boys' brigade' inside the Cabinet and 'young Tory intellectuals' outside.[12] But even after the young M.P.s had become disillusioned with the National Government's pedestrian approach to social and economic problems they felt impelled to hold fast to it for fear of a right-wing Conservative administration 'as bent on losing India . . . as their predecessors were on losing the American colonies, and more concerned to stamp on Socialism than to counter Socialism with constructive policies' which would 'bring the party to disaster in twelve months.' After three years of the coalition the *Spectator* concluded: 'If the choice is to be between a Conservative Government pure and simple and a further term of the National Government the decision must be for the latter.'[13]

Some young Conservatives hoped that this dilemma could be avoided by the creation of a new centre party. These were men who disliked the dogmatic socialism of the Labour party, but who wanted a more vigorous attitude than that displayed by the National Government, men who wanted to save capitalism from itself by remedying its worst abuses. The most outspoken of these was Harold Macmillan, who represented the depressed constituency of Stockton-on-Tees. In the summer of 1935 he described to the House of Commons the unhealthy situation created by the National Government:

Although the English people may want a policy of the Left Centre and even of the Centre, although they may want a policy far more advanced, far more ambitious, far more risky if you like, than any upon which this Government will embark, there is no political mechanism by which they can obtain it. The only Government that can be formed is one which must depend for its support upon the parties of the Right. That seems to me to be a very dangerous situation. At all events it puts an enormous responsibility upon the Prime Minister [Baldwin] and those who have faith in him. . . . If the people find that they cannot get what they want through the ordinary groupings of Parliamentary movements, through the ordinary

[11] Memorandum: Invitation to Join Mr. Baldwin's Government. Written by Sir Austen Chamberlain on 21 and 22 Dec. 1935. Sir Austen Chamberlain Papers (hereafter cited as A.C.), Box 41, folder 125.

[12] Feiling, *Life of Neville Chamberlain*, pp. 199–200.

[13] 'The Next House of Commons', 12 Oct. 1934.

Parliamentary machine, they may be driven ultimately to other means, and if they are, the Prime Minister and his colleagues will be the only true begetters of revolution.[14]

In July 1936 Macmillan, who had asked his electors for freedom to criticize the government at the 1935 general election, resigned the Conservative whip to sit as an independent M.P. For a year he devoted his energies to the Next Five Years Group, an association of reform-minded thinkers which he hoped to turn into 'some kind of Popular Front, wide enough to embrace Progressive Conservatives, Radical Liberals, and those members of the Socialist Party who were prepared to work for a limited objective'.[15] When this proved impossible he returned to the Conservative fold following Neville Chamberlain's accession to the prime ministership.[16]

Macmillan's statement and actions reveal the frustration of the National Government's most energetic supporters and the impregnability of the administration. No wonder Sir Austen Chamberlain, dining with a group of young Conservatives in 1934, found them embracing a variety of views 'from something indistinguishable from Fascism on the one hand to extreme Pacifism and Socialism on the other. They gave me the impression of extreme *malaise* and uncertainty, a groping after something which eludes their grasp. They need a clear call and bold leadership. I don't see any sign of their getting it at present.'[17] An objective analyst might have concluded that the National Government had won its huge majorities by astute management on transitory issues and that it would be lucky to repeat these victories. But such an observation was seldom made, except optimistically by members of the Opposition. Perhaps people felt that what the Administration had achieved twice it could repeat indefinitely. Certainly no one expected it to lose the general election anticipated in the autumn of 1939. There was, rather, a widespread conviction that the National Government was no temporary coalition but a permanent feature of British political life. In the course of a tribute to R. B. Bennett, a former

[14] 9 July 1935. 304 H.C. Deb. 5s., col. 238.

[15] Harold Macmillan, *Winds of Change 1914–1939* (London, 1966), p. 487.

[16] His letters to the party leaders declining and reaccepting the whip were printed in *The Times*, 8 July 1936 and 31 July 1937.

[17] Sir Charles Petrie, *The Life and Letters of the Right Hon. Sir Austen Chamberlain* (London, 1939 and 1940), ii. 398.

Canadian Prime Minister, in 1939 Winston Churchill wistfully remarked that 'Canada was a country of party government like we had in the days when Britain was rising to be a leading power'.[18] Lord Francis Williams was more direct when he wrote that after 1931 'Britain had its own respectable version of single-party rule'.[19] This situation might have continued indefinitely if Clement Attlee had not been determined to return to party politics in 1945.

The National Government's crushing majorities made it virtually impossible to defeat the Administration in the House of Commons. (In the division which forced Neville Chamberlain's resignation it had a majority of 81.) It also made the Government's supporters hesitate to make a complete break with their party. Whenever there was serious disagreement within the National party in this period there was talk of some M.P.s splitting off and joining the opposition. Nothing ever came of it. Discontented Tories were not anxious to take the irrevocable step of breaking party ties to face an uncertain, and probably short, political future. Far better to stay on the Government side of the House in the hope of a reconstructed Cabinet which would include some of the critics. Nor was the Labour party particularly eager to take in disaffected Conservatives, who would be more of an embarrassment than a source of strength. A divided governmental party suited their interests much better.

Winston Churchill, who had crossed the floor of the House of Commons on a couple of opportune occasions, recognized the conditions within which dissenters had to operate in the 1930s. He always went out of his way to affirm his credentials as a genuine Conservative, usually by rousing attacks on the economic and imperial views of the socialists. At the same time, as the Liberal and Labour parties came to share his outlook on foreign affairs, he made favourable references to the change, thereby keeping open a life-line to the left. Events proved the wisdom of these tactics: when Chamberlain resigned in 1940 the only candidates considered to succeed him were Conservatives and Churchill found himself in the happy position of being a Conservative who was acceptable to the Labour party. Had he broken with his own party earlier he might have ruined his chances of

[18] Reported in *The Times*, 20 Apr. 1939.

[19] Lord Francis Williams, *A Pattern of Rulers* (London, 1965), p. 1.

becoming Prime Minister. But then it was never Churchill's aim to break the party but rather to capture it in good working order.

In addition to factors peculiar to the 1930s the usual pressures of party whips and the appeal to group spirit were employed to deter criticism. Loyalty, it has been said, is the Conservatives' secret weapon; and so long as Baldwin was their leader it proved more effective than coercion. Earl Winterton, a long-time member of the House and a critic of the Government's defence policy, explained the difficulty of trying to introduce a critical note into the soothing atmosphere created by Baldwin. The present parliament, Winterton said, reminded him of

> a comfortable middle-aged club, the majority of whose members think it rather bad form to criticise the committee, and especially the deservedly popular chairman, who has been there so long that he has become almost an institution. They are inclined to argue that although he does make mistakes, one ought to forgive him because of his past services. So they look upon those minority members of the club who are not wholly satisfied with the conduct of affairs as self-seekers, merely anxious to be on the committee themselves.[20]

The device of buying off critics with office was conspicuously neglected in the 1930s; so much so that by the time war broke out most people were convinced that the ablest Conservatives were sitting on back-benches. No doubt the chief reason for this neglect was that the Government's majority was never seriously threatened by the dissenters. The most outstanding attempt to buy off a critic occurred during the Hoare–Laval crisis, when Baldwin hinted to Sir Austen Chamberlain that he could become Foreign Secretary if he supported the Government; but this was probably not a genuine offer. The other cases in which this device was used are also inconclusive. Towards the end of 1936 Sir Philip Sassoon, the Under-Secretary of State for Air, asked Ronald Cartland, one of the young critics, if he would become his Parliamentary Private Secretary; but Cartland, suspecting that this rather cheap offer originated in the Whips' office, refused. On the other hand, Earl Winterton jumped at the offer of the Chancellorship of the Duchy of Lancaster. As he recalled in his memoirs: 'The only thorn in this Lancastrian rose for me was that having become a Minister, I had to resign the chairmanship of a Select

[20] 10 Nov. 1936. 317 H.C. Deb. 5s., col. 757.

Committee of the Commons on Financial Resolutions.'[21] Once inside the Cabinet Winterton stood loyally by the Government, despite stories of his disagreements on foreign policy that reached his friends outside. The bigger guns, who would have commanded more important offices from which they could have exerted considerable influence, were not taken into the Administration. Perhaps it was felt that their nuisance value was less outside, even when they were attacking the Government, than inside, where they would have been a major disruptive force.

Despite their critical attitudes the leading dissenters maintained close personal and social relations with their leaders and they were informed of policy decisions by Cabinet Ministers and senior civil servants. Sir Austen Chamberlain kept in touch with the Foreign Office and was regularly consulted by the Foreign Secretary of the day. Winston Churchill was even invited by Baldwin to join the Committee of Imperial Defence on Air Defence Research and his views were privately considered in Downing Street during the major crises. Ostensibly these contacts did not limit the dissenters' freedom to criticize the Government, and Churchill robustly denied that they did,[22] but by taking them into its confidence the Cabinet must have blunted the edge of their criticism. At any event it put them in a different position from members of the Opposition.

In attacking the Government the critics pressed into service all the traditional justifications of dissent. Basing their argument firmly on the outmoded constitutional theory that M.P.s are elected as individuals rather than as members of a party, they asserted the Burkean claim to be representatives, not delegates, elected to exercise their own judgement on issues as they arose. 'I do not hold the opinion that hon. Members should vote as their constituents direct them,' declared Robert Boothby. 'I think that hon. Members have a duty to take into consideration what they believe to be in the best interests of the country as a whole.'[23] Winston Churchill maintained that this was imperative in view of the National Government's enormous majority. Contemptuously rejecting the idea that 'the only place from which words of warning and words of controversy should come is the

[21] Earl Winterton, *Orders of the Day* (London, 1953), p. 227.
[22] Winston S. Churchill, *The Gathering Storm* (Boston, 1948), p. 150.
[23] 13 Apr. 1932. 264 H.C. Deb. 5s., col. 873.

diminutive representatives on the Front Opposition Bench,' he admonished

> the great Conservative majority which not only fills [the House of Commons] but bears the whole brunt of the responsibility, that if it were thought that we were careless of our duties and did not examine these matters with great attention; if it were thought that Members were liable to be driven this way and that by the guidance of my hon. Friend on the Front Bench and the other Whips, not only would this Parliament, from which so much was hoped by our loyal working people, pass away in derision, but the very gravest injury would have been done to the structure of Parliamentary institutions altogether.[24]

According to Churchill and the other critics Parliament was a deliberative assembly in which policy was actually formulated, not a rubber stamp for the decisions of the executive. But this seemingly cogent rationalization for an independent attitude on the part of private M.P.s was no match for party pressure; and Churchill himself, when in office, took a different attitude towards those who dared to quibble about his decisions.

The three leading Conservative back-benchers in the early 1930s were Winston Churchill, Sir Austen Chamberlain, and Leopold Amery. It has often been argued that the National Government's foreign policy would have been more successful if they had been included. This is debatable, considering their records as foreign policy critics, but in any event they were left out for what seemed good reasons at the time: Chamberlain because he asked to be excluded; Churchill for his stand on India and his attempt to seize the party leadership; and Amery for his strong and unpopular imperial views. When the country's leaders were trying to construct a harmonious team from former opponents Churchill and Amery were not likely to prove very helpful. But they were not left out for their attitudes towards foreign affairs; nor were they, in the first instance, critics of the Administration's foreign policy.

The most spectacular and persistently hostile M.P. was Winston Churchill. In January 1931, eight months before the National Government was formed, he had resigned from the Shadow Cabinet over Baldwin's decision to endorse more self-government for India. This was a clear bid for the party leader-

24 14 Dec. 1932. 273 H.C. Deb. 5s., cols. 380–1.

ship. Churchill was well aware that Baldwin's Indian policy was unpopular in the party and that many members were suspicious of his lethargic conduct as Leader of the Opposition. And so long as the party was in opposition, with die-hards safely ensconced in safe constituencies making up the greater part of its strength, Churchill's chances of success were bright. Indeed within a month of the break the party's chief agent told Neville Chamberlain that perhaps a majority leaned towards Churchill and suggested: 'It would be in the interests of the Party that the Leader should reconsider his position.'[25] Had the Conservatives remained in opposition for a full term, with a general election in 1933 or 1934, Churchill might well have captured the party; but all these plans were ruined when the National Government was formed and right-wing Conservatives were swamped by an influx of moderate M.P.s. When these latest recruits refused to listen to his siren song Churchill grumbled bitterly: 'I thought myself that there was a good deal of exaggeration about the crisis which arose last August and September—and a certain amount of manipulation.'[26]

In the campaign preceding the 1931 general election the Administration made some inept moves to keep Churchill out of the House of Commons. Despite the electoral arrangement made by the parties comprising the coalition, a Liberal, pledged to support the Government, was nominated in his constituency; and on the eve of the poll the Liberal leader, Sir Herbert Samuel, sent a message urging his election and Churchill's defeat. Ramsay MacDonald also got involved in an acrimonious correspondence with Churchill for making some pointed remarks about the latter's policies as Chancellor of the Exchequer. But, much to the embarrassment of the Cabinet, Churchill was returned for his safe suburban London seat by a majority of almost 5,000 over his Liberal opponent.

When Parliament met Churchill understandably turned up in a truculent mood, informing the leaders of the coalition that the circumstances of his victory entitled him to adopt an attitude of 'perfect independence' towards them:

My attitude will be one of discriminating benevolence, but I shall not fail to warn them, in good time and quite plainly, upon any

[25] Feiling, *Life of Neville Chamberlain*, p. 185.
[26] 4 May 1932. 265 H.C. Deb. 5s., col. 1175.

occasion when I see them falling short, either by neglect or by action, of the course which is appointed for them. I shall do my best in that way to contribute to what we all hope will be their successful conduct of affairs.

Turning to his own leader Churchill taunted him for keeping the coalition going when he could have formed a Conservative administration:

During the years I worked with him . . . if there was one doctrine that my right hon. Friend inculcated upon me more than any other, it was his abhorrence of coalitions . . . It is certainly surprising to find him now the champion coalitionist, though doubtless for a very sound reason. I am sure no one is more aware of the dangers of such a course than my right hon. Friend, and I am sure he will be reminded of those dangers whenever he should chance to walk across the portals of the Carlton Club.[27]

The political cycle had come full circle in less than a decade: Baldwin, who had done so much to pull down the Lloyd George coaltion which Churchill had vigorously defended, was now the *de facto* leader of the National Government, while Churchill was its chief opponent.

Although Churchill's chances of wresting the leadership from Baldwin had practically disappeared at the 1931 election he kept at his task like a punch-drunk fighter. The only possible explanation of these futile activities is that Churchill was determined to secure the backing of a powerful wing of the Conservative party if he could not win the leadership itself. Gathering the party die-hards around him he led their attacks on the socialist tendencies of the government, the Statute of Westminster (which would open the way to complete independence for Eire—a name, incidentally, which Churchill despised), disarmament and, above all, the Government of India Bill. *The Economist* commented on their shrewd concentration on the last issue:

In choosing India as the issue best calculated to dissociate the Conservative Party from Mr. Baldwin and break up the National Government, Mr. Churchill and his die-hard supporters chose wisely and well. To surrender our Empire in India! To give way to sedition! How many true Conservatives breathe with a soul so dead as to be deaf to such an appeal as this![28]

[27] 11 Nov. 1931. 259 H.C. Deb. 5s., cols. 130–1.
[28] 'Notes of the Week', *The Economist*, 1 July 1933.

At every stage of the discussion, which took up most of the 1931–5 parliament, Churchill delivered unwearying attacks on the bill and asserted his conviction that the subcontinent could never aspire to dominion status. As he put it in one of his less elegant rhetorical passages:

It is impossible because the condition of India, of the country in which they live, the political, social, cultural, racial, religious conditions of that country are such that any attempt to apply the democratic institutions of Australia and Canada rigidly and pedantically to India would produce measureless tyranny and misery ending in bloodshed and probably utter confusion.[29]

In his tooth-and-nail resistance to this measure Churchill came up with the charge that Sir Samuel Hoare, the Secretary of State for India, and Lord Derby, an old friend of Churchill's and a pillar of the Conservative party in Lancashire, had persuaded the Manchester Chamber of Commerce to change its brief from opposing more self-government for India to supporting it.[30] When the charge was rejected by the Committee of Privileges Churchill's prestige fell to the lowest point in the decade. His attempt to dispute the decision in the House of Commons simply provoked denunciations from fellow Conservatives who feared and distrusted him. 'The power of that menace is not decreasing,' said one of them, 'it is increasing in geometrical progression downwards. It has now become atavistic.'[31] Leopold Amery, who disagreed with Chuchill's stand on India, seized this golden opportunity to lay a clever trap to expose Churchill's motives:

At all costs he had to be faithful to his chosen motto: *Fiat justitia ruat coelum.*
Mr. Churchill: Translate it.
Mr. Amery: I will translate it into the vernacular: If I can trip up Sam, the Government's bust.[32]

But Churchill did not confine his campaign to the House of Commons. At the party's annual conference he would whip up the emotions of the rank and file on India, but here he was defeated by Baldwin's less flamboyant but more persuasive

[29] 3 Dec. 1931. 260 H.C. Deb. 5s., col. 1289.

[30] The matter was raised by Churchill as a question of privilege in the House of Commons on 16 April 1934 and was referred to the Committee of Privileges, which reported back to the House on 13 June 1934.

[31] J. P. Morris, 13 June 1934. 290 H.C. Deb. 5s., col. 1789.

[32] 290 H.C. Deb. 5s., col. 1738.

rhetoric: 'However brilliant was the unflagging force of Churchill's offensive, it was Baldwin's combination of humanity, common sense and quiet confidence that invariably won the day.'[33] Frustrated here, Churchill turned to electoral means to stop the bill and pull down Baldwin. In February 1934 he and the India Defence League (an organization financed by the Indian princes to resist any increase in the central government's power at the expense of their own) campaigned vigorously for Admiral Sir Roger Keyes, a right-wing Conservative who was endorsed without much enthusiasm by administration.[34] Flushed by the magnitude of their success the group went further in the following year, promoting Randolph Churchill as the unofficial Conservative candidate in a Liverpool by-election. 'The Young Chevalier' backed by 'the Old Pretender'[35] managed to split the Conservative vote and ensure the return of the Labour candidate; but this proved a Pyrrhic victory for the elder Churchill. Some of his constituents, tired of their member's eccentric conduct, passed a resolution deploring his

> consistent opposition to the National Government in the House of Commons, and further desires to point out to Mr. Churchill that the position of the India Defence League in connection with the Wavertree [division of Liverpool] election creates a highly dangerous precedent for the adoption of an Independent Conservative candidate in the Epping Division, who would undoubtedly now be welcome by many loyal supporters of Mr. Baldwin and the present Government.[36]

[33] Viscount Templewood, *Nine Troubled Years* (London, 1954), p. 102.

[34] Sir Roger Keyes (1872–1945) was a professional naval officer whose personal courage and inspired leadership of the submarine service in the First World War, and even more his audacious (though unsuccessful) attempt to blockade the German submarine bases of Zeebrugge and Ostend in April 1918, made him a popular hero. But in the reaction against the war the fame of such commanders suffered and by 1934 Baldwin and MacDonald were well aware of the political cost of supporting such a candidate or even numbering him among their followers. In 1943 Keyes was elevated to the peerage as Baron Keyes of Zeebrugge and Dover.

[35] *The Times*, leading editorial, 8 Feb. 1934. After this election Randolph Churchill continued his political adventures, apparently without the support of his father and the India Defence League. In March 1935 he supported an independent Conservative candidate (and ex-Fascist) against the official candidate, Duncan Sandys, soon to be his brother-in-law, but with little success: the candidate polled only 2,700 votes. In February 1936 Churchill was unsuccessful again when he ran against Malcolm MacDonald, a cabinet member and son of the former Prime Minister.

[36] Reported in *The Times*, 9 Feb. 1935.

This declaration brought to an abrupt end Churchill's attempt to capture the Conservative party in this way. In any event the issue on which he had tackled Baldwin was about to pass from the political scene. In July 1935 the Government of India Act reached the statute books without a single concession to Churchill and his eighty followers. A month later Churchill informed his constituents that he was now busy urging the Government to secure a sane and stable parliament at the next general election and encouraging it to look to the defences of the country and the empire, maintain world peace, and assist the special (depressed) areas.[37]

The sincerity of Churchill's views on India are not open to question, but this was a problem he approached emotionally and rhetorically and on which he had no special knowledge or understanding. His whole attitude was bound up with his general nostalgia for the palmy days of the Victorian Empire, as they were embalmed in the works of imperialist writers in the late nineteenth and early twentieth century. Paying tribute to Rudyard Kipling (who died in 1936) Churchill said:

> The structure and pageant of British rule in India gave him his first and main inspiration. To read with faithful eye Kipling's Indian stories, short or long, is to gain a truer knowledge of that great episode, the British contact with India, than will be found in the many ponderous blue-books, or in much of the glib, smooth patter which is now in fashion.[38]

It is also clear at this remove that the difference between Baldwin and Churchill was simply one of degree, and that they were both mistaken in thinking that a strong British position in India could be maintained. Baldwin and the moderate Conservatives believed that

> By going forward boldly with India to-day you may keep India in the Empire, and as generations go by and further advances are made you will find her a loyal part of the British Empire, co-operating with us and we with her; and I believe equally that if we do not advance to her the right hand of fellowship, a generous right hand, then I

[37] Reported in *The Times*, 26 Aug. 1935.

[38] Reported in *The Times*, 18 Nov. 1937. Churchill's imperial ideas are discussed in Herbert L. Stewart, 'The "Imperialism" of Winston Churchill', *Public Affairs*, vol. xiii, no. 4, pp. 15–24; and in Harry W. Porter, 'Churchill and the Empire', *South Atlantic Quarterly*, vol. li, pp. 222–34.

believe in the lifetime of many in this room we shall lose the great Empire and lose it forever.[39]

The die-hards, on the other hand, were convinced that India could be kept in the Empire only by force. But *The Times*'s leader-writer was not alone in finding 'a steadying difficulty in distinguishing between Mr. Churchill's apparent readiness to destroy the Government and his claim to be the saviour of India'.[40]

In his role as leader of the die-hard opposition Churchill did not confine himself to attacks on Indian policy. He also demanded rearmament, which Lord Beaverbrook characterized as 'simply another Churchillian stunt to impress himself on the public. Once more he had taken up a cause, the ultimate object being power.'[41] Occasionally too, if less enthusiastically, he denounced the Administration's feeble domestic policy:

When I heard the statements about the duck pond—no, it was the paddle-pool—and the rope mats, and the renovation of archaic Roman bridges, I thought of those men sitting in their cottages, in the distress that falls upon them, and I am bound to say that I think that speech must have been a great shock, a very great and insulting shock to them, coming as it did from a Prime Minister who, in the first instance, led the Socialist party into office on the claim that he could cure—virtually cure—unemployment.

Churchill's prescription here as elsewhere was 'more grip, more mental energy, more resourcefulness . . . by those who have those great powers, and who are in charge of our destinies'.[42] And he could always count on a laugh from all corners of the House when he poked fun at Ramsay MacDonald:

Here I say little of the Prime Minister's oratorical style. We are familiar with it here. We know that he has, more than any other man, the gift of compressing the largest number of words into the smallest amount of thought. We have heard him on so many topics, from India to unemployment and many other matters, providing us with an inexhaustible flow of vague, well-sounding exhortation, the

[39] Stanley Baldwin addressing the annual meeting of the Bewdley Division Unionist Association in Worcester, 29 April 1933. Reported in *The Times*, 1 May 1933.

[40] *The Times*, leading editorial, 3 June 1933.

[41] Kenneth Young, *Churchill and Beaverbrook: A Study in Friendship and Politics* (London, 1966), p. 121.

[42] 16 Feb. 1933. 274 H.C. Deb. 5s. cols. 1233–4.

precise purpose of which is largely wrapped in mystery and which, as far as can be discerned, can be understood differently in different quarters, according to taste.[43]

In the light of these activities it would be misleading to think, as Churchill implied in *The Gathering Storm*, that he addressed himself single-mindedly to foreign affairs in the early 1930s. On the contrary, foreign dangers did not rank very high in his order of priorities. Towards the end of 1934 he told his constituents that the two most important tasks facing the Conservative party were—not foreign policy but 'first . . . to defeat the policy of abdication at the centre in India, and the second is to beat the Socialists. I hope that we shall get rid of the first and then all join together for the second. That is what I am working for.'[44] But his other questionable activities did affect his credibility when he turned to foreign policy in the second half of the decade. As late as October 1938, when Churchill was mourning the fate of Czechoslovakia, John McGovern of the Independent Labour party reminded the House of Commons of the days when Sir Samuel Hoare had been engaged in giving more self-government to India and Churchill's

talk then was that no democratic Government should be given to India in any shape or form. He talked last night about pagan Germany, and said that we must not bargain with them. . . . His love of democracy is, to my mind, a very unreal one. Some people get slogans to suit the times and I think in the right hon. Gentleman's slogan last night he was simply speaking with his tongue in his cheek.[45]

If Churchill's company and causes inspired distrust, his olympian attitude towards his fellow M.P.s was hardly calculated to win him any friends. As a senior privy councillor he could stroll into the House at any time and claim the right to intervene in the debate while more junior members sat for hours, often in vain, hoping to catch the Speaker's eye. Frequently these interventions were simply for self-advertisement or to upbraid the Government for its general shortcomings. On one famous occasion George Lansbury, the Christian pacifist Leader of the Opposition, became so enraged by these antics that he burst out:

[43] 23 Mar. 1933. 276 H.C. Deb. 5s., cols. 544–5.
[44] Reported in *The Times*, 9 Nov. 1934.
[45] 6 Oct. 1938. 339 H.C. Deb. 5s., 531.

I consider it sheer audacity and effrontery on the part of the right hon. Gentleman to walk into this Chamber at this hour of the night and standing up bully the Government. A Minister has the right to speak, but the right hon. Gentleman the Member for Epping comes in and claims the right to speak. Who is he to demand that right? I will tell the right hon. Gentleman what ought to have been told him long ago, and it is that he usurps a place in this House as if he had a right to walk in, make his speech, walk out and leave the whole place as if God Almighty had spoken. There have been statesmen in this House of high intellectual qualities, but they have never treated the House of Commons in the contemptuous manner that the right hon. Gentleman has treated it, for he never listens to any man's speech but his own.[46]

Such was Churchill's reputation in these years that he had only two close followers, Brendan Bracken and Robert Boothby. Bracken followed Churchill in all his policies; Boothby, more discriminating, supported the government on India and remained loyal to Neville Chamberlain much longer than Churchill. To these two M.P.s must be added Duncan Sandys, who entered the House of Commons in March 1935 and married Churchill's daughter, Diana, six months later. The die-hards, courted so earnestly by Churchill, were not constant allies. Although they recognized his great gifts as a leader and colourful spokesman for their causes, they also regarded him as an adventurer not to be trusted very far; and they were hardly reassured by the record of a man who had returned to the party as recently as 1924 after a twenty-year sojourn among the Liberals, who had played a prominent part in breaking the power of the House of Lords, and who had given the welfare state a powerful push. Furthermore, many of the imperialists had been mollified by the introduction of protection in February 1932 and imperial preference later in the year—an act which gladdened their hearts all the more as it led to the resignation of Sir Herbert Samuel and his followers and made the Government more homogeneously Conservative. With the passage of the Government of India Act the bond between Churchill and the die-hards was finally severed and they went their separate ways: he to concentrate on the criticizing the Administration's foreign policy, they to support it.

Compared to Churchill, Sir Austen Chamberlain and Leopold Amery were positively drab and mere grumblers about the

[46] 26 May 1932. 266 H.C. Deb. 5s., col. 684.

National Government's policies. Until his death in 1937, however, Chamberlain was unquestionably the most respected Conservative back-bencher. It was to him, not Churchill, that the young M.P.s turned for guidance and leadership. 'He is the Elder Statesman,' one of them wrote; 'the back benches have given him what the Front Bench never did—disciples.'[47] A former leader of the party, Sir Austen had been appointed First Lord of the Admiralty when the National Government was formed; but following the general election in October 1931 he had surrendered all claim to office, partly to give the young men a chance, partly to ensure that his half-brother became Chancellor of the Exchequer, and partly because he was disappointed at not being offered the Foreign Office.[48] From his position outside the Government Chamberlain kept a close watch on foreign affairs and commanded the respect of all sections of the House when he spoke on these matters. But although he was often dissatisfied with the Government's foreign policy, and his prestige was certainly such that he could have organized a group of dissenters, he never intrigued or caballed. His scrupulous sense of loyalty, his determination to do nothing that would prevent Neville Chamberlain from succeeding Baldwin as the party leader and his unfailing courtesy combined to ensure that his strictures would be moderate and reasonable. Nor did Sir Austen have any of the brutal, self-confident qualities necessary for the leader of a group of rebels. Leopold Amery's judgement of him, though cruel, is substantially true: 'I am afraid life has been full of disappointments for him; but then he has never really had sufficient confidence in himself, and, at bottom, there has not really been enough of himself to have confidence in. Nature intended him for a good lieutenant and eventually an elder statesman.[49]

Amery himself was more vigorous than Chamberlain but

[47] Ronald Cartland to his sister, 1936. Quoted in Barbara Cartland, *Ronald Cartland* (London, 1941), p. 70.

[48] Petrie, *Life and Letters of Sir Austen Chamberlain*, ii. 386. Writing to his sister Sir Austen said: 'I *know* (tho' no one else seems to in the country) that I could have done service in the F.O. which no one else can do; but from the moment that was seen to be out of the question, there was no other place that could not be as well or better filled by a younger man, and it is not good for the party or for the country that opportunity should be lacking for them to gain experience.' A.C., Letters to Hilda and Ida Chamberlain, 1928–31 (8 Nov. 1931).

[49] Diary entry, 4 Nov. 1931. Quoted in Amery, *Unforgiving Years*, p. 71.

duller than Churchill. According to his own account he was left out of the National Government because his protectionist views were abhorrent to Philip Snowden, the free-trade Chancellor of the Exchequer.[50] In fact Amery, a man of strong dogmatic ideas about the Empire and imperial free trade, had been playing Joseph Chamberlain to Baldwin's Balfour for the last two years. Baldwin, however, realized that the day had gone when Joseph Chamberlain's dream of the Empire as a closed economic unit could be implemented, and he also knew that the high tariffs which this would involve were unacceptable to the electorate and to many members of the Conservative party. No doubt he welcomed the opportunity to exclude this forceful and tiresome advocate from the new government. Amery for his part simply kept up his activities from a back bench. He also travelled to the Ottawa conference in 1932 where imperial economic matters were being discussed. He so embarrassed his own government by encouraging the Dominions to press for a complete system of Empire free trade, however, that Neville Chamberlain, a less enthusiastic guardian of his father's vision, accused him point-blank of wrecking the conference.[51] Apart from imperial matters, however, Amery was no particular foe of the Government until Hitler's seizure of Austria in March 1938. But his imperial obsession and dominating personality ensured that he would not be offered a place in the Cabinet.

The National Government came in for considerable criticism from these three back-benchers, but until the middle of the decade little of it had to do with foreign policy. Even after 1935, when foreign affairs assumed a larger role in political discussion, the Administration had little to fear from a combined assault on the part of these three M.P.s. Not only was it difficult to devise an effective alternative to the Government's course, but also their individual views of what the Government should be doing were too different, and often mutually exclusive, for them to combine for an attack.

[50] Diary entry, 4 Nov. 1931. Quoted in Amery, *Unforgiving Years*, p. 62.
[51] Ibid., p. 86.

2. Appeasement and Its Opponents

UNTIL the end of 1938 'appeasement' was the most noble term in the diplomatic vocabulary. Far from carrying its later connotations of weakness, fear, and retreat in the face of bluff it suggested accommodation, conciliation, and the removal of just grievances. The very idea that it could mean 'craven immorality' rather than 'virtuous endeavour' simply did not occur to most Englishmen in the 1930s.[1] It is true that in 1932 Winston Churchill denounced it as 'some word which is smooth and which hides the actual truth' but he was objecting to its use to characterize the Government's Indian policy. '26,600 people', he went on, 'have been sentenced to various terms of "appeasement".'[2] The first person to take exception to appeasement in foreign affairs was Clement Attlee who charged in 1937: 'The policy of this Government throughout, right on from 1931, has always been to try and appease the aggressor by the sacrifice of weaker States, but the more you yield to the aggressor the greater his appetite.'[3] But this was simply a straw in the wind. It was not until Munich that people began to inquire closely as to its precise meaning. Thereafter the term fell like Lucifer never to rise again, though there was at first some attempt to distinguish between true and false appeasement.[4] Eleanor Rathbone, an independent M.P., defined appeasement in its new sense as 'a clever plan of selling your friends in order to buy off your enemies—which has the danger that a time comes when you have no friends left, and then you find you need them, and then it is too late to buy them back.'[5] In the face of such attacks *The Times* newspaper, which had done so much to defend the National Government's foreign

[1] Lord Vansittart, *The Mist Procession* (London, 1958), p. 430.

[2] 29 Apr. 1932. 265 H.C. Deb. 5s., col. 764.

[3] 21 Oct. 1937. 327 H.C. Deb. 5s., col. 76.

[4] Leopold Amery, for example, wrote: 'The wider issue [between Germany and other countries] will not be averted, but only brought far closer by any policy of Danegeld masquerading as appeasement or restitution.' 'Germany's Colonial Demands' in *Germany—What Next?* (Penguin Books, 1938), p. 204.

[5] Address to the University of Manchester graduates who made up part of her constituency (Miss Rathbone was the M.P. for the Combined English Universities), 24 Feb. 1939. Reported in the *Manchester Guardian*, 25 Feb. 1939.

policy, sounded the retreat: '"Appeasement" has become one of the counters of current politics. Yet it is a misleading term, with its false implication that peace does not demand reciprocity, and it might well disappear'.[6] Even Neville Chamberlain made a vain attempt to dissociate himself from appeasement after Hitler's seizure of Prague, admitting that the term was not a happy one or 'one which accurately describes its purpose'.[7] Thereafter politicians used appeasement as an abusive epithet with which to stigmatize their opponents' policies. Ironically it was Winston Churchill who tried to redeem it in 1950 when he pointed out: 'Appeasement from weakness and fear is alike futile and fatal. Appeasement from strength is magnanimous and noble and might be the surest and perhaps the only path to world peace.'[8] No one followed his lead.

The later connotations of appeasement should not obscure the fact that in the inter-war years it was the expression of a battle-scarred generation's faith and hope that negotiation and accommodation could replace war as a means of settling disputes between countries. This naturally appealed most to radicals and pacifists, who denied that Germany had been solely responsible for the First World War; who believed that the conflict could have been avoided by mediation and good will; who maintained that the war had solved nothing; who claimed that Germany had been unjustly treated at the peace conference; and who put their trust in universal disarmament and the League of Nations as the present mediator in international affairs and potential world government. But these feelings were not restricted to left-wingers. It was Neville Chamberlain, the Conservative Prime Minister, who declared that 'In war there are no winners. There is nothing but suffering and ruin for those who are involved and even if we ourselves were not involved with our world-wide ramifications of trade and finance, we could not fail to be involved in the consequences of war and the destruction of property which sooner or later must react upon ourselves.'[9] And Sir John Simon (a Liberal indistinguishable from a Conservative by this time) who told his constituents shortly after he was appointed to the Foreign Office that

[6] Editorial, 'How Much Art Thou Sorry?', 9 Dec. 1938.
[7] Speech at Birmingham, 17 Mar. 1939. Reported in *The Times*, 18 Mar. 1939.
[8] 14 Dec. 1950. 482 H.C. Deb. 5s., col. 1367.
[9] 24 Mar. 1938. 338 H.C. Deb. 5s., cols. 1399–1400.

the days when the efforts of the Foreign Secretary were directed to the preserving of select rival alliances were gone. The days when he was constantly watching the tipping of the scales, what was called the balance of power, were ended. . . . The essence of our foreign policy to-day is that we should endeavour to make our full contribution to focusing the moral force of public opinion upon international problems.[10]

Conservatives, of course, were hardly living for the day when national boundaries would disappear and all mankind would live at peace under the League of Nations. But they were anxious to avoid another conflict which would destroy the country's social structure and reduce its position in the world even further —'bring an end to civilization' as the current phrase was. When war appeared as a disaster rather than a golden opportunity to increase the country's strength the old guide-lines of foreign policy seemed to be of little help. J. L. Garvin, the editor of the *Observer* and a persistent advocate of appeasement, never tired of inveighing against those traditionalists who merely re-iterated 'stiff pedantries and bleak negatives' that could only lead to another 'catastrophe of nations'. Instead he called for 'fresh minds, liberated action and reformed policy'.[11] Appeasement was, in a very real sense, a symptom of Britain's decline as a leading world power, a tacit recognition that her position was no longer secure and a defensive strategy to preserve as much as possible in an era of challenge and change.

The fundamental difference between Conservative and left-wing appeasement was that the former was based more on considerations of power than morality. Radicals advocated concessions on the grounds of justice, while Conservatives were more inclined to favour concessions as an alternative to disruptive force; but moral considerations were not entirely absent from their calculations. Because they stressed power rather than morality, however. Conservatives styled their brand of appeasement 'realistic' to distinguish it from the 'idealistic' appeasement of the left. Indeed the terms 'realism' and 'appeasement' were practically synonymous for Conservatives in the 1930s and the leaders of the National Government took special pride in their

[10] Speech to the Spen Valley Chambers of Commerce, 20 November 1931. Reported in *The Times*, 21 Nov. 1931.

[11] 'The Key of the World', *Observer*, 21 Mar. 1937. This was the last in a series of four articles entitled 'War for What?'.

claim to be realists. Their critics charged that this realism was nothing more than cynicism or a complete disregard for morality and decency; but it is interesting to notice that the term escaped the fate of appeasement, perhaps because the latter bore the brunt of the attack at the end of the decade.

The best contemporary analysis and intellectual defence of appeasement was that produced by E. H. Carr on the eve of the Second World War. Although he was overtaken by events and the publication of a book which offered a sophisticated defence of Munich shortly after the outbreak of war was hardly well timed, *The Twenty Years' Crisis* remains a brilliant account of what the appeasers were trying to do. Carr himself could take comfort in Hegel's proverb, 'The owl of Minerva flies at dusk'.

Carr's basic theme is that change is inevitable in international affairs because the relative power of countries is constantly shifting. Those which are becoming stronger demand concessions, while those which are declining have demands made on them. The usual method of adjustment is war; but the bloodshed and devastation, which do not alter the ultimate outcome, could be avoided if statesmen would abandon their rigid positions and considerations of national prestige and honour in favour of a more flexible approach based on a recognition of change and a willingness to negotiate their differences in a peaceful fashion. Carr quoted with approval Neville Chamberlain's defence of an empirical approach to foreign affairs:

> Surely if you are going to have a policy you must take the particular situations and consider what action or inaction is suitable for those particular situations. That is what I myself mean by policy, and it is quite clear that as the situations and conditions in foreign affairs continually change from day to day, your policy cannot be stated once and for all, if it is to be applicable to every situation that arises.[12]

Once the inevitability of change and the futility of trying to prevent it were recognized the way would be open to replace war by diplomatic bargaining. This had already occurred in domestic affairs:

> In the latter part of the nineteenth century and the first part of the twentieth the 'have nots' of most countries steadily improved their position through a series of strikes and negotiations, and the 'haves', whether through a sense of justice, or through fear of revolution in

[12] E. H. Carr, *The Twenty Years' Crisis 1919–1939* (London, 1939), p. 27.

the event of refusal, yielded ground rather than put the issue to the test of force. This process eventually produced on both sides a willingness to submit disputes to various forms of conciliation and arbitration, and ended by creating something like a regular system of 'peaceful change'.

If this were applied to international relations,

> once the dissatisfied Powers had realised the possibility of remedying grievances by peaceful negotiation (preceded no doubt in the first instance by threats of force), some regular procedure of 'peaceful change' might gradually be established and win the confidence of the dissatisfied; and that, once such a system had been recognised, conciliation would come to be regarded as a matter of course, and the threat of force, while never formally abandoned, would recede further into the background.[13]

Carr guarded himself against the charge that this was simply a doctrine of 'might is right' by claiming that in every dispute there must be some agreement about what is right and reasonable. But he also pointed out that this agreement would be ineffective unless the aggrieved country were strong enough to demand respect for its claims. In Germany's case, for example,

> the mass of political opinion in Great Britain and Germany (and in most other countries) agreed for many years that a criterion of justice and injustice could properly be applied to the Versailles Treaty; and there was a surprisingly considerable, though far from complete, consensus of opinion about the parts of it which were just and unjust respectively. Unfortunately, Germany was almost wholly deficient for fifteen years after the war in that power which is, as we have seen, a necessary motive force in political change.

As a result Germany had become '—not wholly without reason—almost wholly disillusioned about the role of morality in international politics'.[14] This unhelpful attitude could have been prevented if concessions had been made earlier, and in a better spirit, by the 'have' countries.

The ideas delineated by Carr were those which underlay the appeasers' approach to foreign affairs. Though it can easily be shown that the leaders of the National Government were pushed along by events and forced to recognize *faits accomplis* more often than they entered into genuine negotiations or made

[13] Ibid., p. 272.
[14] Ibid., p. 281.

carefully reasoned concessions, the conviction that change was inevitable, and peaceful change preferable to war, made them willing to acquiesce in the unilateral actions of the dictators and certainly sapped any inclination to resist them. As Lord Halifax explained to the House of Lords, it was not England's business to stop or even resist change but rather to ensure that 'no change should be made in Europe'—he might have said the world—'by violence or something approaching violence, that might lead to incalculable consequences'.[15] Leopold Amery, echoing Disraeli, pointed out that Britain's historical role was to be a mediatory and moderating power, trying to ensure that inevitable changes were made without war or that war was tempered as much as possible.[16] And it is significant that three of the Foreign Secretaries in the 1930s, Sir John Simon (1931–5), Sir Samuel Hoare (1935), and Lord Halifax (1938–40), had made their reputations by appeasing the Indian demands for more self-government.[17] These three, along with Neville Chamberlain who proudly identified his foreign policy with the conciliatory Liberal imperialism of his youth, made up the 'Big Four' who controlled foreign policy in the last years of the decade.

This connection between imperial and foreign policy, which was not confined to the leaders of the National Government, had important consequences for the Conservatives' approach to European affairs. Most of them continued to operate on the nineteenth-century assumption that Britain was, or should be, a great imperial power only marginally concerned with events on the Continent. This conviction that they could afford to take a detached view of European developments prevented them from realizing the potential danger to Britain from continental changes.

[15] 16 Mar. 1938. 108 H.L. Deb. 5s., col. 178.

[16] 2 May 1938. 335 H.C. Deb. 5s., col. 564.

[17] Sir John Simon was chairman of the Simon Commission which was set up in 1927 and reported in 1930, recommending: (1) an enlarged electorate in India; (2) a conference between the representatives of the British government, the government of India, and the ruling princes to decide the future form of the central government. Sir Samuel Hoare, as Secretary of State for India, was responsible for drawing up the Government of India Bill and piloting it through Parliament. Lord Halifax (as Lord Irwin: he succeeded to his father's title in 1934) was Viceroy in India from 1926 to 1931. In the 'Irwin declaration' of 1929 he stated that the natural issue of India's constitutional progress was dominion status.

Sophisticated imperialists like Leopold Amery, who still hoped to fulfil Joseph Chamberlain's ambition of making the Empire and Commonwealth a closed economic system, advocated their own form of appeasement which was designed to preserve and strengthen the Empire (thereby maintaining Britain's position in the world), solve Europe's economic and political problems and remove the most likely cause of war. This ambitious scheme was based on the premise that small national economic units were an anachronism in a world dominated by the United States and the Soviet Union, each of which had huge internal markets and resources. In order to survive the smaller countries would have to combine or co-operate to form larger units.[18] The British Commonwealth and Empire, with its common institutions and traditions, was an obvious unit; another was Europe west of Russia; and a third was the part of Asia surrounding industrialized Japan. Once the world was recognized into these large, self-sufficient groups, war, which was largely the result of economic rivalry, would be practically eliminated.

As far as the Continent was concerned the imperialists were particularly concerned to see some kind of co-operation in Central Europe, the 'earthquake zone', whose instability threatened to drag Europe into another major conflict like the Great War of 1914–18.[19] An economic and political union, which would contain adequate materials and markets, would turn the area into an important factor in the stability of the Continent.[20] As it was quite clear that these countries, left to themselves, were unwilling and incapable of devising some larger framework for their own mutual benefit, some English observers concluded that German domination would be preferable to the current unstable situation. Duncan Sandys, soon to be one of the opponents of appeasement, expressed the enlightened view of Central European problems in his maiden speech in the House of Commons on 2 May 1935. The ideal solution, he said, would be a Danubian Economic Federation among the successor states, or possibly a union with Hungary under a restored Habsburg monarchy. 'But, failing this, even a union with Germany would be preferable to the indefinite prolongation of the present dangerous state of

[18] L. S. Amery, 5 Feb. 1936. 308 H.C. Deb. 5s., col. 250.

[19] J. L. Garvin, 'Wanted—A New Policy', *Observer*, 14 Mar. 1937.

[20] Sir Edward Grigg, *Britain Looks at Germany* (London, 1938), p. 50.

8214871 D

uncertainty.'[21] And over two years later Leopold Amery was maintaining that 'any local arrangements of cooperation that Germany can achieve with Eastern Europe and with the colonies of all the colony-owning European powers . . . would contribute more than anything else towards a peaceful settlement in Europe'.[22] From the British standpoint Germany's role in bringing order to Central Europe was not only desirable but almost inevitable. This was the traditional area of German expansion; and considering her vitality in those depression years it would be foolish, and perhaps also dangerous, to frustrate her natural activity. The German minorities in the countries to the east and south of her borders were one more reason for allowing Germany to rehabilitate the region while solving the racial grievance. Mesmerized by conditions which had produced the First World War, Conservatives believed that the state of Central Europe presented a greater threat to European peace and order than the Nazi regime or the rapid increase in German armaments and territory.

German domination of Central Europe was also expected to bring some other benefits. The creation of a strong Middle Europe under German leadership would provide an effective bulwark against the expansion of Communist Russia. For J. L. Garvin this was reason enough for Britain to support the plan.[23] Another advantage would be that Germany's preoccupation with reconstructing the area would make it less likely to threaten the peace elsewhere. And perhaps this preoccupation would end the demands that Britain return the former German colonies which she had held under mandate from the League since the end of the First World War.[24] With Germany's Empire on the Continent and Britain's beyond the sea there was no reason why the two should ever clash. 'If we are for world peace in earnest,' counselled Garvin, 'we must refresh our imaginations, broaden our minds, and brace our moral courage. No jealous nor frightened motives should daunt or deter us. Let the German race, in its turn, have a mission.'[25] This is not to say, however,

[21] 2 May 1935. 301 H.C. Deb. 5s., col. 598.

[22] 'The Problem of the Cession of Mandated Territories in Relation to the World Situation' (Address at Chatham House, 20 Oct. 1936), *International Affairs*, vol. 16 (1937), p. 16.

[23] 'The Key of the World', *Observer*, 21 Mar. 1937.

[24] See L. S. Amery, *The German Colonial Claim* (London, 1939), *passim*.

[25] 'Wanted—A New Policy', *Observer*, 14 Mar. 1937.

that the British Government would stand aside cynically while Hitler conquered the countries to the east and the south. On the contrary, the British leaders insisted that change be effected by peaceful means. This insistence on peace, coupled with an acceptance of revision in Central and Eastern Europe and the optimistic assumption that the problems of that area could be dealt with without repercussions elsewhere, explains the calmness with which Hitler's annexation of Austria was received in Conservative circles. 'Some people', John McGovern of the Independent Labour Party charged, 'liken it to the development of the great trusts and combines in industry, commerce and banking, which gradually swallow the small man and say that we must expect the same policy to be pursued abroad by the large nations swallowing the small nations.'[26] It also goes a long way towards explaining the support for the Munich agreement which did not lack champions at the time. 'What Mr. Chamberlain did he did because it was right,' Scrutator wrote in the *Sunday Times*, 'not because we were unable to do anything else. And—this for our critics in Germany—it follows that in seeking to make ourselves stronger we have no wish to reverse our policy at Munich, but rather to confirm and strengthen it.'[27]

Much of the Conservative anti-French feeling in these years came from France's unwillingness to accept the view that events in Eastern Europe should be allowed to take their 'natural' course. France's obsessive and, from the British point of view, groundless, fear of Germany and her diplomatic engagements in the east which were designed to encircle Germany, threatened to drag Britain into a war to maintain the very *status quo* she wished to see altered. Even the most adamant isolationist-imperialists recognized that the territorial integrity of France and the Low Countries, which constituted the outer bulwarks of Britain's defences, were vital interests which could not be compromised;[28] but the very fact that France would have to be rescued if she got into trouble made the British suspicious of

[26] 24 Mar. 1938. 333 H.C. Deb. 5s., col. 1475.

[27] Scrutator, 'Parliament and Defence', *Sunday Times*, 30 Oct. 1938.

[28] As late as May 1938 Sir Edward Grigg, a prominent backbench imperialist, was arguing that Britain must retain absolute discretion to act as she thought right in any crisis short of invasion of France. Grigg, *Britain Looks at Germany*, p. 34.

every French move. Scrutator explained the difference between the outlooks of the two countries in 1935:

The underlying assumption of French policy in Eastern Europe is that the blessings are worthless in the West without some form of physical restraint on what Germany may do in the East, and that every local disagreement must be a world interest and every war a world war. It is a hard doctrine, especially for this country, which has no real interest in Eastern Europe, has no intention of taking an active part in defending a peace settlement in which she has ceased to believe and is, in addition, asked to compromise what might be some fair prospect of safety at home.[29]

As for the Franco-Soviet pact of 1935, a major attempt to counter Germany's strength with Russian assistance, Sir Austen Chamberlain reported that many right-wing Conservatives regarded it as 'almost a betrayal of Western Civilization'.[30]

Conservative dislike of the League of Nations also stemmed from the obligation of its members to help any of their number which was attacked. This pedantic legality, they claimed, actually put obstacles in the way of international accommodation and ensured that any war would become a world war. Had the principles of the League been applied rigidly in the past, Leopold Amery argued, the modern world would never have developed:

The Turkish Empire would still have to be maintained. India, whatever the chaos might be, as long as there was some decrepit representative of the Mogul surviving there owing his subscription to Geneva, would remain intact. . . . The realities of the world depend upon the necessities of government, of order and development, and whenever nations internally or externally are incapable of fulfilling those functions, they will go down against other nations whose need for peace and for development demand that there shall be order.[31]

In another speech against relying on the League in the event of attack he half-contradicted the assertion that the League prevented change: 'If we were the victims of unprovoked aggression to-day we might as well call on the Man in the Moon for help as make a direct appeal to the League.'[32] Amery was by no means the only Conservative who resented the League's challenge to

[29] *Sunday Times*, 31 Mar. 1935.

[30] Sir Austen Chamberlain to Count Vladimir d'Ormesson, 28 Mar. 1936. A.C. 41, folder 125.

[31] 27 Feb. 1933. 275 H.C. Deb. 5s., col. 82.

[32] 11 Mar. 1935. 299 H.C. Deb. 5s., cols. 100–1.

national sovereignty, disliked its association with international socialism and believed that its aims were hopelessly utopian as well as undesirable. And in attacking the international organization many Conservatives felt they were dealing an indirect blow to their political opponents, who put their hopes for the future in the League.

Conservative suspicion of the League of Nations Union, an organization for publicizing and gathering support for the League itself, was more justified. Even the moderate and courteous Sir Austen Chamberlain was moved to exclaim that the executive, of which he was a member, was composed of 'some of the worst cranks I have ever known and led by [Lord Robert] Cecil, they are ready to proclaim the proper solution of every problem and to dictate indifferently to His Majesty's Government or to the League how it should be handled'.[33] The average Conservative, noticing the Union's vigorous advocacy of pacifism and disarmament, regarded it with the same jaundiced eye that his counterpart twenty-five years later turned on the Campaign for Nuclear Disarmament. Leading members of the party, however, were more sensitive to its popularity and effective propaganda. 'We cannot afford to allow this mass of people to be captivated entirely by other parties', wrote Sir Austen Chamberlain, 'because they think we are uninterested or unfavourable to the League of Nations.'[34] In order to keep up appearances Chamberlain, who had acquired the reputation of a strong League of Nations man while Foreign Secretary, was persuaded by the party leaders and whips to join the Union's executive in 1932.[35] Having made this gesture to the Union's supporters Stanley Baldwin, himself an honorary vice-president, was careful not to commit his party any further. When he was invited to address a Union meeting in Birmingham he replied in his evasive fashion:

I should be reluctant to add to my work by an extra speech on Saturday night: but further than that, I have always avoided these meetings of the League, except one which I addressed in the Albert Hall—or maybe two. There is so much I dislike in the Union propaganda and I should have to steer between the Scylla of cursing

33 Sir Austen Chamberlain to Lord Tyrrell, 13 Feb. 1933. A.C. 40, folder 122.

34 Id. to F. S. Oliver, 3 Aug. 1933. Ibid.

35 Id. to Lord Tyrrell, 13 Feb. 1933; to F. S. Oliver, 3 Aug. 1933. Ibid.

them and the Charybdis of mush and poppycock, and I might be wrecked on either!

So I will beg you to say how I recognise the honour due me in asking but in view of heavy commitments . . . Thank you.[36]

After winning the 1935 election on a platform of supporting the League and collective security the National Government then seized on the 'failure' of the organization to deal with the Abyssinian problem as a pretext for repudiating collective security as unworkable. Sir Austen Chamberlain was allowed to resign from the Union's executive and Lord Milner's widow wrote expressing her relief that his name would no longer be used 'for the purposes of the Angells and Noel Bakers. They will now be left without conservatives and patriotic liberals and will appear in their true colours as disrupters of our country.'[37] Despite their ambiguous talk of 'reforming' the League (perhaps out of existence) Conservatives used its moribund condition to taunt their opponents. 'It is no good going on repeating "the League",' sneered Neville Chamberlain. 'We have to find practical means of restoring peace to the world.'[38]

One of the most important reasons that Conservatives did not want to become involved in a system of collective security was the fear that Britain might find herself fighting to defend Soviet Russia against Germany; and Conservative dislike and distrust of the U.S.S.R. in this period was as axiomatic as the Labour party's admiration.[39] Although many Conservatives liked neither the Nazi nor the Communist system, on balance they preferred Nazism, which did not present any great threat to the existing social order. Sir Edward Grigg wrote in May 1938:

[36] Stanley Baldwin to Sir Austen Chamberlain, 17 Feb. 1933. A.C. 40, folder 122.

[37] Lady Violet Milner to Sir Austen Chamberlain, 28 June 1936. A.C. 41, folder 125.

[38] 21 Oct. 1937. 327 H.C. Deb. 5s., col. 166.

[39] The importance of anti-Communism as a motive of British policy has been the subject of much dispute. Margaret George in *The Warped Vision: British Foreign Policy 1933–1939* (Pittsburgh, 1965) argues that the obsession with Communism prevented the British leaders from perceiving the Nazi danger. This has been disputed by Donald L. Lammers, who claims that 'the truth of the "Anti-Red hypothesis" (to give it its true name) has not been demonstrated—and, indeed, that there are some good (if not conclusive, grounds for thinking it false'. *Explaining Munich: The Search for Motive in British Foreign Policy* (Stanford, 1966). George has the better argument, on balance, though she presents it in an exaggerated form and a sensational manner.

In this Country Conservatives prefer the German system to the Russian because it is nationalistic in spirit and does not seek to undermine the unity of other nations by dividing them on class lines against themselves. But the Russian ideology, reinforcing the doctrine of Marx in a thousand insinuating forms, has undoubtedly turned much Socialist thought into the anti-patriotic channels which Jaurès denounced.[40]

Two years earlier a group of Conservatives, fearing that the Franco-Soviet pact would be extended to include Britain following the invasion of the Rhineland, put the following motion on the House of Commons's order paper:

That this House looks confidently to His Majesty's Government to eschew any military or other commitments which have the appearance of an alliance between Great Britain and France and the Soviet Union and adheres firmly to the desire for close relations between Great Britain, Germany, and France, which was stressed by the Prime Minister in this House on 23 June.[41]

This antipathy towards the U.S.S.R. lasted right into the Second World War, but it is significant that the National Government played down its unwillingness to work with that country whenever Germany appeared menacing and revived it once the danger passed. 'One could make a chart,' said Clement Attlee in the spring of 1939, 'almost like a chart of a patient in a hospital, showing the movement towards some kind of agreement with Russia going up and down, not dependent on the will of this Government, but on the course of external events. Temperature is very low while events do not seem to be very dangerous, but at the least sign of crisis it rises rapidly.'[42]

The prejudice against the Soviet Union completely undermined the National Government's claim that it had no aversion to working with governments of different political complexions and would not allow the pacification of the world to turn on such irrelevant considerations as admiration or dislike for the regimes with which it had to deal. Taking an objective, relativist, and realistic view, leaders of the National Government were fond of asserting that the citizens of other countries were entitled to

[40] Grigg, *Britain Looks at Germany*, p. 14.

[41] *Notices on Motions, Questions, and Orders of the Day*, 29 June 1936. Other names were added on 1 and 6 July, bringing the total number of subscribers to 48.

[42] 19 May 1939. 347 H.C. Deb. 5s., col. 1834.

choose their own form of government without reference to the British standard; but in practice the British leaders disliked some regimes more than others. They had considerable sympathy and even admiration for the Italian system; less for the German, though they hoped that in time it would mellow and mature along Italian lines;[43] but for the Russian system there was nothing but thinly disguised fear and hatred. Neville Chamberlain, who was so proud of his personal contacts with Hitler and Mussolini, never made any attempt to deal directly with Stalin.

These are the elements of Conservative thought which the leaders of the National Government shared and the general framework of ideas within which appeasement was developed. Until the eve of the war these views were championed not only by politicians but also by such influential journalists as J. L. Garvin in his weekly *Observer* editorial, 'Scrutator' in the *Sunday Times*,[44] Geoffrey Dawson and Robert Barrington-Ward, the editor and assistant editor of *The Times*, and a host of others.[45] However the actions of the British Government in these years are appraised it cannot be denied that its approach was in harmony with the bulk of informed opinion and widely accepted ideas about the aims and methods of foreign policy. Even the Opposition stood closer to the Administration's position than its apologists cared to admit later. In February 1938 Arthur Henderson Jr., speaking for the Labour party, told the House of Commons: 'There is no hon. Member on this side of the House who has any objection to the policy of general appeasement to which the Prime Minister referred. The sooner the nations of the world can come together in an attempt to deal with the political and economic problems which confront civilization to-day the more likely we shall be to avoid the conflagration which appears to many people to be inevitable.'[46] Appeasement cannot be dis-

[43] This view was held even by Sir Austen Chamberlain. Petrie, *Life and Letters of Sir Austen Chamberlain*, ii. 394.

[44] The weekly 'Scrutator' article was written by Herbert Sidebotham, who had previously been on the staff of the *Manchester Guardian, The Times*, and oher journals. He also contributed a series of light essays to the *Daily Sketch* under the name 'Candidus'. Sidebotham began writing the 'Scrutator' articles in 1921 and continued to his death in 1940.

[45] Garvin was in close contact with Neville Chamberlain at this time, as he was writing the life of Joseph Chamberlain. Geoffrey Dawson was a close friend of Stanley Baldwin, Neville Chamberlain, and Lord Halifax.

[46] 21 Feb. 1938. 332 H.C. Deb. 5s., col. 86.

missed simply as a reflex decision to follow the line of least resistance in response to events for lack of a well thought-out policy. The leaders of the National Government were no better but no worse than the general run of politicians, and their goals were as well defined as those of most governments, even if events did get ahead of them with alarming frequency. Nor can the 'defence' of appeasement as a necessary expedient to buy time for rearmament be taken seriously. That was a justification invoked only when the Administration's conduct could not be defended on any other grounds. And the rearmament, even in the spring and summer of 1939, was not very impressive.

Certain that events were unfolding in a satisfactory manner and that their diplomatic activities were contributing to this happy situation, the leaders of the National Government refused to accept the fatalistic attitude that Britain was on a collision course with Germany in which no accommodation was possible. This optimism, while explicable, seems unwarranted, defensive, and contrived, to a later observer. In every crisis the British Government chose the optimistic interpretation of what was at best an ambiguous event, uncritically accepted the dictators' assurances about their future conduct and considerably exaggerated their own achievements. The Anglo-Italian agreement of 16 April 1938, which recognized Mussolini's conquest of Abyssinia and gave him a free hand in Spain in return for his 'goodwill', and the surrender of the Irish treaty ports, hardly seem like diplomatic triumphs; but at the time Neville Chamberlain boasted to the House of Commons:

> I should imagine that it would be necessary to go a very long way back in our Parliamentary history to find another occasion on which it has been possible for a Minister in the course of a single week to put forward for the approval of the House two agreements between this country and another country, each of which constitutes the termination of a long and painful difference.[47]

By the reasonableness and commonsense of its pronouncements, too, the Cabinet managed to create the impression that affairs were in competent hands. When the Government recognized the necessity of doing something about rearmament in 1934 Stanley Baldwin confided to the House of Commons in his monosyllabic way: 'I am also certain, I have said so before, that there is no

[47] 5 May 1938. 335 H.C. Deb. 5s., col. 1071.

danger in the near future before this country. There may be less danger than we imagine, and the preparations we are making now are in more than ample time.'[48] This assurance, while it gave rise to later charges that the National Government had misled the country about foreign dangers, was certainly sufficient for most M.P.s at the time. 'So much are hon. Members reassured,' Winston Churchill exclaimed in 1937, 'that it is a matter of public comment that it is difficult to keep a House when the gravest matters are being discussed.'[49]

To criticize an Administration which could present its policies in such comforting terms and which commanded an overwhelming majority of loyal adherents was no easy task. Yet while eighty Conservative back-benchers were willing to resist the Government of India Bill to the utmost of their abilities in these circumstances, only twenty could be induced to abstain from the division on Munich. Part of the difference, of course, was due to the fact that foreign affairs were more ambiguous than the Indian issue, on which every member had a clear opinion. In Hitler's case, for example (and it would have been easier for the critics and the Government if there had been only one dictator threatening the international order), every demand and every move until the seizure of Prague could be interpreted either as an attempt to redress the legitimate grievances of a dissatisfied major power or as one more step in a programme of unlimited German expansion.[50] The German demand for equality of armaments seemed reasonable enough, especially since the victors in the First World War had not disarmed. The reoccupation of the Rhineland in 1936 also seemed justified: the Germans, after all, were simply going into their own back yard and the move was accompanied by impressive-sounding guarantees about their future conduct. Austria in 1938 was an independent, German-speaking country which, notwithstanding the treaty of St. Germain, should be allowed to decide its own relationship with the adjoining Reich. And when Hitler claimed the German-speaking part of Czechoslovakia following the absorption of Austria he could appeal to

48 18 May 1934. 289 H.C. Deb. 5s., col. 2141.

49 4 Mar. 1937. 321 H.C. Deb. 5s., col. 578.

50 Hans J. Morganthau, *Politics Among Nations: The Struggle for Power and Peace*. 2nd edn. (New York, 1955), pp. 63–4.

the principle of self-determination enshrined in the treaty of Versailles. Despite the plan laid down in *Mein Kampf* (no complete version of which was available in English), only adamant Germanophobes maintained the compromise was impossible between Germany and the other countries of Europe. The xenophobic *National Review*, for instance, declared at the end of 1932:

It makes not a tattle of difference to us what sort of German politicians are in power. Whoever they are, they will work unceasingly to recover their pre-war frontiers, they will continue to rearm, whatever they may promise, and they will be the consistent enemies of peace and good European order as they have been since Prussia acquired the hegemony of the German peoples.[51]

But this despairing attitude did not commend itself to most of those who were concerned with foreign policy as directors or commentators. With only slight exaggeration it might be said that there were no anti-appeasers before Munich. Certainly there was less fundamental disagreement over foreign policy within the Conservative party than some memoirs would suggest.

Even those who stand out as the strongest opponents had more doubts and hesitations than they cared to admit later. Anthony Eden, for example, told Harold Nicolson three weeks before the reoccupation of the Rhineland that in seeking to avert another war he was 'prepared to make great concessions to German appetites provided they will sign a disarmament treaty and join the League of Nations. His idea is to work for this during the next three years and then suddenly to put it before the League.'[52] Eden was more specific in his remarks to the cabinet:

Are we prepared, for instance, to recognize that Germany should have special trading privileges in certain areas, e.g., the Danube Basin? Are we prepared to surrender our most-favoured-nation right in order that this may be brought about? Are we prepared in certain circumstances to consider a guaranteed loan to Germany? Are we prepared to consider the return to Germany, under mandate or otherwise, of even one of the colonies taken from her during the war? Are we prepared, more particularly if the German Government

[51] 'Episodes of the Month', Dec. 1932. The journal reiterated its position after Hitler became Chancellor: 'Whether Brüning, von Schleicher, Hitler or any other, German or Austrian, is the Chancellor of the Reich, we have to deal with an enemy to European peace.' 'Episodes of the Month', Mar. 1938.

[52] Harold Nicolson, diary entry, 13 Feb. 1936. Harold Nicolson, *Diaries and Letters 1930–1939*, ed. Nigel Nicolson (London, 1966), p. 243.

devalue the mark, to resist the probable pressure from interested parties in this country demanding the further exclusion of German goods from the British market? Are we prepared to consider with France and Belgium the abandonment of the demilitarised zone? Are we prepared, in fact, to approach Germany with proposals to collaborate so far as possible in a new period of European tranquillity and economic reconstruction, instead of as hitherto waiting for her 'claims' and 'repudiations'?[53]

These reflections were inspired by Sir Robert Vansittart, the Permanent Under-Secretary at the Foreign Office, to whose memorandum they were attached. Vansittart, whose name became practically synonymous with anti-Germanism in the Second World War, had been privately urging treaty revision since the beginning of the decade.[54] By 1936 he had reached the conclusion that there was no point in 'trying to be friends with Germany and at the same time insulting her, à la Duff Cooper, and that she will never be content until she regains her lost colonies. If we ever want lasting peace we must restore them to her.'[55] He was even more conciliatory towards Italy.

The most adamant opponent of any colonial appeasement was Leopold Amery, who maintained that 'there is no case which can be regarded, on closer examination, as justifying the German demand for colonial retrocession, and, on the other hand, an overwhelmingly strong case for the native populations concerned, and, secondly, on the grounds of our own safety and existence as an Empire, against any concession to that demand.'[56] But Amery had no objection to appeasing Germany at the expense of Central and Eastern Europe though he deplored the means by which Hitler acquired those areas. And until the end of the decade he was an eloquent spokesman for Italy's grievances. In the light of this record it is hard to understand A. L. Rowse's claim that Amery was 'consistently opposed to appeasement: throughout the whole of that deplorable decade he was more right than any other front-bench figure [*sic*], even than Churchill with whom

[53] Anthony Eden, *Germany: Memorandum by the Secretary of State for Foreign Affairs*, 11 Feb. 1936. Cab. 24/260.

[54] See Sir Robert Vansittart, *An Aspect of International Relations in 1931*, 14 May 1931. Cab. 24/221.

[55] Sir Henry Channon, diary entry, 7 July 1936. Sir Henry Channon, *Chips: The Diaries of Sir Henry Channon*, ed. Robert Rhodes James (London, 1967), pp. 68–9. See also the diary entry for 26 Feb. 1937.

[56] Amery, *The German Colonial Claim*, p. 175.

he fought side by side in vain'.[57] In fact Churchill and Amery were usually opposed on foreign policy until Munich and even afterwards they did not work very closely together.

Churchill himself delivered a powerful indictment of appeasement in 1936, when he accused the Government of continuing 'to adhere to a policy which was adapted to one set of circumstances after an entirely different set of circumstances had supervened'. Unable to leave this eloquent charge alone he added: 'They persisted in spite of all we could say to the contrary. I suppose they resented the warnings which were given, although the warnings which I gave to the House were sober warnings and friendly warnings.'[58] Yet only two months before Hitler came to power Churchill had laid down the principle: 'The removal of the just grievances of the vanquished ought to precede the disarmament of the victors.'[59] Nor was this simply an empty formula to support his demands for rearmament: in the same speech Churchill revealed that he had in mind such grievances as Transylvania and the Danzig Corridor. It was not until the invasion of the Rhineland that he emerged as a firm opponent of appeasing Germany; and even afterwards he continued to hope that Hitler would settle down and become a good European. Like most Conservatives too, he favoured conciliating Mussolini so that Britain could count the powerful Italian state among its friends.

All this does not mean that there were no Conservatives who were troubled by the deteriorating international situation and by the National Government's handling of foreign affairs. But it does indicate that very few critics opposed the Administration continuously and that the dissenters had no well-thought-out position when a crisis struck. Even more than the Government they were caught unprepared by events and reacted to them in an *ad hoc* manner. This was brought home to Basil Liddel Hart during the course of a dinner with Duff Cooper, Winston Churchill, J. F. C. Fuller, and Viscount Trenchard on 14 February 1936. Afterwards he reflected:

A very stimulating evening yet it had a rather depressing effect. For here one had several of the outstanding men in the realm of defence for the past generation—much bigger minds certainly than the

[57] A. L. Rowse, *All Souls and Appeasement* (London, 1961), p. 1.
[58] 10 Mar. 1936. 309 H.C. Deb. 5s., col. 2005.
[59] 23 Nov. 1932. 272 H.C. Deb. 5s., col. 89.

present heads of the Services—yet much of the discussion was chaotic, some times rhetorical rather than reasoned, and often marked by an obvious failure to grasp the point. Much of the talk showed clearly the want of a scientific habit of thought in past study and a lack of precision of thought in treating the points now.[60]

The critics of appeasement did, however, have certain common attitudes and assumptions which lay behind their approach to foreign affairs. The feature which most distinguished them from most members of the Conservative party was their Francophilia. Sir Austen Chamberlain, who professed to love France 'like a woman', was probably the most prominent Francophile in the House of Commons, but Winston Churchill with his cry 'Thank God for the French Army', Duff Cooper, and Brigadier-General E. L. Spears were not far behind. Their disposition naturally led them to share the French suspicion of Germany. When Hitler came to power and began issuing his threats they adopted the position that German grievances could not be considered under such conditions and urged the former allies to stand by the treaty of Versailles which many Englishmen felt was morally bankrupt. Sir Austen Chamberlain, who had never seriously been affected by misgivings about the treaty, consistenly maintained that the settlement was no worse than that concluded at the end of any major war. On one typical occasion he replied to a critic who disagreed with him: 'It is very easy to criticise the Treaty of Versailles and call it a dictated peace. Will my hon. Friend tell me what treaty following upon a war was not a dictated peace?'[61] Effective though this might have been in debate it was no real answer to those who felt they were living in a new diplomatic era. Nor were those who believed in the justice of Germany's claims, regardless of her present ruler and political system, moved by General Spear's denial of those claims at the end of 1933: 'To talk of Treaty revision now is like throwing matches into gun-powder.'[62]

To protest that appeasement was the wrong course to take in existing circumstances was one thing; to devise an alternative policy to replace it quite another. The obvious alternative, which formed the basis of the dissenters' case, was the traditional

[60] B. H. Liddell Hart, *Memoirs* (London, 1965), i. 305–6.
[61] 21 Dec. 1933. 284 H.C. Deb. 5s., col. 1533.
[62] 21 Dec. 1933. Ibid., col. 1517.

argument that Britain must preserve the balance of power in Europe as a guarantee of its own security. This was best articulated by Winston Churchill at a meeting of the Conservative party Foreign Affairs Committee in March 1936: 'For four hundred years the foreign policy of England has been to oppose the strongest, most aggressive, most dominating Power on the Continent, and particularly to prevent the Low Countries falling into the hands of such a Power.' He laid particular stress on the continuing relevance of that doctrine:

I know of nothing which has occurred to alter or weaken the justice, wisdom, valour and prudence upon which our ancestors acted. I know of nothing which has happened to human nature which in the slightest degree alters the validity of their conclusions. I know of nothing in military, political, economic, or scientific fact which makes me feel that we might not, or cannot, march along the same road.

Churchill was careful to point out that this was not a specifically anti-German policy:

The question is not whether it is Spain, or the French Monarchy, or the German Empire, or the Hitler régime. It has nothing to do with rulers or nations; it is concerned solely with whoever is the strongest or the potentially dominating tyrant. Therefore, we should not be afraid of being accused of being pro-French, or anti-German. If the circumstances were reversed, we could equally be pro-German or anti-French. It is a law of public policy which we are following, and not a mere expedient dictated by accidental circumstances, or likes and dislikes, or any other sentiment.[63]

Nevertheless, the practical conclusion to be drawn from this doctrine was that Britain should become more involved in European affairs and direct its efforts to building an alliance to contain Germany. But the National Government had not the slightest intention of opposing German expansion in the east or dividing Europe into two armed camps like those which had lurched into war in 1914. Churchill's audience probably also reflected that the policy he was advocating had involved the country in a series of major continental wars since the time of Elizabeth I. For most people the problem was not to prepare for the next round in this seemingly endless cycle but to find a way of escaping the historical pattern.

[63] Churchill, *The Gathering Storm*, pp. 207–8.

In order to make their policy more acceptable the Conservative critics tried to incorporate it into the framework of the League of Nations. Here again they took the French view of the League as a Concert of Europe designed to maintain the peace with the support of the member states' armies rather than the left-wing view that it was the mediator and potential government for the whole world or the conventional Conservative view that it was at best a forum for discussion and the adjustment of minor disputes. General Spears, who advocated armed collective security throughout the decade, warned that an unarmed League was like the Amphictyonic League which had met at Delphi to talk and could do little else. Ultimately this led to the domination of Greece by Rome, a strong external power. 'Hon. members would do well to ponder that episode.'[64] But while younger members like Spears and Paul Emrys-Evans might argue that machinery was now at hand to stop aggression, as it had not been in 1914, this was not a case which most Conservatives could accept. Though they were always willing to support rearmament for the defence of Britain and the Empire they were not convinced that either was in danger from Germany's empire-building on the Continent. As nationalists and imperialists they were also unwilling to surrender any of the country's sovereignty to the League which, in their mind, could never stand for anything but pacifism, disarmament, and world socialism. Nor were they convinced by the distinction between an alliance for peace and a coalition directed against Germany. On the eve of the war Churchill tried to refute this impression:

> I shall be told, 'But this is the encirclement of Germany.' I say, 'No, this is the encirclement of an aggressor.' Nations who are bound by the Covenant can never, however peaceful they may be, menace the peace and independence of any other state. This is the essence of the conditions which bring them together. To form a war combination against a single state would be a crime. To form a combination for mutual defence against a probable aggressor is not only no crime, but the highest moral duty and virtue. We ask no security for ourselves that we are not prepared to extend to Germany.[65]

But again it must have seemed that he was a bellicose advocate

[64] 13 Dec. 1933. 284 H.C. Deb. 5s., col. 461.

[65] Speech at the Manchester Free Trade Hall, 9 May 1939. Winston S. Churchill, *Blood, Sweat, and Tears* (New York, 1941), p. 24.

of preventive war who did not realize that a new era had dawned in international affairs. *The Times* said of the critics after Munich: 'They still believe in power politics: they have learned nothing from 1914 and nothing from 1919.'[66]

The Conservative advocates of armed collective security did nothing to endear themselves to the rest of the party by their attitude towards the Soviet Union. It is true that some of them, like Harold Macmillan and Robert Boothby, admired the planned Russian economy and that in 1937 Winston Churchill declared that he preferred Communism to Nazism, although 'I hope not to be called upon to survive in a world under a Government of either of these dispositions' ('You would not', called out James Maxton),[67] but they were no less anti-Communist than their colleagues. They were, however, more willing to swallow their dislike of the Russian dictatorship and, like the French, consider the U.S.S.R. an acceptable ally for restraining Germany. While they were not enthusiastic about a close connection between Britain and the Soviet Union they did argue that the vital interests of the two countries did not conflict at any point and that Russia sorely needed peace to deal with her internal problems.[68] Since the U.S.S.R. was too preoccupied with domestic matters to pose an international threat, the British Government should not ignore or reject the advances of a major power concerned to maintain the peace. But above all the dissenters were determined that Britain should not be manœuvred into an anti-Russian crusade promoted by Germany[69]—an aspiration exactly contrary to that of most Conservatives. Nevertheless it must be recorded that there was no really vocal group urging the Government to make overtures to the Soviet Union before Munich.

Looking back on the 1930s the policy that Winston Churchill christened 'arms and the Covenant' seems an impressive and obvious alternative to appeasement. It has certainly been commended highly by historians. But the radical departure from Conservative orthodoxy in that decade which it involved explains why so few members of the party and they only late in the decade,

[66] Editorial, 'A Drive for Peace', 19 Oct. 1938.
[67] 14 Apr. 1937. 322 H.C. Deb. 5s., col. 1063.
[68] Winston Churchill, 13 July 1934. 292 H.C. Deb. 5s., col. 732.
[69] Paul Emrys-Evans, 5 Nov. 1936. 317 H.C. Deb. 5s., col. 330.

8214871 E

adopted it. Winston Churchill did not become its champion until 1936; Sir Austen Chamberlain went to his grave unconverted in 1937; so that for the most part it was promoted by young, relatively obscure members, who carried little weight in the party. And the fact that the Liberal and Labour parties came to adopt a similar policy made it doubly suspect to the other Conservatives.

II. THE CRISES

3. Dangers Seen and Unseen

SCARCELY had the National Government been formed than an international crisis was created by Japan's seizure of the nominally Chinese province of Manchuria on 18 September 1931. This event is often identified as the first step on the road to the Second World War: the Western Democracies, it is argued, by failing to stop Japan and to support the League of Nations in taking a firm line against the aggressor, created a precedent for Hitler and Mussolini and neglected the opportunity to build up the machinery for collective security that could be used against them. But at the time of the seizure British politicians were too concerned with domestic problems to pay much attention to foreign affairs at all, much less to developments in an obscure corner of the Far East. The Government was preoccupied with attempts to balance the budget by cutting salaries, pensions, and unemployment benefits. As a result of the reduction in naval pay there was a 'mutiny' (more accurately, passive resistance) in the fleet at Invergordon on 15 September. Six days later the country went off the gold standard in spite of the fact that the National Government had been formed to 'save the pound'. These exciting events ensured that few people appreciated the significance which *The Economist* attached to the Manchurian episode: 'China is relying, in this crisis, on the League Covenant and on the Kellogg Pact, and if these instruments are not proved to be effective in this test, what are the prospects of international economic reconstruction by co-operative effort? This, surely, is the heart of the matter.'[1] Only later, when all possibility of effective action had faded, did the debate over Manchuria really wax hot: and then there were loud cries for moral and economic sanctions against Japan.[2]

The leading members of the Conservative party, without exception, believed that Japan had good grounds for its action. Pointing out that 'to treat China as a political unit is to betray the most complete ignorance of everything pertaining to the Far East',

[1] 'The League and Manchuria', *The Economist*, 17 Oct. 1931.

[2] For a carefully documented study of this phenomenon see R. Bassett, *Democracy and Foreign Policy: A Case History: The Sino-Japanese Dispute 1931–33* (London, 1952).

the *Saturday Review* claimed that 'every schoolboy knows that the only part of the Chinese Republic where life and property are safe is where they are protected by Japanese bayonets'.[3] Most Conservatives regarded Japan as a traditionally friendly country whose co-operation was essential to the maintenance of the British empire in the Far East, a guarantor of stability and order in that part of the world and 'a force against Bolshevism in China and revolutionary Nationalism in India'.[4]

Sir Austen Chamberlain, who acted as the National Government's conscience on foreign affairs, began by supporting Japan's seizure of Manchuria. Britain, he maintained, had 'every reason to remember with pride and satisfaction' its association with the island race of Japan, 'in some of whose circumstances we can see so great a likeness to our own'. While recognizing that his own country, as a member of the League of Nations, had to take its part in judging the case and 'bringing the moral influence of the world to bear on Japan', he hoped that the Administration would do 'nothing to prevent the restoration to the full of the old Anglo-Japanese friendship'.[5] Chamberlain's sympathies gradually shifted from Japan to China as the situation developed in Manchuria, but he continued to oppose any unilateral British disapproval of Japan's action. In particular he warned members of the Opposition to refrain from urging the country to thrust itself into the struggle between China and Japan—'and thrusting it with no international mandate and as no part of any common international action'.[6]

Winston Churchill had none of Sir Austen's hesitations. He supported wholeheartedly a move which would bring law and order to one province of the crumbling Chinese empire: 'It is in the interests of the whole world that law and order should be established in Northern China. Anarchy and Communism had caused widespread misery to countless Chinese people.' Arguing that 'China is in the same state that India would be in if the guiding hand of British rule were withdrawn', he had 'no doubt whatsoever that the Northern Province of China, to which Japan gives a very considerable measure of orderly government, is the

[3] 'Half a League Backwards', 31 Oct. 1931.
[4] 'Notes of the Week', *Saturday Review*, 7 Jan. 1933.
[5] 22 Mar. 1932. 263 H.C. Deb. 5s., col. 912.
[6] 27 Feb. 1933. 275 H.C. Deb. 5s., col. 69.

least unhappy of all the provinces of China at the present time'. He also warned against any British involvement on either side: 'It is necessary for us to secure an open door for our trade and a fair chance for our merchants. A clear-sighted policy should be able to secure that without any risk that would involve war'.[7]

Those Conservatives who disliked the League of Nations took comfort from Japan's action in striking a blow at the hated institution. 'A modicum of good sense and clear sight', exulted the *Saturday Review*, 'should have taught the League to keep its fingers from between the hammer of Japan and the anvil of China.'[8] The Lytton Commission and the League's hostile attitude towards Japan appeared as unwarranted intrusions into the affairs of a major power; and nationalistic Conservatives were not anxious to create precedents of that kind. Leopold Amery maintained:

> Had it not been for the League of Nations, Japan and China might long ago have come to some reasonable accommodation in Manchuria, and Japan would have been contented to ask for a good deal less than she is going to ask and going to get today. I venture to say that if China is plunged into a disastrous war with Japan, is it largely due to her misguided reliance upon the League of Nations.[9]

The *Saturday Review* also made Conservative flesh creep by invoking fears of Communism: 'Behind China, it may be noted, stands Russia, whose soldiers have already been found fighting in the uniforms of the Celestial Army'.[10]

The hapless Sir John Simon, who became Foreign Secretary in November 1931 (Lord Reading having held the office since August), had no choice but to keep the country out of any danger of war. Pressing domestic problems, combined with indifference or hostility towards China, precluded any serious talk about using force or taking any steps which might result in military action. As Scrutator wrote in the *Sunday Times*: 'The reason this country did not invoke sanctions against Japan in Manchuria was that neither the Government nor the people were so vitally interested in Manchuria's political future as to run risks

[7] Address to his constituents at Waltham Cross, 27 February 1933. Reported in *The Times*, 28 Feb. 1933.

[8] 'Notes of the Week', 1 Oct. 1932.

[9] 27 Feb. 1933. 275 H.C. Deb. 5s., col. 83.

[10] 'No Manchurian Adventures', 14 Nov. 1931.

for it. Sanctions would have meant war, and had war come it would have been the most unpopular and, possibly, one of the most disastrous in our history.'[11] But Simon's cautious conduct earned him nothing but abuse from all sides. The *New Statesman* compared his 'complacency' to that of a policeman 'who watches a street fight and talks hopefully of the probability that sooner or later the combatants will leave off fighting and the stronger keep the spoils'.[12] The liberal Conservative *Spectator* also expressed annoyance that Simon was not taking a firmer stand at Geneva: 'Has he been urging that the plain implications of the Covenant should be followed, and if so in what quarters has he met with resistance? Or has he been merely working for some compromise formula that would save Japan's face and deprive China of the support she has a right to expect from her fellow signatories of the Covenant and the Kellogg Pact?[13] On the other hand, Simon was criticized by right-wing Conservatives for dealing with the League at all. The *English Review* which had found it a 'source of satisfaction that a man of his ability should be appointed to the Foreign Office,'[14] soon became Simon's bitter opponent: 'Perhaps the very qualities which have made him a great advocate unfit him in some measure for the office of Foreign Secretary. He appears to treat an international problem as if it were a brief, and he displays a complete lack of interest in the psychology of those with whom he is dealing.'[15]

While the League was dying in the night unmourned by those who later tried to revive it, a more important event occurred closer to home when Adolph Hitler became Chancellor of Germany on 30 January 1933. This evoked little concern from British observers at the time. Indeed the *New Statesman* was arguing as late as 1935 that Japan presented a more serious threat to peace than Germany: 'What a rearmed Germany might do, if the world fails to organise for peace, ten or fifteen years hence, is beyond the range of our vision. Our case is rather that a conflagration on any scale is conceivable within the next two or three years only if Japan gives the signal.'[16] This was not the

[11] 20 May 1934.
[12] 'Current Comments', 26 Mar. 1932.
[13] 'Paris and Manchuria', 28 Nov. 1931.
[14] 'Foreign Affairs', Dec. 1931.
[15] 'Current Comments', Apr. 1933.
[16] 'Policy and Armaments', 16 Mar. 1935.

last occasion in the decade in which concentration on one development helped to obscure the significance of the next.

One of the reasons that Hitler was not taken seriously at first was that he seemed to be the captive of his political associates. *The Economist* doubted that Hitler could keep his place in the saddle with 'Freiherr von Papen perched on the cropper behind him and digging in his East-Prussian spurs. For the steed is the German people—a mighty, apocalyptic beast which is just realising that it has recovered its strength.'[17] The *Spectator* thought the Administration would soon collapse and, 'in no way directly affected by the change in Germany, we can watch impending developments in the hope, if in no great confidence, that they may somehow make for stability. It is as well that Hitlerism should be put to the ultimate test.'[18] But the most remarkable prediction came from the *New Statesman*: 'We shall not expect to see the Jews exterminated, or the power of big finance overthrown. There will doubtless be an onslaught on the Communists; but if it is pressed to extremes it will provoke a powerful resistance, and may even result in a "united Marxist front" which will give the Nazis and their allies more than they bargained for.'[19] Even after Hitler had established his dictatorship there was less apprehension among Conservatives than among Liberals or Labourites. Sir Charles Petrie, writing in the right-wing *English Review*, observed complacently, 'Revolutions are messy affairs, but in contrast with those in Russia, France and Spain, the Nazi assumption of power was peaceful in the extreme.'[20] At the other end of the party the *Spectator* was alarmed at the disappearance of individual liberty in Germany: 'All the guarantees of the constitution have been suspended, and no one knows for how long. Methods, not merely of suppression but of brute force, are to be employed against the Government's enemies . . . Equally repugnant to all sense of decency is the renewal of the characteristic Nazi attack on the Jews to whom much of the prosperity and culture of modern Germany is due.' But the journal remained confident that a democratic Germany would re-emerge even though 'there is a chapter of force to live through first, and force wielded by incompetents can be a tragic business'.[21]

[17] 'Hitler in the Saddle', 4 Feb. 1933.
[18] 'Hitlerism on Trial', 3 Feb. 1933.
[19] 4 Feb. 1933.
[20] 'Foreign Affairs', Aug. 1933.
[21] 'News of the Week', *Spectator*, 3 Mar. 1933.

Many people were genuinely puzzled about the new Germany. Anthony Crossley, a young Conservative M.P., told the House of Commons shortly after Hitler came to power that he had seen some things on a visit to Germany that he would have liked to see copied in Britain: the files kept on the unemployed and their qualifications, the food canteens, and the labour exchanges.[22] A year and a half later another back-bencher, Robert Bower, reported on his return form Germany: 'Above all, Nazism is a movement of youth. Have we been so successful in solving our lesser post-War problems that we can afford to be unsympathetic to a genuine effort of German youth to repair in its own way a shattered world for the condition of which it is in no way responsible?'[23]

Sir Austen Chamberlain saw in Germany a confirmation of his worst fears about that country. Characterizing this new German nationalism as 'the worst of the all-Prussian Imperialism with an added savagery, a racial pride, an exclusiveness which cannot allow to any fellow-subject not of "pure Nordic birth" equality of rights and citizenship within the nation to which he belongs', he asserted that Europe could not afford to listen to Germany's pleas for revision and equality. 'Are you going to discuss with such a Government the Polish Corridor? The Polish Corridor is inhabited by Poles; do you dare put another Pole under the heel of such a Government?'[24] Chamberlain's remarks were warmly applauded by various sections of the House but his audience soon recovered from its passing indignation with Nazi Germany, and the talk of revision, equality, and justice for that ill-treated country was soon revived. As for Sir Austen, he continued to make these kind of speeches in the vain hope that they would induce the Nazis to follow the more moderate line of Italian Fascism.[25]

Winston Churchill's attitude towards Nazi Germany was more ambiguous. While recognizing the threat which such a country posed to European peace he was also fascinated by the character and accomplishments of Hitler. In 1935 he wrote:

> Although no subsequent political action can condone wrong deeds, history is replete with examples of men who have risen to power by

[22] 2 Mar. 1933. 275 H.C. Deb. 5s., col. 666.
[23] Letter to the editor of *The Times*, 19 Sept. 1934.
[24] 13 Apr. 1933. 276 H.C. Deb. 5s., col. 2759.
[25] Petrie, *Life and Letters of Sir Austen Chamberlain*, ii. 394.

employing stern, grim and even frightful methods, but who nevertheless, when their life is revealed as a whole, have been regarded as great figures whose lives have enriched the story of mankind. So may it be with Hitler.[26]

And in 1937 he observed: 'One may dislike Hitler's system and yet admire his patriotic achievement. If our country were defeated I hope we should find a champion as indomitable to restore our courage and lead us back to our place among the nations.'[27] Churchill's fascination with the German dictator did not, of course, make him 'pro-Hitler' like many Conservatives or lead him to the conclusion that Hitler could or should be appeased. Indeed, the reaction of Churchill, Chamberlain, and a few other back-benchers to Nazism was to deny the case for treaty revision and to advocate a form of containment.

Churchill, who devised the slogan 'arms and the Covenant', was no sudden convert to the policy it described. He had shown no enthusiasm for the League during the Manchurian crisis. In fact during the first few years of the decade he followed a rather orthodox isolationist line, trusting that Britain could keep out of European affairs and rely on the French army to keep the peace there. Developing the case for the closest possible co-operation between the English-speaking peoples in 1932 he asserted that Britain should not undertake any further engagements on the Continent beyond those which the United States would be prepared to support—in practical terms, none.[28] And in the same speech he warned against the folly of expecting too much from the League: 'He is a bad friend to the League who would set it tasks beyond its compass.' In March 1933 he was still arguing against Continental involvements, claiming that he would rather see the country have far larger defence estimates and be free to choose its own course than do anything about rearmament that would commit it to a closer association with France.[29] In November of that year he announced his conversion to a new policy and took the occasion to attack those who mocked the League because it had been incapable of dealing with the situation in the Far East. Its failure there did not mean that it could

26 'Hitler and His Choice', in Winston S. Churchill, *Great Contemporaries* (London, 1937), p. 261.

27 17 Sept. 1937. Winston S. Churchill, *Step by Step* (London, 1937), p. 170.

28 23 Nov. 1932. 272 H.C. Deb. 5s., col. 91.

29 14 Mar. 1933. 275 H.C. Deb. 5s., col. 1819.

not function perfectly well as a Concert of Europe. In the existing condition of Europe every policy involved risk, but

> the least risk and the greatest help will be found in recreating the League of Nations, not for the purpose of fiercely quarrelling and haggling about the details of disarmament but in an attempt to address Germany collectively, so that there may be some redress of the grievances of the German nation and that it may be affected before this period of re-armament reaches a point which may endanger the peace of the world.

According to Churchill's son, who edited *Arms and the Covenant*, this speech marks the beginning of Churchill's 'advocacy of the League as an effective instrument for the maintenance of peace.'[30] But the force of this appeal was weakened by his demand for re-armament so that the country could be safe in its neutrality—'a neutrality from which, as I have said before, we should not be drawn except upon the conscience and the will of the overwhelming mass of our people'.[31]

For the next year and a half Churchill's speeches were a mixture of support for the League and freedom of choice for Britain. In March 1934 he was still upholding the case for complete independence in foreign policy:

> These are not the times when we can afford to confide the safety of our country to the passions or to the panic of any foreign nation which may be facing some grave and desperate crisis. We must be independent. We must be free. We must preserve our full latitude and discretion of choice. In the past we have always had this fundamental independence.[32]

In July 1934 he made his first really ringing endorsement of the League as an agency for keeping the peace in Europe:

> I have been trying for the last few years to seek out for myself what would be the best way of preventing war, and it has seemed to me that the League of Nations should be the great instrument upon which all those resolved to maintain peace should centre, and that we should all make our contribution to the League of Nations . . . I cannot see how better you can prevent war than to confront an aggressor with the prospect of such a vast concentration of force,

[30] Winston S. Churchill, *Arms and the Covenant*. Speeches compiled by Randolph S. Churchill (London, 1938), preface.

[31] 281 H.C. Deb. 5s., cols. 141–3.

[32] 8 Mar. 1934. 286 H.C. Deb. 5s., cols. 2064–5.

moral and material, that even the most reckless, even the most infuriated leader would not attempt to challenge these great forces.[33] But it was not until Hitler seized the Rhineland that Churchill became the League's forceful champion. Such support as he did give the League in the early 1930s, however, did something to redeem Churchill from the disrepute into which he had fallen as a result of his opposition to the Government of India Bill. At the beginning of 1934 Clement Attlee compared Churchill's views favourably with those held by Sir John Simon,[34] and a year later R. H. Bernays of the Liberal party was so impressed by Churchill's speeches on the 'grandeur of the peace system at Geneva' that he hoped to see him become a vice-president of the League of Nations Union.[35] Both these comments were made while Churchill was still fighting the Government of India Bill. Once that incubus had fallen away Churchill and the Opposition drew closer together on foreign policy.

The most formidable obstacle to the formation of a group favouring collective security within the Conservative party was the attitude of Sir Austen Chamberlain. This highly respected back-bencher was as moderate in his support for the League as he was in all things. He regarded it as a strong moral force, perhaps the best hope for a better world in the future, but certainly not an organization which should have the power to coerce its members. Even when he realized that some overwhelming force was needed to restrain Hitler, the author of the Locarno treaties preferred to see 'collective security' achieved through regional pacts, underpinning the general League structure with 'agreements among nations in a particular region, whose fates are so knit with one another that they cannot be indifferent to what happens in that area and who on any aggression in that area will be found ready to help in the repression of the aggressor'.[36] Although Chamberlain gave this restricted meaning to 'collective security' his habitual use of the term gave the impression that he believed in a general system of collective security within the framework of the League. The fact that he meant something less simply added to the confusion at the time of the Abyssinian crisis.

[33] 13 July 1934. 292 H.C. Deb. 5s., cols. 730–1.
[34] 6 Feb. 1934. 285 H.C. Deb. 5s., cols. 1003–4.
[35] 31 May 1935. 302 H.C. Deb. 5s., cols. 1446–7.
[36] 11 Mar. 1935. 299 H.C. Deb. 5s., col. 75.

The change in attitude towards the League after Hitler's rise to power also produced a different outlook towards the Soviet Union. In 1932 Winston Churchill painted a grim picture of the threat which that country posed to European peace:

We must also remember that the great mass of Russia, with its enormous armies and its schools of ardent students of chemical warfare, poison gas, its tanks and appliances, looms up all along the Eastern frontier of Europe, and that the whole row of small States Finland, Estonia, Latvia, Lithuania, Poland—not a small State, but for this purpose in the line—and Rumania, are under the continued preoccupation of this enormous, and to them, unfriendly Russian power. It may be that there is no danger, but I expect that if we lived there we should feel rather uncomfortable about it.[37]

Once having decided that Germany was the greater threat, however, Churchill's attitude changed abruptly. When Russia's admission to the League of Nations was being discussed in 1934 he told the House of Commons:

I notice that for some time the speeches of Mr. Litvinoff had seemed to give the impression, which I believe is a true one, that Russia is most deeply desirous of maintaining peace. It is not enough to talk about her as 'peace-loving' because every Power is peace-loving always. One wants to see what is the interest of a particular Power and it is certainly in the interests of Russia, even on grounds concerning her own internal arrangements, to preserve peace.[38]

For the rest of the decade, as each German crisis arose, Churchill continued to point to the U.S.S.R. as a valuable counterweight to Germany. While he disliked the social and governmental structure of the Soviet Union, and no one doubted his strong anti-Communism, Russia was not the 'Red bogey' for him that it was for most Conservatives.

On the same day in 1934 that Churchill spoke so favourably of the U.S.S.R. Robert Boothby, who 'for many years past supported the closest possible relations, both political and economic between this country and Russia', also welcomed that country's entry to the League. 'I believe,' he said, 'that that will be a very great stabilizing force in the world at a very critical moment in all our affairs.'[39] The following year Lord Cranborne, Anthony

[37] 13 May 1932. 265 H.C. Deb. 5s., col. 2352.
[38] 13 July 1934. 292 H.C. Deb. 5s., col. 737.
[39] 13 July 1934. Ibid.

Eden's Parliamentary Private Secretary and heir to the Marquess of Salisbury, asked permission to make a personal speech in order to impress on the House of Commons his conviction that Russia was an important factor in European stability. Dismissing the 'German idea of a military Russian peril' as 'an absolute myth' he argued that the Soviet Union was engaged in a great economic and social enterprise which would absorb its attention for years to come:

Her whole energies are occupied at present with that experiment, and she will not consider, as I understand it, anything likely to endanger that experiment. The greatest hindrance to her internal experiment would undoubtedly be war, and therefore I believe Russia is at the present time firmly against war. Nor is that the only reason. She really has no incentive to go to war.[40]

The same views were also found in the *Spectator*. In February 1934 the journal detected a new attitude towards Russia,

a sporting, or—shall we say?—philosophic desire to see the best that the Russians can make of the system they have adopted—a desire to keep the ring and give her the opportunity to try out her great experiment and show the world how it works. We have not made so big a success of our own affairs that we can afford to ignore what is being done in a different way elsewhere; and a country which has dared to take the dangerous chance may surely have stumbled upon some discoveries which might be applicable even to our own so different system.

The *Spectator* explained Russia's more friendly attitude as a response to Japanese imperialism in the Far East, a challenge which would be more serious to an isolated country than to one on good terms with the Western Powers.[41] It was hardly surprising that the journal believed that the act of faith necessary to admit the U.S.S.R. to the League of Nations was justified: 'Russia's admission to the League may conceivably hurt the League more than it helps it. But all the present indications are that the Assembly States were consulting their own interests no less than Russia's when they cast their votes on Tuesday.'[42]

Die-hard Conservatives, of course, did not share this optimistic appraisal of the Soviet Union. The *English Review*, not without

[40] 2 May 1935. 301 H.C. Deb. 5s., cols. 627–8.
[41] 'Britain and Russia—A New Start', 23 Feb. 1934.
[42] 'Russia at Geneva', 21 Sept. 1934.

Schadenfreude, declared that its admission to the League had dealt a crushing blow to the international organization: 'It was at least regarded, in a homely idiom, as a club which demanded certain standards of conduct in its members and was prepared, if not to insist upon them, at least to make it as unpleasant as possible for those who fell short of them.[43] The *Saturday Review* believed that Russia's admission to the League was 'simply another of Stalin's tricks whereby he hopes to get the backing of the League of Nations in his quarrel with Japan', and castigated the Foreign Secretary for dashing off to Geneva to welcome home the prodigal: 'Why should this country allow Sir John Simon to help pull the fat out of the fire for the benefit of the Bolshevists and further jeopardise our relations with our old ally Japan?'[44]

Right-wing criticism of Sir John Simon for welcoming the U.S.S.R. to the League was simply the last in a series of charges levelled at him from all sides of the coalition. A brilliant lawyer who could always see both sides of every case and offer sophisticated, and seemingly specious, reasons for taking no action at all, Simon was widely distrusted for his smooth platitudes and intellectual agility. In a typical summing-up at the end of one debate he said: 'The Government and their supporters have no reason to be dissatisfied with the general tenor of the Debate. A little criticism does not do any harm. Parliamentary government depends on it. . . . The critics answer one another.'[45] No wonder Neville Chamberlain commented in his diary: 'Simon's weakness has given rise to much criticism. . . . The fact is that his manner inspires no confidence, and that he seems temperamentally unable to make up his mind to action when a difficult situation arises.'[46] This weakness provoked an outburst in the House of Commons from Richard Law, a young Conservative backbencher and son of Bonar Law, the former Conservative leader. 'It is, obviously, quite right to point out the difficulties,' said Law, 'but I would be more satisfied that the Government were going into these problems as deeply as I think they ought to be gone into, if he would point out sometimes some of the advantages which must in any reasonable contingency accrue from these

[43] Douglas Jerrold, 'Current Comments', Oct. 1934.
[44] 'Notes of the Week', 8 Sept. 1934.
[45] 30 July 1934. 292 H.C. Deb. 5s., cols. 2442–3.
[46] Jan. 1934. Quoted in Feiling, *Life of Neville Chamberlain*, p. 249.

policies.'[47] But it was not merely the Foreign Secretary's personality and manner that provoked his critics. He was also blamed by the left-wing supporters of the National Government for not dealing effectively with Japan and for the failure of the disarmament conference; and by the right-wingers for dealing with the League of Nations at all, thereby jeopardizing the country's sovereignty.

In the spring of 1935 there was rare unity within the ministerial ranks for getting rid of Simon. As the international situation became more serious M.P.s felt they could no longer 'listen to appeals to remember the consequences that might accrue from disturbing the existing balance of Party representation. . . . In spite of the fact that [Simon] is an excellent platform apologist of the general record of the Government, and is therefore useful to Government Liberals, even the Simonites demonstrate little enthusiasm for him.'[48] In April a group of seventy Conservative M.P.s protested against keeping Simon at the Foreign Office; and Stanley Baldwin admitted to Sir Austen Chamberlain that the cabinet no longer had any confidence in him.[49] A month later Sir Austen was writing that Simon had become a positive danger and could be removed by the back-benchers if Chamberlain would take the lead; but he added, characteristically: 'I won't though asked to do so.'[50] No revolt materialized, perhaps because Baldwin moved Sir Samuel Hoare to the Foreign Office on becoming Prime Minister on 7 June. Hoare came to the post with laurels earned while piloting the Government of India Bill through the House of Commons, but within six months he too was faced with an uprising from the back benches.

47 8 Nov. 1934. 293 H.C. Deb. 5s., col. 1390.

48 'News of the Week', *Spectator*, 17 May 1935.

49 Sir Austen Chamberlain to Ida Chamberlain, 6 April 1935. A.C., Letters to Ida and Hilda Chamberlain, 1935–7. (Hereafter cited as A.C. Letters.)

50 Sir Austen Chamberlain to Hilda Chamberlain, 5 May 1935. Ibid.

4. Mussolini or the League

THE first open challenge to the international order after Japan's seizure of Manchuria came not from the new Nazi regime in Germany but from Italy. In contrast to Hitler's lightning moves Mussolini made no attempt to hide his preparations for the attack on Abyssinia from the rest of the world. A clash between Italian and Abyssinian troops on 5 December 1934 gave him a pretext for action but the war itself did not begin until 3 October 1935. The intervening ten months, during which the Italian dictator noisily assembled his forces, gave the other European countries ample time to consider how they were going to meet this challenge to the League's authority and how they intended to prevent war between the two member-states. But the diplomatic gestures designed to stay Mussolini's course came to nothing. The Duce was determined to have his colonial triumph at the expense of Abyssinia and he was convinced, correctly as it turned out, that no effective steps would be taken to restrain him. The ten months between the Wal Wal incident and the commencement of the war did not suffice for the British Government, the most important member of the League, to formulate a clear, consistent policy for averting war or one that could withstand the domestic and external pressures once the fighting had begun. In fact the crisis revealed that the Cabinet and its supporters were subject to fatal divisions and hesitations.

From the outset everyone recognized that the issue between Italy and Abyssinia was not an isolated quarrel but a real test for the League of Nations system. As Sir Austen Chamberlain pointed out: 'It is a question whether all the efforts which have been made since the War to establish a new public law and a new standard of conduct between nations are to be abandoned at the first test or are to be asserted, and by the assertion of them strengthened.'[1] *The Economist* prophesised that if the failure to deal promptly with Japan were followed by the failure to deal with the simpler problem in Africa the very existence of the

[1] 5 Dec. 1935. 307 H.C. Deb. 5s., col. 351.

League would be jeopardized.[2] The Abyssinian crisis was a touchstone for the National Government's handling of foreign affairs and the attitude of Conservative back-benchers for the rest of the decade.

Discussing the attack on Abyssinia in the light of later events it was easy for Winston Churchill to pontificate: 'Mussolini's designs upon Abyssinia were unsuited to the ethics of the twentieth century. They belonged to those dark ages when white men felt themselves entitled to conquer yellow, brown, black, or red men, and subjugate them by their superior strength and weapons.'[3] But the merits of Abyssinia's case were less obvious at the time. A primitive, badly governed, slave-holding country, it was not regarded by anyone as a blameless suppliant for justice. Churchill himself said, three weeks after the war had begun: 'No one can keep up the pretence that Abyssinia is a fit, worthy and equal member of a league of civilised nations. The wisdom of British policy was shown in our opposing their admission [to the League of Nations] and the unwisdom of the Continental countries, who now bitterly regret what they did, was shown in its admission.'[4] Even the *New Statesman* agreed that the Abyssinian Empire was 'a barbarous affair. It is doubtless not governed in accordance with the best European ideas. It contains a number of unruly tribal chieftains. It has not purged itself of the abomination of slavery.'[5] The intrinsic merits of Abyssinia's case, however, were largely irrelevant to the dispute between those who felt that the issue should be solved through the League of Nations and those who felt that a compromise could be worked out directly between Britain, France, and Italy (at Abyssinia's expense) and then presented to the League for ratification.

Socialists, who had detested Mussolini and his system for over a decade, welcomed the confrontation between the Italian dictator and the League, but it is significant that Clement Attlee, the new leader of the Labour Party, did not believe in a combination of League powers to defeat Italy. 'I do not believe that you can destroy Fascism, or any other form of government by attack from without. I think it will fall by its own inherent rottenness.'[6]

[2] 'Notes of the Week', 25 May 1935.
[3] *The Gathering Storm*, pp. 165–6.
[4] 24 Oct. 1935. 305 H.C. Deb. 5s., col. 365.
[5] 'Mussolini's Challenge', 18 May 1935.
[6] 22 Oct. 1935. 305 H.C. Deb. 5s., col. 35.

The Labour party was by no means agreed about the use of force in international affairs; even the meaning of 'collective security' called forth a lively debate among its members. Most Labourites were convinced that moral and economic sanctions would be sufficient to force Italy into line—as they might have been had they been applied.

The Conservative party was thrown into greater consternation by Mussolini's action. The Italian dictator had many admirers among right-wing Conservatives and there were even more within the party who were anxious to retain the goodwill of what they regarded as a leading military power in case of trouble from Germany. The *National Review,* looking at the matter in pre-1914 terms, maintained that Britain had 'no interests in Abyssinia save the guarding of the sources of the Nile'. On the other hand, 'we have great interests in Europe, and it is important to us, who have no army, that Italy should not be weakened by Colonial difficulties'.[7] Sir Charles Petrie, writing in the *English Review,* argued that a free hand in Abyssinia was a small price to pay for Italian troops on the Brenner Pass; and he accused Germany of fomenting trouble in Africa 'in the hope, not only of distracting Italian attention from Central Europe, but also of making bad blood between Italy, France and ourselves. Those who may be inclined to question this would do well first of all to ask themselves why the Wilhemstrasse has sent one of its ablest diplomats to Addis Ababa.'[8] It could also be argued that the Italian desire to seek revenge for the humiliation of Adowa was as understandable as the British determination to reconquer the Sudan after the fall of Khartoum.[9] Moreover, the Italian annexation of Abyssinia would bring law, order, and European civilization to a backward corner of the African continent. But whatever might be thought of the morality or wisdom of an attack 'not essentially different from any other wars of colonial conquest such as the French operations in Morocco before the war', Leopold Amery saw no reason why its success or failure should disturb the general peace.[10] Here, as far as right-wing Conservatives were concerned, was a clear-cut case for British non-involvement

[7] 'Episodes of the Month', June 1935. [8] *English Review,* March 1935.

[9] Leopold Amery, 23 Oct. 1935. 305 H.C. Deb. 5s., cols. 192–4.

[10] Address at the Conway Road Schools, Sparkbrook, 8 Oct. 1935. *Unforgiving Years,* Appendix D, p. 421.

Consistent with their view of the League of Nations as an agency for settling minor disputes between small countries, Conservative isolationist-imperialists maintained that the dispute should be left to the countries directly concerned. To submit the case to Geneva, far from preserving peace, would probably transform the conflict into a major international war. The prominent right-wing Conservative, Sir Henry Page Croft, charged that the formerly pacifist defenders of the League who now clamoured for action against Mussolini 'never told the people that the League of Nations was to be the instrument for war. You have always said that it was an idealistic institution where you hoped you would find the nations of the world coming together to find arbitration and agreement.'[11] It was not hard to detect, as *The Economist* did, a 'gleeful *Schadenfreude*' among those Conservatives that the League and collective security were breaking down. ' "Then", they tell us, "we shall be back in the good old pre-War days; and, after all, the British Empire did not do so badly for itself in the nineteenth century." '[12] But few were so passionate in their hatred as Lady Houston, the wildly eccentric owner of the *Saturday Review*, who telegraphed Mussolini:

English patriots present their homage to Mussolini the greatest patriot in the world—for his aim for Italy is to build up and achieve —while the British politician's aim is to drag down and destroy the British Empire. English patriots hope Mussolini will stand fast and dam [*sic*] the League of Nations—*which only exists to enable Russian Bolshevism to destroy civilization.*[13]

Many right-wing Conservatives shared Lady Houston's general sentiments, though they hesitated to express them in such categorical terms.

Such was the change in public opinion since the Manchurian episode, however, that the die-hard Conservatives found themselves bracketed with left-wing pacifists in their demand that no action be taken to defend Abyssinia against the Italian attack. No doubt Leopold Amery was able to raise some kind of cheer from his constituents when he declared that he was 'not prepared to send a single Birmingham lad to his death for the sake

[11] 24 Oct. 1935. 305 H.C. Deb. 5s., col. 415.
[12] 'British Interests', 31 Aug. 1935.
[13] *Saturday Review*, 31 Aug. 1935.

of Abyssinia',[14] but the tide of public and political opinion was against him. When he tried to develop his views in the House of Commons just before it was dissolved for the general election his Conservative colleagues were so embarrassed that one of them, Sir John Withers, moved 'that the Right Honourable Gentleman be no longer heard.'[15] Lloyd George, a few minutes later, tried to make some political capital by charging that Amery's speech 'undoubtedly represents a very considerable body of opinion on the Conservative side of the House', but he was met by cries of 'no' from the Government benches.[16] Amery recalled in his memoirs: 'It was the only speech I have ever made when I have felt that almost the whole House was actually hostile and when even the few who really agreed at heart wished that I had held my peace, or at any rate hesitated to express their agreement openly.'[17] Only at the other end of the political spectrum did the right wing Conservatives find some support among the extreme socialists who regarded the dispute as 'an Imperialist quarrel between Britain and Italy'[18] and among the pacifists who denounced war sanctions 'either by the League of Nations or unilaterally by our own Government'.[19] Moderate and left-wing Conservatives believed, in the words of the *Spectator*, that the League would be dead

in fact if not in name if its principles are deliberately betrayed by countries like Great Britain and France in order that a war of aggression and aggrandizement by Italy against another member of the League may be condoned. Whenever the League stands by its principles it gains influence and authority. Whenever it abandons them it is ignored and contemned.[20]

Popular enthusiasm for the League of Nations, which swept the country in 1935 was largely a product of the 'Peace Ballot' launched by the National Declaration Committee, which was

[14] Reported in *The Times*, 9 Oct. 1935.

[15] 23 Oct. 1935. 305 H.C. Deb. 5s., col. 195. The *Hansard* reporter represented Sir John as saying: 'May I move that the Question be now put?'. But as Amery pointed out, this was obviously out of place in the middle of a three-day debate. Amery, *Unforgiving Years*, p. 178.

[16] 23 Oct. 1935. 305 H.C. Deb. 5s., col. 196.

[17] *Unforgiving Years*, p. 178.

[18] John McGovern of the Independent Labour Party, 22 Oct. 1935. 305 H.C. Deb. 5s., col. 94.

[19] George Lansbury, 22 Oct. 1935. 305 H.C. Deb. 5s., col. 66.

[20] 'News of the Week', 5 July 1935.

backed by the League of Nations Union, in November 1934. Great excitement was generated during the campaign to impress the Government with the amount of support for the League in the country. People were asked:

1. Should Great Britain remain a Member of the League of Nations? (Yes, 11,090,387; No, 355,883; Doubtful, 10,470; Abstentions, 102,425)

2. Are you in favour of an all-round reduction of armaments by international agreement?
(Yes, 10,470,489; No, 862,775; Doubtful, 12,062; Abstentions, 213,839)

3. Are you in favour of the all-round abolition of national military aircraft by international agreement?
(Yes, 9,533,558; No, 1,689,786; Doubtful, 16,976; Abstentions, 318,845)

4. Should the manufacture and sale of armaments for private profit be prohibited by international agreement?
(Yes, 10,417,329; No, 775,415; Doubtful, 15,076; Abstentions, 315,345)

5. Do you consider that, if a nation insists on attacking another, the other nations should combine to compel it to stop by
(*a*) economic and non-military measures?
(Yes, 10,027,608; No, 635,074; Doubtful, 27,255; Abstentions, 855,107; Pacifist, 14,121)
(*b*) if necessary, military measures?
(Yes, 6,784,368; No, 2,351,981; Doubtful, 40,893; Abstentions, 2,364,441; Christian Pacifist, 17,482)[21]

During the latter part of the polling—the results were announced on 27 June 1935—Mussolini's preparations for the Abyssinian war gave the Peace Ballot greater point and reinforced the movement to support the League.

The Peace Ballot was somewhat misleading in that it omitted the crucial question of rearmament to make collective security effective, doubtless because the organizers felt that Britain had enough arms, in conjunction with other countries, to deter any aggressor. In any event the answers to the fifth question indicate that most League enthusiasts believed that economic sanctions could be invoked without the risk of war. More questionable was the National Declaration Committee's refusal to circulate with the Ballot a blue paper drawn up by Sir Austen Chamberlain and some of his friends to point out the shortcomings of the Ballot and to counter the green paper which the polling agents

[21] Dame Adelaide Livingstone, *The Peace Ballot: The Official History* (London, 1935).

were already distributing on behalf of the Union for Democratic Control. When Sir Austen persisted the organizers decided to circulate neither paper. This transparent action to influence the results of the poll simply increased Chamberlain's contempt for the pretentiousness and extremism of the Union and made it only a matter of time until he resigned from the executive. The National Government managed to get through the general election with the name of their most prominent and respected backbencher on the Union's notepaper but in the spring of 1936 he resigned because he could not agree with the other members that sanctions against Italy ought to be continued.[22] This dispute between Chamberlain and the Union probably reinforced his reluctance to support a vigorous and uncompromising League policy.

Interpreting the Peace Ballot in precise political terms may have been difficult, but the message that eleven million voters had indicated their support for the League was one which no politician could afford to ignore.[23] Right-wing Conservatives might attack the Ballot, but the results impressed more moderate members of the party and the administration. 'Henceforth', remarked the *Spectator,* 'there can be no reasonable doubt about the conviction of the mass of the people of this country; no Government will dare to flout public opinion by flouting the League, or by refraining from efforts to secure agreed disarmament and collective sanctions against peace-breakers.'[24] Any intention the Government might have entertained of conciliating Italy at Abyssinia's expense was killed for the time being when the National Declaration Committee made public its figures.

Three weeks before the results of the Peace Ballot were announced the National Government was reconstructed. Stanley Baldwin took over the prime ministership, while Ramsay MacDonald succeeded him as Lord President of the Council. As Baldwin had been the leading figure in the Cabinet since the 1931 general election this made little practical difference except that he now had the responsibility as well as the power. In the sphere

[22] Sir Austen Chamberlain wanted to make his resignation final at the beginning of May but was persuaded by Professor Gilbert Murray to withhold it until 23 June. Sir Austen to Gilbert Murray, 23 June 1936. A.C. 41, folder 125.

[23] 21,997,054 people voted in the general election of 1935. David Butler and Jennie Freeman, *British Political Facts 1900–1960* (New York, 1963), p. 124.

[24] 'The Peace Ballot', 28 June 1935.

of foreign affairs an ingenious compromise was devised. Sir Samuel Hoare replaced the ill-starred Sir John Simon as Foreign Secretary while Anthony Eden, who had been Lord Privy Seal, moved up to the newly created post of Minister for League of Nations Affairs. Hoare, who had been offered the viceroyalty of India—and probably wished he had taken it before the year was out—accepted the Foreign Office at the insistence of older Conservatives who were suspicious of Eden's emotional championship of the League. After Hoare's recent experience in conciliating the various Indian factions these Conservatives now hoped that he would put his talents to better use in bringing France and Germany together.[25] At the same time the politically astute Baldwin, well aware of Eden's prestige in the country, persuaded the young Minister to accept the new arrangements in spite of his complaints about 'dyarchy' and perhaps his disappointment at not being offered the Foreign Office. To soothe Eden's feelings even more the Prime Minister assured him that the division of responsibility for foreign affairs would be only temporary.[26] Fortunately for the Government the differences between Hoare and Eden did not become obvious until the general election was safely won.

Most political observers welcomed the Cabinet changes and Eden's promotion was taken as a sign of the Government's firm commitment to the League of Nations. Surveying the new Administration *The Economist* concluded that it would have a strong diplomatic team.[27] Indeed it was only the extreme Conservatives who objected to the new appointments: the *Saturday Review* for example characteristically denounced Sir Samuel Hoare as 'an obedient Party tool' and upbraided Baldwin for his failure to introduce a real Conservative policy. 'With his mealy-mouthed democratic internationalism, he believes we can escape from danger by talking, compromising, and by relying on the League of Nations. His Government is one of shufflers and twisters of which he is the worst.'[28] Less hysterically, Leopold Amery, who had supported Hoare's Indian policies, wrote that the new Foreign Secretary would have 'his work cut out clearing

25 Templewood, *Nine Troubled Years*, p. 108.
26 Eden, *Facing the Dictators*, pp. 242–3.
27 'Changes in Downing Street', 15 June 1935.
28 Kim, 'Baldwin's Road to Ruin', 15 June 1935.

up the mess into which Eden has got us over Abyssinia'. Amery looked forward to September when Eden would be sent to Geneva 'with orders to unsay all his high talk about coercing Italy to respect the "collective system" '.[29]

When the new Ministry was formed it was hard to say what attitude it would adopt towards the Abyssinian dispute. Eden's elevation pointed to some effort to stop Mussolini through the League, but at the Stresa conference in April the British Government had deliberately passed up the opportunity to deter Mussolini from his course; and on 17 May Sir Eric Drummond, the British ambassador in Rome, told the Cabinet that Mussolini would not give way to pressure from the League and that war could only be avoided by forcing Abyssinia to grant economic concessions to Italy.[30]

In his maiden speech as Foreign Secretary Hoare did nothing to shed any light on the Government's position. He talked in vague terms about a system of collective security under the League, 'whether it be a near or a far prospect', and asserted his country's willingness to share in the responsibility for such a system. 'But', he hedged, 'when I say collective responsibility, I mean collective responsibility.' He then went on to express sympathy with Italy's overseas ambitions and saw no reason why that should be the cause of war: 'We have surely found in the past that it is possible to adjust differences of this kind without recourse to war, and I am not prepared even now to abandon any chance that may present itself for averting what I believe will be a calamity.' Above all he urged M.P.s to dismiss from their minds

> the rumours, altogether without foundation, that we have asked the French Government to join in a blockade of Italy and that we ourselves are preparing some isolated form of coercion against the country which has been our friend since the Risorgimento. We stand for peace, and we will not abandon any reasonable chance that may offer itself for helping to prevent a disastrous war.[31]

This was hardly a ringing endorsement of the League, or anything else for that matter. But then it was not intended to be: Hoare was keeping his options open because the Government had not decided how to handle the problem.

[29] Diary entry, 7 June 1935. Amery, *Unforgiving Years*, p. 168.
[30] Cab. 23/81.
[31] 11 July 1935. 304 H.C. Deb. 5s., cols. 517–20.

After Parliament had risen for the summer and the prospect of war had increased, the new Foreign Secretary and the Minister for League of Nations Affairs turned their full attention to the Abyssinian problem. To assist them in their attempt to find a policy they called in the leaders of the Opposition parties and Sir Austen Chamberlain, Winston Churchill, and Lord Robert Cecil. Attlee, Lansbury, Samuel, Cecil, and Chamberlain all urged a policy of collective security based on Anglo-French co-operation.[32] Churchill and Lloyd George, on the other hand, stressed the dangers of action against Italy. Churchill afterwards remembered saying that the Foreign Secretary was '*justified in going as far with the League of Nations against Italy as he could carry France*; but I added that he ought not to put any pressure upon France because of her military convention with Italy and her German preoccupations; and that in the circumstances I did not expect France would go very far'.[33] Hoare's recollection of the conversation was somewhat different. While Churchill doubted that the French would go as far as economic sanctions he added: 'That is no reason for not pressing them. The real danger is Germany and nothing must be done to weaken the anti-German front. The collapse of the League will mean the destruction of the instrument that may be chiefly effective as a deterrent against German aggression.'[34] In any event Churchill's advise seems to have been not to attempt anything beyond the mild economic sanctions which the French might be induced to support. After pondering this advice the Cabinet announced on 24 August that it would stand firmly by its obligations to the League of Nations.

Having decided to adopt an unequivocal League policy the National Government lost no time in trumpeting its firm resolve to the country and to the whole world. On 11 September Sir Samuel Hoare electrified the League of Nations Assembly with a carefully prepared statement that had been considered by Neville Chamberlain and approved by the Prime Minister. In categorical terms he told the delegates:

> The attitude of His Majesty's Government has been one of unswerving fidelity to the League and all that it stands for, and the case before us [the Italo-Abyssinian dispute] is no exception, but, on the

[32] Templewood, *Nine Troubled Years*, p. 160.

[33] Churchill, *The Gathering Storm*, p. 169. The italics are in the original.

[34] Templewood, *Nine Troubled Years*, p. 160.

contrary, the continuance of the rule. The recent response of public opinion shows how completely the nation supports the Government in the full acceptance of the obligations of the League membership, which is the oft proclaimed keystone of its foreign policy.

... In conformity with its precise and explicit obligations the League stands, and my country stands with it, for the collective maintenance of the Covenant in its entirety, and particularly for steady and collective resistance to all acts of unprovoked aggression. The attitude of the British nation in the last few weeks has clearly demonstrated the fact that this is no variable and unreliable sentiment, but a principle of international conduct to which they and their Government hold with firm, enduring and universal persistence.[35]

Even Eden and his Under-Secretary, Lord Cranborne, were startled by the tone of Hoare's speech when he showed them the text. They pointed out that this went beyond anything the Cabinet had previously discussed and finally prevailed on a reluctant Hoare to modify his statement somewhat. But apparently they remained mystified by the firmness of the Foreign Secretary's language, especially since the Cabinet had earlier refused to let Eden warn Laval that Britain intended to fulfil its obligations under the Covenant.[36]

There was no reason why Eden and Cranborne should have been puzzled by Hoare's declaration. It is fairly clear that the National Government's decision to give unqualified support to the League was prompted by the public mood as expressed in the Peace Ballot and by the fact that a general election was due before November 1936. Just two weeks after Hoare's speech Neville Chamberlain cynically confided to Leopold Amery that

we were bound to try out the League of Nations (in which he [Chamberlain] does not himself believe very much) for political reasons at home, and that there was no question of our going beyond the mildest of economic sanctions such as an embargo on the purchase of Italian goods or the sale of munitions to Italy. ... If things become too serious the French would run out of things first and we could show that we had done our best.[37]

Baldwin's shrewd decision to adopt a League policy and the

[35] Reported in *The Times*, 12 September 1935.

[36] Eden, *Facing the Dictators*, pp. 292–3. Apparently Hoare himself did not anticipate the 'universal acclamation' with which his speech was received by the League delegates. Templewood, *Nine Troubled Years*, pp. 169–70.

[37] Amery, diary entries. Amery, *Unforgiving Years*, p. 174.

popular support which greeted it, convinced him that he should lose no time in calling a general election for November. Foreign policy was naturally the chief issue; and in its election manifesto the National Government declared:

The League of Nations will remain, as heretofore, the keystone of British foreign policy. The prevention of war and the establishment of settled peace in the world must always be the most vital interest of the British people, and the League is the instrument which has been framed and to which we look for the attainment of these objects. We shall therefore continue to do all in our power to uphold the Covenant and to maintain and increase the efficiency of the League. In the present unhappy dispute between Italy and Abyssinia there will be no wavering in the policy we have hitherto pursued. We shall take no action in isolation, but we shall be prepared to take our part in any collective action decided upon by the League and shared in by its members.

A jarring note was struck in the next sentence in which the Government asserted that it would continue discussions in the hope of achieving 'a just and fair settlement, provided that it be within the framework of the League and acceptable to the three parties to the dispute—Italy, Abyssinia, and the League itself.'[38] Since Italy had already violated the territory of another member-state the British Government's job should have been to help in forcing Italy out of Abyssinia, not trying to devise a compromise, but this feature of the manifesto was overshadowed by the seemingly unambiguous sentences which preceded it.

By making support of the League of Nations the chief plank in the National Government's platform Baldwin completely undermined the opposition's claims. The *New Statesman* gloomily conceded:

In their new role of hundred per cent. Covenanters the Government are happily placed for an election. The Labour Party, which has a constructive peace policy of its own and plenty of ground for criticism of the Government's past, will have difficulty in making an effective appeal to the electorate at a moment when the Government are doing what the Labour Party has always told them to do.[39]

Within the Conservative party the isolationist-imperialists put up some resistance to the new policy. Lady Houston, writing in

[38] *The Times*, 28 Oct. 1935.
[39] 'Comments', 12 Oct. 1935.

her *Saturday Review*, denounced Sir Samuel Hoare for thinking that 'England has a wild desire to be governed by a League of Foreigners—whose languages have to be interpreted to our Foreign Minister and whose expenses must be paid by Great Britain'.[40] And on 15 October Leopold Amery, the most outspoken opponent of sanctions, formed a delegation consisting of almost a hundred members of both Houses to urge the Prime Minister to announce that Britain would not resort to force in the Abyssinian dispute. Baldwin, however, would commit himself no further than to say that he would think over their suggestions 'and said more or less definitely that we were not contemplating any such steps as the closing of the Suez Canal or an actual blockade'. The delegates went away 'depressed and angry', convinced that 'the whole thing figured in his mind as a useful aid to the General Election, and that he had no idea of its repercussions outside'[41]—an odd comment on the Prime Minister's consummate political skill. But much as they disliked the direction Government policy was taking the right-wing Conservatives had little choice but to come to terms with it if they wanted their party to win the election; and even they preferred Baldwin to a Labour government. As for the moderate M.P.s who had been unexpectedly elected in the 1931 landslide, they not only agreed with the new policy but recognized that it increased their chances of re-election.

The two most proment back-benchers, Sir Austen Chamberlain and Winston Churchill, found themselves in a dilemma over the Abyssinian dispute. They both recognized that Germany posed a serious threat to European peace and were reluctant to have attention diverted from it by what they regarded as a minor side-show. But as neither could decide whether Italy or a strong League would be more effective in restraining Germany, though generally favouring the former they vacillated between two policies. This inability to settle on a consistent policy meant that they were unable to give a clear lead to the other back-benchers during the Hoare–Laval crisis; and this failure to put pressure on the Government to continue the course on which it was embarked meant the end of collective security.

[40] 'Hoare's Progress', *Saturday Review*, 21 Sept. 1935.

[41] Amery, diary entry. Amery, *Unforgiving Years*, p. 176. *The Times*, 16 Oct. 1935.

In the spring of 1935, when Mussolini seemed to be committing himself irrevocably to his African adventure, Sir Austen was asked by the Foreign Office to write to his old friend Dino Grandi, the Italian ambassador in London, in order to impress on him informally the British concern about Mussolini's plans. After writing the letter Chamberlain decided to deliver it himself and have a talk with Grandi. Speaking as a 'real friend of Italy and a strong and convinced supporter of Anglo-Italian co-operation' he emphasized the importance of close co-operation between the two countries warning the ambassador that 'if Italy seeks a solution of the troubles which have arisen by armed force, it will have a deplorable effect on British opinion and may give rise to comment, both in Parliament and in the Press, which will inevitably provoke retorts from Italy and must embitter public opinion on both sides'. Chamberlain also pointed out that Italian aggression would weaken public law in Europe and encourage Germany to fresh provocation; and he stressed that

> the friends of Italy cannot view without grave anxiety the prospect of a considerable part of the Italian forces being locked up for an indefinite term in Africa whilst the European situation is so critical and whilst no assurance has been received from Germany that she will respect Austrian independence and refrain from further interference in the internal affairs of that Country.[42]

Although Sir Austen's primary concern was to keep Italy interested in restraining Germany, his frequent talk of collective security made him appear to be a leading supporter of the League in the Abyssinian dispute. In July, for example, he told the House of Commons:

> What is at stake is the system of collective security. We cannot be the policemen of the world—that is an impossible position—but we ought to take our fair share in promoting security in co-operation with other members of the League, particularly with those who in a particular case can give the most effective support and are best situated to uphold its authority. We ought to do that only after discussion in the Council, and if it can be obtained with that authority. But if we do not live up to these obligations, then the whole collective system is gone. It is not merely that it has failed

[42] Sir Austen Chamberlain to Count Grandi, 10 May 1935. A.C. 41, folder 125. The interview took place on 11 May.

to protect Abyssinia; it is that it is a broken reed for any European Power to rely upon.[43]

And on 31 October—two weeks before the election—he declared at a meeting of the League of Nations Association that 'if treaties solemnly signed, covenants freely undertaken, pledges to pursue peaceful regulation of the disputes among nations and to abjure war as an instrument of national policy could be broken and nothing happen then it was idle to pretend that peace could be in any way secure'.[44] These pro-League pronouncements may have been in part expedient concessions to public opinion by Sir Austen Chamberlain but they also reflect his indecision as to the League's value in restraining Germany.

Winston Churchill was in the same quandary as Chamberlain but being more flamboyant he gave his rhetoric free play and delivered strong speeches on every possible side of the question. In the summer and autumn of 1935 he condemned Italy's action, praised the League for taking a strong stand and urged the British Government not to be too prominent in opposing Italy, thereby alienating that country. Even the hard-pressed Abyssinians came in for sympathy and encouragement from time to time:

Abyssinian tribesmen are being attacked by very large Italian armies equipped with all the most terrible weapons of modern science. They are being bombed from the air, bombarded by cannon, trampled down by tanks, and they are fighting as well as they can in their primitive way to defend their hearths and homes, their rights and freedom.[45]

And in a widely publicized address to the City Carleton Club on 26 September he tried to deter Mussolini from his attack on Abyssinia:

Speaking as a true friend of Italy he expressed his surprise that so great a man, so wise a ruler, as Signor Mussolini should be willing, and even eager, to put his gallant nation in such an uncomfortable military and financial position. . . . Unless Italy accepted the good advice of the League of Nations and deferred to its decision such a condition might continue even for years. His experience of war was

[43] 11 July 1935. 304 H.C. Deb. 5s., col. 567.

[44] Reported in *The Times*, 1 Nov. 1935.

[45] Address to his constituents at Chingford, 8 Oct. 1935. Reported in *The Times*, 9 Oct. 1935.

that it took much longer and cost much more than one expected. Italy might one day be grateful to old friends like Great Britain for helping to keep her out of what might be a deadly trap.[46]

When Sir Austen Chamberlain wrote expressing his agreement with this friendly warning Churchill gloomily replied: 'I am glad you approve the line I took about Abyssinia; but I am very unhappy. It would be a terrible deed to smash up Italy and it will cost us dear. . . . If we had felt so strongly on the subject we should have warned Mussolini two months before.'[47]

A couple of days after the Carleton Club speech Churchill followed Chamberlain's example by having a talk with Count Grandi. In their discussion Churchill suggested a meeting of the British, French, and Italian heads of state to 'carry off something' that no one of them could do alone. 'After all', Churchill reported to Sir Robert Vansittart,

> the claims of Italy to primacy in the Abyssinian sphere and the imperative need of internal reform in Abyssinia had been fully recognised by England and France. I told him I should support such an idea if it were agreeable. The British public would be willing to try all roads to an honourable peace. I think there should be a meeting of the three. Any agreement they reached would of course be submitted to the League of Nations. It seems to me the only chance of avoiding the destruction of Italy as a powerful and friendly factor in Europe.[48]

The tone of sweet reasonableness in this conversation and report, the desire to appease Italy in order to maintain her friendship and strength, the blithe disregard of public opinion on the Abyssinian question and the suggestion that something could be 'carried off' and then presented to the League for acceptance, was not significantly different from the agreement reached by Sir Samuel Hoare and the French Prime Minister two months later.

An escape from the dilemma of preserving the League and collective security for possible use against Germany and at the same time maintaining the friendship of Italy lay in the attitude of France. Churchill knew that it was safe to advocate a League policy because it could never be put into effect unless the British

[46] Reported in *The Times*, 27 Sept. 1935.

[47] Churchill, *The Gathering Storm*, p. 174.

[48] Ibid., Appendix A: A Conversation with Count Grandi. Mr. Churchill to Sir Robert Vansittart, 28 Sept. 1935.

Government pressured France to adopt a stiffer line towards Italy. And to guard against this Churchill constantly stressed the value of Italian friendship to France and warned the Government against forcing France to renounce it. 'How strange it is', he wrote to Sir Austen Chamberlain, 'that after all these years of begging France to make it up with Italy, we are now forcing her to choose between Italy and ourselves!'[49] He also advised the Administration to beware, in playing its part in the collective system, lest it become 'a sort of bell-wether or fugleman to gather and lead opinion in Europe against Italy's Abyssinian designs'. Britain, he maintained, was simply not strong enough to be the law-giver and spokesman of the whole world.[50] The contradictions in Churchill's pronouncements, like Sir Austen Chamberlain's, can be explained by the fact that he wanted the best of both courses without the danger that might accrue from a steadfast adherence to one policy.

On 22 October Parliament reassembled for a three-day session before being dissolved for the general election. During this brief meeting the House of Commons debated the international situation, thereby giving every section of the House of Commons an opportunity to rehearse its election arguments.

Sir Samuel Hoare, presenting the Government's case, affirmed the Administration's intention of upholding the policy of collective security and claimed that it was a policy 'not of one party, but of the House as a whole. Indeed, I think I may go further and, when I remember the unprecedented expressions of support, I can claim that not only is it the policy of this House, but it is also the policy of the great majority of men and women in the country as a whole.'[51] The Labour Opposition, apart from the pacifists, could hardly quarrel with this statement and had to content itself with lamely urging the Government to go further and embrace full internationalism.

[49] Winston Churchill to Sir Austen Chamberlain, 10 Oct. 1935. Churchill, *The Gathering Storm*, p. 174.

[50] 11 July 1935. H.C. Deb. 5s., cols. 540–50. The strength of the British navy varied, depending on the presuppositions of the speaker. Those who wished to stop Mussolini felt that it was quite adequate to the task, while those who wished to keep out of the Abyssinian quarrel argued that it was weak and vulnerable to Italian attack. In August Churchill wrote to Hoare expressing his fears about the weakness of the navy; a month later he was warning Grandi about its strength and efficiency. Churchill, *The Gathering Storm*, pp. 170–1 and 173.

[51] 22 Oct. 1935. 305 H.C. Deb. 5s., col. 18.

You cannot follow at one and the same time the system of the League of Nations and the system of old-fashioned Imperialism [said Clement Attlee]. We base our policy on the facts of the modern world, which in our view lead imperatively to subordination of national sovereignties to the League and ultimately to a co-operative commonwealth of the world. We believe that in a state of the world so closely linked as is the world of to-day you must have some authority other than the will of individual Powers.

And while urging the Government to stronger action against Italy Attlee made the usual objections to any increase in the country's defences: 'We are not persuaded in the least that the way to safety is by piling up armaments. We do not believe that in this there is such a thing as national defence. We think that you have to go forward to disarmament, and not to the piling up of armaments.'[52] But while the Opposition might try to score points on the administration John McGovern of the Independent Labour Party was justified in observing that there was

a good deal of shadow boxing going on. There is really no difference of opinion among the three political parties, the Government, the Liberals and the Labour party. They are all agreed on the application of sanctions, some believing that trade and financial sanctions will be all that is required, and others saying that it may entail military sanctions and you will have to be prepared to go the whole hog.[53]

One after the other the supporters of the National Government rose to pay tribute to its wisdom in adopting collective security and to associate themselves with it. Even the right-wing Conservatives had to make the best of a bad situation and find some aspect of their leaders' programme to commend. Leopold Amery took comfort in the fact that the Government had not committed the country to war with Italy and welcomed the decision to step up rearmament:

Let us strengthen our defences and beware how we enter unnecessary quarrels. In the anxious days before us, no one knows how anxious they will be, our one sheet anchor is the strength of the British Navy and its sister services, coupled with a foreign policy, prudent, conciliatory, and non-aggressive, seeking a quarrel with no one, taking part in no unnecessary quarrel, but concerned first and foremost with the security and unity of the British Empire.[54]

52 22 Oct. 1935. Ibid., cols. 35 and 46.

53 22 Oct. 1935. Ibid., col. 90.

54 23 Oct. 1935. Ibid., col. 196.

Sir Henry Page Croft, noting that 'for better or worse' the country was a member of the League, declared that he for one supported the Government's position without hesitation; but the real message of his speech was contained in the passage in which he told the Cabinet that it would get a 'wonderful response from the people' if it took a stand for peace supported by adequate armed forces.[55] Listening to these speeches Lloyd George was not slow to point out the irony of a situation in which those who opposed the Administration in 'the one great policy they have' would get the full support of a rich party while members of the Opposition who were urging collective security would be opposed by all the resources at the Government's disposal.[56]

Sir Austen Chamberlain was in the House during the debate but rather surprisingly took no part in it. Perhaps he was deterred by the difficulty of trying to reconcile his contradictory inclinations in order to present a coherent argument. The difficulties involved in such an enterprise were illustrated in the curious speech delivered by Winston Churchill. Leopold Amery, talking to Churchill before his speech, was dismayed to find that 'his hopes for a League to restrain Germany and his love of a fray decided him, not only to support the Government, but to go beyond it'.[57] But in fact Churchill did not go far beyond Amery's position. After discoursing on German rearmament he dismissed the Abyssinian struggle as 'a very small matter compared with the dangers I have just described'. Making his usual plea for rearmament he annoyed the opposition by claiming that British arms and the League covenant were allied assurances for peace and safety. And against an adamant Foreign Secretary he urged the Government not to abandon the hope of an acceptable compromise:

Perhaps I put it too strongly—that the hope of a satisfactory settlement being reached was not completely dead. Not even that?—that the hope of a satisfactory settlement being reached would always spring eternal in his breast—

Sir Samuel Hoare: I am obliged.

Well, I am sure we should all share the strait-jacketed optimism of my right hon. Friend.

55 24 Oct. 1935. 305 H.C. Deb. 5s., cols. 409 and 420.
56 23 Oct. 1935. Ibid., col. 197.
57 Amery, *Unforgiving Years*, p. 179.

Finally, and most illogically in the light of the rest of his speech, Churchill delivered a Miltonic passage of praise for the League: 'We see a structure always majestic but hitherto shadowy, which is now being clothed with life and power, and endowed with coherent thought and concerted action. We begin to feel the beatings of a pulse which may, we hope, and we pray, some day—and the sooner for our efforts—restore a greater measure of health and strength to the whole world.'[58] It was hardly surprising that Arthur Greenwood, the Labour M.P. who followed this *tour de force,* described it as a characteristic performance:

There are few people in this House who possess his powers of oratory and that highly florid style with which he has succeeded in boxing the compass. . . . The right hon. Gentleman has been trying to have it both ways. I have no doubt that he has perhaps succeeded in justifying his appointment to high office if the worst happens and the National Government is returned.[59]

The Labour party might complain, unconvincingly, that the Administration was following Mussolini's example in fighting the general election on foreign policy in order to divert attention from conditions at home,[60] but since they could offer little choice on the chosen issue, which was dominating public attention, a victory for the National Government was almost a foregone conclusion. But to counter the arguments that the Administration's foreign policy would lead to war Baldwin assured the Peace Society (a pacifist organization) that he felt 'bound over to make the peace'. Seeking to dispel the suspicions aroused by the Cabinet's announcement that it was looking to the country's defences the Prime Minister said:

It does not mean that we look upon force as the judge and law-giver in the affairs of nations. . . . Do not fear that it is a step in the wrong direction. You need not remind me of the solemn task of the League —to reduce armaments by agreement. I know and I shall not forget. But we have gone too far alone and must try to bring others along with us. I give you my word that there will be no great armaments.[61]

Having coppered every bet the National Government confidently waited for the election results.

[58] 24 Oct. 1935. 305 H.C. Deb. 5s., cols. 357–68.
[59] 24 Oct. 1935. Ibid., col. 368.
[60] Arthur Greenwood, 24 Oct. 1935. Ibid., cols. 369–70.
[61] Stanley Baldwin, *This Torch of Freedom* (London, 1935), pp. 338–9. The speech was delivered on 31 Oct. 1935.

Polling was held on 19 November after a remarkably quiet election campaign and the Government was returned with 431 seats. Sir Charles Petrie, writing in the *English Review*, expressed the hopes of the right-wingers in advising Baldwin to interpret his majority as a release from having to take into account every crank and faddist.[62] Lady Houston also urged the Prime Minister to be himself again '—a real Conservative—and be Master in his own House, letting "National" which being interpreted means "International" rest in the oblivion where the electorate have put it'.[63] Baldwin of course had no intention of using his mandate to implement the policies of his die-hard followers. As *The Economist* pointed out: 'So long as the Prime Minister follows his own liberal instincts, he will continue to attract support from many moderate men and women who associate his name with a sincere desire for an unambiguous policy abroad and a more vigorous attack on unemployment at home.'[64] The *Spectator* was more specific, claiming that the electoral triumph was a message to the Government to persist in sanctions and to intensify them until the League's victory was assured: 'On that policy the electors have given an unequivocal verdict, for it is certain that nineteen Opposition members out of twenty are in unreserved agreement with the action the Government has taken.'[65]

It was in this atmosphere of almost unbroken support for the Administration's foreign policy that news of the Hoare–Laval agreement burst on the country, just four weeks after the general election. The exhausted Foreign Secretary, on his way to recuperate in Switzerland, had been induced to make a short stay in Paris, where he had worked out a compromise solution to the Abyssinian problem with the French Prime Minister, Pierre Laval. This projected settlement granted Italy sovereignty over part of Abyssinia and an economic sphere of interest over the rest. While this was less than Mussolini hoped to get, any compromise was unacceptable given the state of British public opinion. When the terms leaked out in Paris on 9 December there was a public outcry in Britain which was naturally reflected in the House of Commons. National M.P.s, and particularly those

[62] 'Foreign Affairs', Dec. 1935.
[63] 'Bravo, Mr. Baldwin', *Saturday Review*, 23 Nov. 1935.
[64] 'Mr. Baldwin's Victory', 23 Nov. 1935.
[65] 'The Election and After', 22 Nov. 1935.

who represented marginal areas, were especially embarrassed by this turn of events, which meant the rejection of the very policy on which they had campaigned and been elected less than a month before.

Stanley Baldwin, whose practice was not to interfere with the decisions of his Ministers, decided to stand by Hoare and ride out the storm. Doubtless the Foreign Secretary would return to England with some shrewd reason for his action that would win over the House of Commons. In the meantime the Prime Minister was embarrassed by a short debate on the matter on 10 December. After listening to the Opposition's indictment of the Government for abandoning its election platform, Baldwin rose to reply. Ill at ease and lacking his usual command of the House he could only point lamely to the difficulties inherent in getting the members of the League to co-operate and hint mysteriously at the reasons which prevented him from making a better case: 'I have seldom spoken with greater regret for my lips are not yet unsealed. Were these troubles over I would make a case and I guarantee that no man would go into the Lobby against us.'[66] This speech, which seemed deliberately misleading, destroyed Baldwin's prestige and influence, which had reached a peak during the election campaign. His public image was not restored until the abdication crisis a year later.[67]

As soon as the details of the Paris agreement were known the Labour party naturally put down a motion demanding that they be repudiated and started preparing for a vote of no confidence in the Government. But even before the Opposition had declared its intention the supporters of the National Government were engaged in a battle on the order paper over the Foreign Secretary's conduct. On 11 December, in response to public opinion, Vyvyan Adams submitted a motion declaring that 'this House will not assent to any settlement of the Italo-Abyssinian dispute which ignores our international obligations under the Covenant of the League of Nations by granting the aggressor state greater concessions after its unprovoked aggression than could have been

[66] 307 H.C. Deb. 5s., col. 856.

[67] Professor Marguerite Potter examines a variety of motives that might have prompted Baldwin's utterance in 'What Sealed Baldwin's Lips?' (*The Historian*, vol. xxvii, no. 1, pp. 21–36). The evidence for her speculation is slender; and the most likely explanation remains that Baldwin expected Hoare to provide a good case on his return.

obtained by peaceful negotiations'.[68] The following day right-wing M.P.s put down two motions commending Hoare's efforts to end the war. One welcomed 'in the interests of this Country and of world peace the constructive efforts of the Government to end the Italo-Abyssinian dispute, and assures it of full support in any practical proposals it may consider necessary to achieve that end'.[69] The other, entitled 'Peace Policy of the Government', expressed approval of the 'declared policy of His Majesty's Government, aiming at the early restoration of peace in Abyssinia and of the preservation of peace in Europe'.[70] Five days later, when the Labour party handed in its motion, no less than fifty-nine National M.P.s signed an amendment altering it to read:

That this House, recognising that the proposals set out in the White Paper for the settlement of the Italo-Ethiopian dispute are unacceptable, urges His Majesty's Ministers to resume the policy outlined in September by the Foreign Secretary at Geneva and overwhelmingly endorsed by this Country at the recent general election.[71]

The signature at the head of this motion was that of Brigadier-General E. L. Spears, the one man who argued for armed collective security throughout the decade. Finally, on the very day of the debate on the Foreign Secretary's conduct, Earl Winterton put down a milder amendment, almost certainly inspired by the party Whips, declaring that 'this House, holding that any terms for settlement of the Italo-Abyssinian dispute should be such as the League can accept, assures His Majesty's Government of its full support in pursuing the foreign policy outlined in the Government manifesto and endorsed by the Country at the recent general election'.[72]

This activity among the back-benchers and in the country put the National Government in a potentially dangerous situation despite its huge majority. Only the die-hards were pleased with Hoare's agreement; and, while it was unlikely that the Administration would be defeated in the House, its majority might be so far reduced that it would feel obliged to resign.

[68] *Notices of Motions etc., 1935–6*, 11, 12, and 16 Dec. 1935.
[69] Ibid., 12 Dec. 1935.
[70] Ibid., 12 and 16 Dec. 1935.
[71] Ibid., 17 and 19 Dec. 1935.
[72] Ibid., 19 Dec. 1935.

Drastic action had to be taken to avoid disaster in the debate on 19 December. On the morning of the 18th the Cabinet debated the matter at considerable length. Apparently they considered this soul-searching so revealing that the minutes were sealed up for twenty years except for a brief moment in 1946 when they were shown to the then Prime Minister, Clement Attlee. The discussion turned on whether the administration could stand behind Hoare, and if so on what grounds, or whether his agreement should be repudiated. Neville Chamberlain spoke on behalf of the Foreign Secretary but most members of the Cabinet felt that it would be political suicide to defend the Hoare–Laval pact, considering the Government's pledges during the general election campaign and Hoare's ringing declaration at Geneva in September. By the end of the meeting Baldwin, who expected the Government's majority to fall to about 100, had not made up his mind what position to take in the debate but 'would stand or fall by what he said on the morrow'. But he must have been impressed by Lord Halifax's argument for Hoare's resignation. The whole moral position of the Government before the world was at stake Halifax pointed out: 'If the Prime Minister were to lose his personal position, one of our national anchors would have dragged.'[73] Later in the day Sir Samuel Hoare was persuaded to resign and the Government's position improved, but it was still possible that someone would marshal the back-benchers to vote against the Administration or induce them to abstain from the division. And even a small defection of its supporters would be humiliating.

The two members who might have organized a back-bench revolt were Winston Churchill and Sir Austen Chamberlain. Fortunately for the Cabinet the unpredictable Churchill was out of the country on a holiday. Looking back later he wished that he had returned: 'I might have brought an element of decision to the anti-Government gatherings which would have ended the Baldwin regime. Perhaps a Government under Sir Austen Chamberlain might have been established at this moment.'[74] Things looked different at the time. Having made his peace with the Conservative party following the passage of the Government of India Act Churchill hoped that he would be offered a

[73] Cab. 23/90B.

[74] Churchill, *The Gathering Storm*, p. 185.

place in the Administration, preferably the Admiralty, following the general election.[75] Hence his support of every position in the Abyssinian dispute and his enthusiastic endorsement of the National Government's election manifesto. But as soon as the results were in, revealing that the Prime Minister was not dependent on his right-wing followers, Baldwin announced that he had no intention of offering Churchill any office. The latter had good reason to be disappointed, though he could afford to be philosophical about it later: 'There was much mocking in the press about my exclusion. But one can see how lucky I was. Over me beat the invisible wings.'[76] Perhaps hoping for better luck in the new year Churchill set out to try his artistic skill in Spain and North Africa. His friends were quite right to advise him to stay away and to argue that he could only harm himself by coming home.[77] While he might have stirred up a political revolt in order to break the National Government it is hard to see how he could have attacked the Hoare–Laval pact in the light of his past utterances. Having urged the Cabinet to find a compromise solution to the Abyssinian war he would have appeared ridiculous leading the pro-League forces, even though political memories are notoriously short. And if there had been a successful revolt while he was out of the country Churchill would almost certainly have been taken into the new Administration.

Sir Austen Chamberlain presented a more formidable challenge to the Government. As soon as the terms of the Hoare–Laval agreement became known the back-benchers flocked to him for a lead. But his course was difficult to predict. While he had made speeches in favour of the League he had said nothing that would qualify him as an opponent of the pact. As late as 15 December he was undecided as to what he should do:

> Laval has behaved treacherously, but I fear Sam Hoare has blundered badly. I don't know what part I shall take in Thursday's debate nor even how I shall vote. Much will depend on the speeches of Hoare and S.B., but they will have an extraordinarily difficult task, for I have never known the political sky cloud over so suddenly nor have I ever seen blacker clouds on the horizon.[78]

Baldwin's chief fear was that Chamberlain would decide to lead

[75] Churchill, *The Gathering Storm*, p. 179.
[76] Ibid., p. 181.
[77] Ibid., p. 185.
[78] Quoted in Petrie, *Life and Letters of Sir Austen Chamberlain*, ii. 404.

the discontented elements in an attack on the Government. Even Hoare's resignation might not be sufficient to apease the back-benchers. The Prime Minister decided to reinsure himself by talking to Chamberlain, whose happiest days had been at the Foreign Office: 'Austen, when Sam has gone, I shall want to talk to you about the Foreign Office.'[79] On the evening before the debate Sir Austen defended the Hoare–Laval agreement as the best of several bad alternatives at a meeting of the Conservative Foreign Affairs Committee; but the feeling against him was so strong that he immediately delivered another condemning it.[80] This seemed to undo Baldwin's work and make it impossible once more to tell what line he would take in the House of Commons the following day.

When the debate began on 19 December Sir Samuel Hoare rose to justify his conduct and to explain his resignation. The House listened in sympathy to the ailing ex-minister[81] as he spoke of the need to maintain Italian friendship and the difficulty of getting other countries (i.e. France) to take their part in the collective system, but M.P.s were not impressed by his speech. As soon as Hoare sat down Clement Attlee, the Leader of the Opposition, moved that the terms of the Hoare–Laval agreement be formally repudiated and demanded the resignation of the National Government so that the country could get back to collective security and full support of the League. It was not only the country's honour that was at stake, he charged, but also the Prime Minister's.[82] Attlee was followed by Baldwin, who was visibly embarrassed, partly by the remarks which had just been addressed to him but also because Sir Austen Chamberlain had not yet announced what position he would adopt in the debate. Addressing himself more to his own followers than to the Opposition Baldwin apologized abjectly for his conduct. Neither he nor his colleagues, he explained, had felt they were betraying their election promises in seeking a compromise solution to the Abyssinian problem. What had convinced him of his error had been 'that deeper feeling which was manifested by many of my

[79] Colvin, *Vansittart*, p. 83.

[80] Templewood, *Nine Troubled Years*, pp. 186–7.

[81] Hoare had broken his nose while skating in Switzerland after his talk with Laval. He appeared in the House with a bandage on it and wits remarked that he had broken his nose to save his face.

[82] 19 Dec. 1935. 307 H.C. Deb. 5s., cols. 2017–30.

hon. Friends in many parts of the country on what I may call grounds of honour. The moment I am confronted with that I know that something has happened that has appealed to the deepest feelings of our countrymen, that some note has been struck that brings back from them a response from the depths.'[83] This amazing admission that the Prime Minister did not know right from wrong until it was pointed out to him by the voters was at least consistent with Baldwin's fundamental belief that the Government ought to respond to the expressed wishes of the country.

The anticipation of Sir Austen Chamberlain's speech was so great that the Speaker called him directly after the Prime Minister instead of choosing a member from the other side of the House. Many M.P.s believed that the fate of the Administration depended on his words. Indeed Chamberlain himself wrote after the debate: 'Had I thought it compatible with the public interest I believe that after S.B.'s miserably inadequate speech and the initial blunder, I could have so reduced his majority as to force his resignation.'[84] In his brief remarks the words which stood out were those in which he denounced Attlee for pointing his finger across the table and charging that the Prime Minister's personal honour was at stake. If that were the issue then decency demanded that the back-benchers rally to their leader's defence: 'Whatever opinion we may hold about what is past, whatever differences of opinion there may be among us as to what ought to be done, that is a challenge which every Member of the National party will resent and resist.'[85] Chamberlain then announced that he would vote for whichever amendment to the Labour motion the Speaker selected. Although it has been argued that Attlee overplayed his hand and lost the opportunity of getting Sir Austen and the other discontented Conservatives to vote against the Government or to abstain,[86] the possibility of Chamberlain taking this course was remote. Baldwin had done his work well and Attlee simply provided Chamberlain with a convenient pretext for marshalling support behind the Administration he expected to join shortly. He, in

[83] 19 Dec. 1935. H.C. Deb. 5s., cols. 2028–9.

[84] Quoted in Petrie, op. cit., ii. 406.

[85] 307 H.C. Deb. 5s., col. 2040.

[86] Cf. Young, *Baldwin* (London, 1952), p. 218; C. F. Brand, *The British Labour Party: A Short History* (Stanford, 1964), p. 196.

turn, saved the back-benchers from the wrath of their constituents without forcing them to compromise their loyalty to their party leaders.

In the excitement of the moment no none noticed that Sir Austen Chamberlain was also advocating a compromise solution to the Abyssinian war. While he welcomed the rejection of the Hoare–Laval agreement he denied that the search for a compromise peace constituted disloyalty to the League or an infringement of the Covenant.

There is nothing in the Covenant to support that argument—not a word. It is essential, while sanctions are in force which are intended to bring about peace, that the League should never lose sight of the fact that sanctions are not an end in themselves, but only a means to that end; and that if that end can be secured by negotiation—as indeed it always must be, for without negotiation it will only be secured by the exhaustion of one party or the other—it is not merely permissible under the Covenant, but it is a duty under the Covenant, to pursue those negotiations.[87]

No doubt Sir Austen looked forward to working for a better compromise than Hoare's when he went to the Foreign Office.

As a face-saving compromise in the debate the Government accepted Lord Winterton's amendment to the Labour party's motion, re-affirming its intention of continuing the foreign policy laid down in its election platform. National M.P.s were able to express their constituent's opposition to the Hoare-Laval pact while voting for their party leaders. The agonizing dilemma of choosing between their constituents and their leaders disappeared. Harold Nicolson, the spokesman for the new diplomacy, who had entered Parliament at the general election rejoiced in his discovery that

this Parliament is not a mere balance of party machines, but is in fact a director and a representative of public opinion, and that through the corridors and lobbies of this House, in a way that outsiders do not realise, public opinion can directly, immediately, and swiftly make itself felt in such a way that the Government become aware of what is really being thought throughout the country.

Nicolson echoed the fears, if not the sensitivity, of many National M.P.s when he told the House of his thoughts when the terms of the Paris agreement were revealed:

[87] 307 H.C. Deb. 5s., col. 2039.

I spent a sleepless night wondering what in all honesty I was to do, knowing that if this White Paper had been published on the 4th November, it would not be I who would be sitting in this House, but my socialist opponent, and I remember wondering and thinking, in stress of conscience, whether I ought not to resign my seat and return my mandate to those who had voted for me.

But it is indicative of the back-bench attitude that so prominent a defender of the League as Nicolson could assert that the British Government's chief concern should not be the preservation of Abyssinian integrity. He defended the Hoare–Laval agreement as 'a very brilliant essay in vivisection.' The real objection was to 'the procedure by which this Pact was negotiated and put through and sent to Addis Ababa' which he denounced as 'a most disgraceful reversion to the very worst of the methods of the pre-war diplomacy, not of this country, but of Italy herself'.[88] An astute observer could have concluded from Nicolson's remarks that as soon as the public lost interest in the Abyssinian war the Cabinet could expect no trouble from its supporters if it decided to abandon Abyssinia and conciliate Italy.

The day after the debate Baldwin, true to his word, asked Sir Austen Chamberlain to call on him to discuss the Foreign Office with 'the same frankness that has always prevailed between us'. The Prime Minister said that he would have 'loved' to have Chamberlain return to the Foreign Office but feared that the work might prove too much.

The Office required iron nerves. The strain of it had broken down Hoare and Vansittart as previously it had broken down Crowe and Tyrrell. No one would believe that my appointment could be more than temporary, or that I should last out the Parliament. He then expatiated at some length on the danger of a man becoming unfit for his work without himself becoming aware of it and illustrated his argument by reference to one of his colleagues in the Government. I could only infer that he thought I should 'crack' (his own word) under the strain, and should persist in continuing the work without realising my mental condition.[89]

At this point Baldwin interrupted his soliloquy to ask Sir Austen for his views on the matter. 'If that is your opinion', he replied, 'it is conclusive.' After a further disquisition on the burdens of

[88] 307 H.C. Deb. 5s., 2077–9.

[89] Sir Austen Chamberlain's version of this conversation to Anthony Eden was: 'He told me I was ga-ga.' Eden, *Facing the Dictators*, p. 534.

office the Prime Minister asked Chamberlain's opinion of Anthony Eden as Foreign Secretary. No doubt taken aback Sir Austen said that he had always thought that his former protégé had 'the makings of a Foreign Secretary', but questioned whether his health was equal to the strain.

When Chamberlain called on the Prime Minister again the following day he found that the latter had decided to appoint Eden to the Foreign Office. Chamberlain was asked to join the Government as a Secretary of State with no specific duties. But after thinking about the offer and discussing it with his wife, Chamberlain, no doubt feeling cheated and bitterly disappointed at not being able to return to the Foreign Office, declined. In his record of these events Sir Austen wrote:

His repeated references to Ramsay MacDonald's condition and to the danger of men becoming senile without being aware of it were offensive in their iterations. I could perceive no prospect of public usefulness in the acceptance of such an offer and so conveyed and I came to the conclusion that what he wanted was not my advice or experience, but the use of my name to help patch up the damaged prestige of his Government.[90]

For the rest of his life Chamberlain maintained correct, if not cordial, relations with 'the worst Prime Minister since that other great and good man, Aberdeen'.[91] And it was hardly surprising that in eulogizing him Baldwin reminded the restive members on the Government benches that Sir Austen's chief characteristic was loyalty: 'It was a loyalty that was shown to his family, to his party, to the House of Commons and to his country. . . . I have never known him let a man down.'[92] Baldwin knew whereof he spoke.

After getting rid of Chamberlain the Prime Minister discussed the Foreign Office with Eden. The latter proposed Lord Halifax for Foreign Secretary but Baldwin did not consider him a good candidate. After lapsing into a contemplative silence for some time Baldwin announced: 'It looks as if it will have to be you.'[93] In this off-hand fashion Eden was invited to redeem the Government from Hoare's blunder.

[90] Memorandum: Invitation to Join Mr. Baldwin's Government. Written by Sir Austen Chamberlain, 21 and 22 Dec. 1935. A.C. 41, folder 125.

[91] Sir Austen Chamberlain to Hilda Chamberlain, 15 Mar. 1936. A.C. Letters.

[92] 17 Mar. 1937. 321 H.C. Deb. 5s., col. 2102.

[93] Eden, *Facing the Dictators*, p. 354.

For most people in the country Eden's promotion was 'the best Christmas present the Prime Minister could have given us'.[94] His well-known enthusiasm for the League of Nations seemed a guarantee for the future: 'It demonstrates the will of the Government, and still more the will of the people, that the foreign policy of Great Britain shall remain based on the League of Nations, and that the policy shall be maintained not only in words, but in deeds.'[95] Right-wing Conservatives, of course, took no comfort in such a guarantee. Eden's appointment, claimed the *Saturday Review*, was 'another extreme surrender to Bolshevism to carry through oil and other sanctions up to the hilt, for Mr. Eden (Litvinoff's mouthpiece) [is] the darling of the Sanctionists, and the protector of the little Powers'.[96] The *National Review* was more optimistic, predicting that in time Eden would be forced to see the real dangers of the situation and turn from the League like Sir Samuel Hoare.[97]

Once the Government had survived the debate on the Hoare–Laval agreement the way was open to pursue the same course by degrees. After Hoare's experience the Administration was careful not to put itself forward too prominently in League affairs. And as the country and the Conservative back-benchers became more apathetic towards the League and even disillusioned by its ineffectiveness in stopping Mussolini the Government began to plead practical difficulties for not taking more vigorous measures against Italy. Really effective sanctions, which would have included oil, were not imposed for fear that they would provoke Mussolini to a 'mad dog' act of revenge against the British fleet in the Mediterranean. Right-wing Conservatives continued their opposition towards any punitive action against Italy and Sir Austen Chamberlain and Winston Churchill soon made it clear that they had no intention of leading any movement to ensure the continuation of sanctions. On 6 April Churchill criticized the Government's policies for falling between two stools: 'We have managed to secure all the disadvantages of both courses

[94] 'Comments', *New Statesman*, 28 Dec. 1935.

[95] 'Mr. Eden and the World', *Spectator*, 27 Dec. 1935.

[96] Kim, 'Sold Again!', 28 Dec. 1935. Two months later the same writer was denouncing Eden as a 'Popinjay in Power': 'A coxcomb. A fop who poses as a big man, drunk with egoism, totally incapable of realising the enormous responsibilities of his high office.' 7 Mar. 1936.

[97] 'Episodes of the Month', Jan. 1936.

without any of the advantages of either. We have pressed France into a course of action which did not go far enough to help the Abyssinians, but went far enough to sever her from Italy.' It was wrong, he said, to lead 'fifty nations up the blind alley of fatuity and frustration. It was a grievous thing, also, to encourage, however indirectly, a primitive population to a desperate resistance and then, in the event, to leave them to their fate.' By taking such a prominent position in imposing sanctions Britain now found itself in a very dangerous situation.[98] When Anthony Eden reminded Churchill that he had told the House of Commons the previous October that he intended to tell his constituents that he would go 'the whole way with the whole lot' in support of sanctions,[99] Churchill claimed that he had meant 'the whole lot of nations, not the whole lot of sanctions'.[100]

Early in May Sir Austen Chamberlain declared that it was foolish and even dangerous to continue sanctions now that Abyssinia had been conquered. Recent experience had proved that economic sanctions were not sufficient to deter a great power, only armed force could do that. Such sanctions as had been applied had neither ended the war nor prevented bloodshed. To go further and expel Italy from the League would only weaken the international organization without forcing Mussolini to give up his spoils. The Duce would not relinquish his new possessions without a fight, which the Labour party was not prepared to face.[101] Perhaps Chamberlain's statement in the House of Commons was prompted by an interview he had had with the Italian Ambassador the day before (5 May), although his biographer claims that he did not reveal what he was going to say in his speech.[102] But the day after his speech Chamberlain wrote to Grandi urging him to impress on Mussolini the value of moderation and wisdom in the hour of victory: 'It is the sharpest test of statesmanship and few indeed have passed it successfully.' Sir Austen suggested that the Italian leader would generate much goodwill if he placed the newly conquered country under a mandate from the League of Nations: 'It would be a great act. If it is too great for him, accept broadly the conditions applying to

98 310 H.C. Deb. 5s., cols. 2481–2.

99 24 Oct. 1935. 305 H.C. Deb. 5s., col. 364.

100 310 H.C. Deb. 5s., col. 2597.

101 6 May 1936. 311 H.C. Deb. 5s., cols. 1769–71.

102 Petrie, *Life and Letters of Sir Austen Chamberlain*, ii. 413.

mandated territories in respect of treatment of natives and the recruitment of armed forces.'[103] Mussolini, of course, had not the slightest intention of compromising his sovereignty in Abyssinia, but Grandi flattered the elder statesman by telling him that Mussolini 'already knows in full detail not only your Speech but all you have done to help the situation and how great has been the weight of your influence in the last few days.' Playing on Conservative hopes for closer relations with Italy the Ambassador dramatically hailed Sir Austen's declaration as a turning-point in the history of Europe: 'It means the new start, the rebuilding, after this momentous year, and, I hope, the beginning of a new and real friendship between our countries.'[104]

Taking his cue from Sir Austen Chamberlain Winston Churchill strengthened his attack on sanctions. He told his constituents that he was not prepared to support the punitive measures 'merely for the purpose of injuring or weakening the Italian people. Unless we are convinced that what we do will be of real practical help to the tribesmen of Abyssinia, we have no right to go further along that path.' He now claimed that the Hoare–Laval agreement had been 'a very shrewd, far-seeing agreement which would have saved the Negus of Abyssinia from ruin before his army was destroyed. The serious thing against it was that it should never have been made by the same Sir Samuel Hoare who had sounded his wonderful trumpet to the League of Nations scarcely three months before.'[105] No mention here of the solemn pledges made by the National Government at the general election.

With the two senior back-benchers taking this tack Neville Chamberlain, the Chancellor of the Exchequer, began urging his colleagues to abandon sanctions. The matter was discussed at Cabinet meetings on 27 and 29 May. Anthony Eden argued that sanctions were having considerable effect but Chamberlain maintained that they should be ended to get Italy back into the League, secure assurances about its future conduct, and revive its interest in restraining Germany. Baldwin, however, while he shared the view that sanctions should be lifted, had no intention of being caught in the same trap twice in less than six months.[106]

103 Sir Austen Chamberlain to Count Grandi, 8 May 1936. A.C. 41, folder 125
104 Count Grandi to Sir Austen Chamberlain, 8 May 1936. A.C. 41, folder 125
105 Reported in *The Times*, 9 May 1936.
106 Cab. 23/84.

In order to force a decision on the Prime Minister by showing that sanctions were no longer popular among back-benchers Neville Chamberlain planted a calculated indiscretion on the subject into a speech he delivered to the 1900 Club on 10 June. 'I did it deliberately,' he wrote afterwards, 'because I felt that the party and the country needed a lead, and an indication that the government was not wavering and drifting without a policy. . . . I did not consult Anthony Eden because he would have been bound to beg me not to say what I proposed.'[107] In his address the Chancellor declared that it would be 'the very midsummer of madness' to continue sanctions. They had been tried and failed; and as sanctions involved the risk of war the experiment had demonstrated that countries were unwilling to fight unless they were actually threatened.[108] Chamberlain's move turned out even better than he expected: in introducing the speaker Robert Horne, a former Chancellor of the Exchequer and now a Conservative back-bencher, had invited the Government to end sanctions: 'When there is a corpse in your midst it is better to bury it.'[108] Perhaps the typical moderate Conservative attitude had been summed up a month before when Sir Hugh O'Neill, a Conservative member of the League of Nations Union, told the House of Commons that the League had not only failed but was 'doomed, damned and dead. . . . At the General Election I supported the League of Nations as it was then constituted, because I believed it was possible for it to do something. I am now convinced that in the greatest crisis it has ever had to face it has proved incapable of accomplishing what it set out to accomplish.'[109]

Although the Opposition was furious when the National Government announced its intention of terminating sanctions on 18 June, there was little stir among its own supporters. They accepted without a murmur the curious argument that Britain should take the lead in removing sanctions since it had taken the lead in imposing them. When the Labour party introduced a motion on 23 June censuring the Administration for abandoning

[107] Diary entry, 17 June 1936. Feiling, *Life of Neville Chamberlain*, p. 296.

[108] Reported in *The Times*, 11 June 1936.

[109] 6 May 1936. 311 H.C. Deb. 5s., col. 1778. Such was the loss of faith in the League following the Italian conquest of Abyssinia that the League of Nations Union found it difficult to collect subscriptions. N. Wood, 'Winning Over the Waverers', *Headway*, Mar. 1937.

its policy, only two Conservatives voted against the Government, Vyvyan Adams and Harold Macmillan (who then resigned the party whip to sit as an independent Conservative). Others who might have been unhappy about the withdrawal of sanctions were reassured by ministerial statements that the League would be 'reformed', though it was never spelled out whether this meant strengthened or, as the die-hards hoped, reformed out of existence.

'So ended the years of delusion in this country,' wrote Leopold Amery with satisfaction twenty years later. 'So also ended the League of Nations, killed by the wishful thinking of sincere but misguided enthusiasts and by the interplay of our party politics.'[110] Now that the policy of collective security had been abandoned and was in disrepute it was difficult for any Conservative to advocate such a solution to international problems without exposing himself to the ridicule of his colleagues. After the Abyssinian fiasco most of the National Government's internal critics were too convinced that the League had failed to expect an effective barrier to German expansion to be created within its framework. As the potential danger from Germany increased they demanded that the Government act to build a defensive alliance against that country. But, by failing to press the Administration to stand by the policy it had announced in September 1935, the back-benchers were not only in a weak position to demand resistance to Germany but they were also largely responsible for breaking the instrument which could have been used to restrain Hitler. Baldwin would certainly have continued the policy of collective security within the framework of the League if his supporters had kept up the pressure. Most M.P.s, of course, were not much concerned about foreign affairs unless the Government's conduct produced strong feeling in their constituencies, but those who made foreign policy their speciality failed to give their colleagues any real alternative to acquiescing in the course, because they in turn were unable to make up their minds as to whether they should support the League or appease Mussolini. And when they did arrive at a firm decision it was one which undercut their later advocacy. It was difficult for people like Winston Churchill, who had helped to persuade the back-benchers that sanctions were foolish, to claim shortly after

[110] Amery, *Unforgiving Years*, p. 190.

that the best hope of peace lay in supporting the League and collective security.

The Abyssinian affair had other repercussions on the foreign policy debates in the next few years. Mussolini's rapid conquest of Abyssinia convinced the British Government and most of its supporters that Italy was a great military power, making them even more eager to curry the Duce's favour so that his mighty forces could be used to deter Hitler from aggression. Mussolini's activities in Abyssinia and his intervention in the Spanish Civil War also diverted attention from Germany's rearmament and territorial demands. Not until the seizure of Prague in March 1939 was the German dictator's conduct judged in the same light as Mussolini's. In the shadow of Italian wickedness Hitler was able to continue his rearmament, seize the Rhineland and Austria, and accept the German-speaking areas of Czechoslovakia from a grateful Britain and France, before any large body of suspicion was aroused in England. At least until Munich more people saw Mussolini rather that Hitler as the principal peace-disturber.

Meanwhile, both the old system of diplomatic alliances against a nation which threatened to overthrow the balance of power in Europe, and the new League system, had been discredited. The British Government continued to deal with each crisis as it arose on the principle of non-involvement unless it presented a challenge to British interests in the narrowest sense.

5. Crying Wolf: The Reoccupation of the Rhineland

ONE of the interested observers of the argument over sanctions was Adolf Hitler, who concluded that if Britain and France were unwilling or unable to stop Mussolini they would be even less likely to resist German reoccupation of the Rhineland, which had been declared a demilitarized zone in 1919 and accepted as such by Germany in the Locarno treaties of 1925. On Saturday, 7 March 1936 Hitler suddenly marched his troops into the area; and when his gamble paid off he was able to confront his doubting generals with a clear triumph of his intuition over their fears and hesitations, thereby spiking opposition to other daring moves in the future. With the subsequent fortification of the Rhineland Germany was secure from attack in the west in the event of a move to the east. But the true significance of the invasion did not become obvious until Hitlers' designs on his eastern neighbours became more evident. At the time it was accepted as a minor territorial adjustment and a justifiable move on Germany's part.

British indifference to the reoccupation of the Rhineland was in startling contrast to the uproar that had developed when Mussolini began his preparations for attacking Abyssinia. This time, said the Conservative M.P. Emrys-Evans, 'I received no notice of great Albert Hall meetings of protest, when agreements were broken, when the Covenant was defied, when Locarno was smashed.'[1] Not only did the speed of Hitler's move catch the country off guard but it was also accompanied by impressive-sounding guarantees for the future: a twenty-five-year Western non-aggression pact, bilateral treaties with Germany's eastern neighbours, and the prospect of Germany's return to the League at some future date. The olive branch effectively hid the sword, at least for the time being. Hardly anyone in England was prepared to put Germany's action on the same plane as Italy's. Hugh Dalton, speaking for the Labour party, claimed that public opinion drew

[1] 23 June 1936. 313 H.C. Deb. 5s., col. 1654.

a clear distinction between the actions of Signor Mussolini in resorting to aggressive war and waging it beyond his frontiers and the actions, up to date at any rate, of Herr Hitler which, much as we may regard them as reprehensible, have taken place within the frontiers of the German Reich. The public here draws that distinction, and it is a very proper distinction.[2]

The *Spectator* maintained that there could be 'no question of League-imposed sanctions where there has been no resort to war. And this country could not join in military measures when there has been no such action by Germany as would in itself endanger the peace.'[3] Supporters of the League of Nations had no intention of letting public attention be diverted from Italy's crimes by Germany's petty larceny. *Headway*, the League of Nations Union's magazine, warned against forgetting Abyssinia in the flurry over Locarno: 'The supporters of the League must not allow such a tragedy. Italy is making war; Abyssinians are dying in defence of their country. Germany has not made war; no life has been lost because of her action. The League has done its duty in blaming Germany. Now it must return its attention to Italy.'[4]

For many people Hitler's action simply removed one of the major humiliations imposed by the bankrupt Versailles treaty. The reoccupation of the Rhineland was a sign that Germany had substantially regained that equality of status for which she had agitated so long and which enlightened opinion in England had advocated since the end of the First World War. As the *Spectator* put it:

That the Rhineland should be no longer demilitarised is a small thing in itself; no one ever supposed that mark of inequality could be permanent. No one is disposed to moralise over-much about Germany's repeated breaches of the Treaty of Versailles. Her right

[2] 26 Mar. 1936. 310 H.C. Deb. 5s., col. 1454. Writing about the Rhineland crisis in 1940, however, Dalton claimed: 'The British Softies were quite happy . . Others, of whom I was one, were not at all happy. We spoke publicly of the deep concern felt by all Germany's neighbours at her massive and menacing rearmament. We urged the organisation, in Eastern as well as Western Europe, of collective security against German aggression. But we recognised, frankly and regretfully, that British public opinion was not prepared to react with energy against this particular treaty violation.' Hugh Dalton, *Hitler's War* (Penguin Books, 1940), p. 65.

[3] 'Does Germany Mean Peace?', 20 Mar. 1936.

[4] 'News and Comment', Apr. 1936.

to equality has been generally recognised in principle and it only remains to apply it in the remaining details.[5]

But if no one was prepared to deny Hitler's case his methods gave some cause for alarm. Lloyd George, no opponent of Hitler at this point, said in his vivid fashion that Hitler had 'organised a torch-light procession through a powder magazine, and there has nearly been a very shattering explosion.'[6] But here again there were many who were willing to overlook the way in which Germany had redressed her grievances in the hope that the way was now open for a period of better understanding between Germany and the rest of Europe. 'The essential is to get discussion started on Hitler's positive proposals', said the *Spectator*.[7] *The Times,* two days after the reoccupation, hailed the move as 'A Chance to Rebuild'. And the organ of the League of Nations Union was positively ecstatic about the possibilities which now opened up: 'Is March 1936 a turning point in world history? It may prove so. Already the signs are being read hopefully and even confidently by some experienced observers who are seldom the dupes of their desires. They say that the unhappy and most unhappily prolonged chapter of post-war resentments and suspicions is closed.'[8]

But amid these expressions of confidence in the future there were a few shadows of suspicion that lengthened with the passage of time. 'The future of the world would be easier to predict if anyone except Herr Hitler himself knows what reliance can be placed on Herr Hitler's word,' wrote the *Spectator*. His fine proposals for the future would 'evoke new hopes of the re-establishment of confidence and security in Europe *if* Herr Hitler could be depended upon to keep his word, which he has just spectacularly demonstrated that he cannot.'[9] This, of course, was the nub in trying to assess all Hitler's actions. A week later the *Spectator* returned to the theme:

Nothing in Herr Hitler's peace proposals, except his suggestion of Germany's return to the League, is inconsistent with the theory that Germany wants peace in the west with a view to freeing her for action in the east. Hitler proposes a non-aggression pact with France

[5] 'The German Challenge', 13 Mar. 1936.
[6] 26 Mar. 1936. 310 H.C. Deb. 5s., col. 1481.
[7] 'News of the Week', 13 Mar. 1936.
[8] 'Hopes of a Brighter Day', *Headway*, Apr. 1936.
[9] 'The German Challenge', 13 Mar. 1936.

which would immobilise France if Germany were at war with Russia. He offers no non-aggression pact to Russia.

If Hitler wanted his promises to be accepted, the journal concluded, he should accompany them with some concrete evidence of his good faith.[10] But these doubts and hesitations were obscured by the more general reaction: 'After all, they are only going into their own back-garden.'[11]

The complacency with which the reoccupation of the Rhineland was received in England was due in some measure to strong anti-French feeling in the country at the time. Sir Austen Chamberlain described it in a letter to Count Vladimir d'Ormesson. Right-wing politicians, who regarded the recent Franco-Soviet pact as 'almost a betrayal of Western Civilization' were afraid that the country would be dragged into war as a result of French diplomatic activity in Eastern Europe. There was no doubt, he wrote, that Britain was united 'in the determination to join in the defence of France and Belgium against any invasion. To set against this, however, there is a great fear of France's entanglements and a general feeling that the occupation of the demilitarized zone by Germany was a certainty sooner or later and that it is useless to cry over spilt milk.' Moderate and left-wing opinion, while less critical of France's agreement with Russia, 'reproaches her with slackness in applying sanctions to Italy and contrasts the claims of France for strong action about the Rhineland, where no blood was shed, with her apathy in regard to the slaughter in Abyssinia'.[12] Politicians of every shade could unite in regarding the German action as a kind of divine retribution for France's diplomatic sins in the last few months.

With practically all political opinion in England hostile to France there was little likelihood that the British Government would allow itself to be persuaded by France to take action against Germany. Stanley Baldwin, still recovering from the acute humiliation brought on him by the Abyssinian dispute, was determined to avoid a repetition of the experience in this latest crisis. Happily for him his inclination not to intervene was reinforced by the attitude of his followers and the Opposition.

[10] 20 Mar. 1936.

[11] This remark, usually attributed to Lord Lothian, is quoted in Churchill, *The Gathering Storm*, pp. 196–7.

[12] Sir Austen Chamberlain to Count Vladmir d'Ormesson, 28 Mar. 1936. A.C. 41, folder 125.

Two days after the invasion of the Rhineland Harold Nicolson reported: 'General mood of the House [of Commons] is one of fear. Anything to keep out of war.' And the next day: 'The country will not stand for anything that makes for war. On all sides one hears sympathy for Germany. It is all very tragic and sad.'[13] When Eden broached the issue of force the Prime Minister made it clear that Britain would not support any French military action against Germany.[14] And when the matter of Anglo-French staff talks came up Baldwin warned his Foreign Secretary of their unpopularity among the Conservative back-benchers: 'The boys won't have it.'[15]

At the very moment of the invasion the Prime Minister, under pressure from his party to do more about rearmament, was brooding over the possible candidates to head the new Ministry of Defence. Winston Churchill's chances were not unhopeful, even though he had been passed over for the Admiralty a few months before. His claims were supported by Sir Austen Chamberlain but just as strongly opposed by Neville Chamberlain. The latter argued that Churchill's entry would alarm the liberal and moderate supporters of the Government who regarded his exclusion as a pledge against militarism; but the prospect of having to fight Churchill for the party leadership when Baldwin retired also weighed with the Chancellor of the Exchequer.[16] As it turned out it was Hitler's invasion of the Rhineland that dashed Churchill's chances. On 13 March it was announced that the Solicitor General, a minor figure best remembered for his part in the debates on Prayer Book reform, had been appointed Minister for the Co-ordination of Defence. 'Inskip would create no jealousies,' wrote Neville Chamberlain. 'He would excite no enthusiasm but he would involve us in no fresh perplexities.'[17] Churchill's unoriginal comment was that this was the most remarkable appointment since Caligula made his horse consul.[18] The *Saturday Review*, taking up his case, criticized the Prime Minister for not appointing Churchill to prove his seriousness

[13] Diary entries, 9 and 10 Mar. 1936. Nicolson, *Diaries and Letters*, pp. 248–9.
[14] Eden, *Facing the Dictators*, p. 358.
[15] Ibid., p. 407.
[16] Feiling, *Life of Neville Chamberlain*, p. 278.
[17] Diary entry, 11 Mar. 1936. Macleod, *Neville Chamberlain* (London, 1961), p. 193.
[18] Amery, *Unforgiving Years*, p. 196.

about rearmament: 'Mr. Baldwin likes to surround himself with spineless sycophants and nancyfied nobodies; like many other vain man he cannot tolerate the man who calls a spade a spade.' But at the same time the magazine also warned Churchill to concentrate on rearmament and 'NOT IN THE SAME BREATH ADVOCATE OUR BEING TIED TO THE CARTWHEEL OF THE LEAGUE OF NATIONS.'[19]

Although the House of Commons was prepared for a two-day defence debate on 9 and 10 March, an ideal opportunity to discuss the reoccupation of the Rhineland, M.P.s of all parties were quite willing to leave the matter to the Government and it was scarcely mentioned in the debate. The Prime Minister managed to get through a long speech on defence and its relation to collective security without a single reference to the Rhineland. The Labour party was more concerned with the iniquity of unilateral British rearmament than with Hitler's latest move. And Winston Churchill was inhibited from making a damaging attack on the Administration by the fact that he was being considered for the Ministry of Defence and his performance in the debate might influence the Prime Minister's decision. According to Neville Chamberlain he suppressed the critical speech he had prepared,[20] delivering instead a speech defending and encouraging the Cabinet in its rearmament efforts.

It was not until 26 March that the House of Commons held a debate on the invasion of the Rhineland. By that time nothing that could be said in the House would have the slightest effect on what had happened or induce the Government to take steps towards evicting the entrenched German troops from the formerly demilitarized zone. For almost three weeks M.P.s had voluntarily refrained from discussing the matter so that the Government would not be embarrassed in its talks with the other Locarno powers and in the League of Nations. But this unusual political restraint was really a reflection of the general conviction that nothing could or should be done about the *fait accompli*. Indeed at the Cabinet meeting on 25 March Anthony Eden had urged that the Government ought to combat this complacency in the following day's debate. The opportunity should be taken

to enlighten public opinion which was assuming that Germany was

[19] Kim, 'Baldwin's Contribution to National Defence—Inskip!', 21 Mar. 1936.
[20] Diary entry, 11 Mar. 1936. Macleod, *Neville Chamberlain*, p. 193.

the 'white sheep' and not the 'black sheep' . . . Another idea which ought to be combatted was the prevalent one that the occupation of the Rhineland was no threat to France. It was a threat because so long as the Rhineland was demilitarised the Germans, in order to invade France through Belgium as in 1914, would have to use large forces to hold the Rhineland and their striking force would be reduced. After occupying the Rhineland they could fortify it, hold the frontier with a relatively small force, and greatly increase their striking force on the northern bank.[21]

Eden had good cause to be concerned about the reaction to the invasion of the Rhineland. Even Harold Nicolson, one of the best-informed diplomatic observers in the House of Commons, was unable to decide what course the British Government should adopt. He was well aware that the French had a good case for arguing that the Germans ought to be repelled from the Rhineland: 'We know that Hitler gambled on this coup. We know Schacht told him it would lead to financial disaster, that Neurath told him it would create a dangerous diplomatic situation, and that the General Staff told him that if France and Great Britain acted together there would be no chance of resistance.' But now that the German troops were in the Rhineland the British Government was in a dilemma:

If we send an ultimatum to Germany, she ought in all reason to climb down. But then she will not climb down and we shall have war. Naturally we shall win and enter Berlin. But what is the good of that? It would only mean communism in Germany and France, and that is why the Russians are so keen on it. Moreover the people of this country absolutely refuse to have a war. We should be faced by a general strike if we even suggested such a thing.

In the circumstances Nicolson concluded the only course open to Britain was to 'swallow this humiliation as best we may, and be prepared to become the laughing stock of Europe. I do not mind that very much. We can rebuild our shattered name. But it does mean the final end of the League and I do mind that dreadfully. Quite dreadfully.'[22] Nicolson did not mention that if the League had been supported properly in the Abyssinian crisis Hitler might well have hesitated to challenge a smoothly functioning collective system.

[21] Cab. 23/83.

[22] Harold Nicolson to Victoria Sackville-West, 12 Mar. 1936. Nicolson, *Diaries and Letters*, pp. 249–50.

At the beginning of the debate on the Rhineland Anthony Eden thanked the members of the House of Commons, the press, and the public for their restraint in the period since the invasion. He then went on to describe the bland and unobjectionable aims of the Administration:

First to avert the danger of war, second, to create the conditions in which negotiations can take place, and third, to bring about the success of these negotiations so that they may strengthen collective security, further Germany's return to the League and, in a happier atmosphere, allow these larger negotiations on economic matters of armaments which are indispensable to the appeasement of Europe to take place.[23]

These were goals which appealed to a wide political spectrum, from the Labour party to right-wing Conservatives. Indeed no extreme Conservative bothered to speak in the debate. Not only were they indifferent to the reoccupation but they also regarded it as a natural consequence of sanctions which had shown Hitler that Italian support for Locarno was dead. As the *National Review* put it:

Sanctions were always bound to kill Locarno by the breach they made between the guarantors of that instrument, England and Italy, and it was a very curious form of blindness on the part of the Locarno enthusiasts which made them believe that sanctions against Italy could be applied without injury to the Streseman–Briand–Chamberlain plan.[24]

Hitler's latest move was something of a blessing for die-hard Conservatives, as it gave them a strong argument for dropping sanctions; and they took comfort from the fact that the Government was taking steps towards rearmament. Meanwhile Leopold Amery praised the 'self-restraint' of France—reinforced by the lack of British support—which had prevented a European conflagration on 7 March: 'In a position of immense difficulty France has endeavoured to meet her obligations towards the League and to pay some regard to the future of Europe.'[25]

The only significant opposition to the Government came from the traditionalists among its followers, who believed that treaties must be adhered to and who worried about the threat which Germany's action posed to the balance of power in Europe.

[23] 26 Mar. 1936. 310 H.C. Deb. 5s., col. 1446.
[24] 'Episodes of the Month', Apr. 1936.
[25] 6 May 1936. 311 H.C. Deb. 5s., col. 1824.

Winston Churchill, his lips unsealed by the Government's decision to dispense with his services once more, was articulate about the Administration's general and specific shortcomings in the sphere of foreign policy. Reviewing the period since the National Government had taken office he declared:

Five years ago all felt safe, five years ago all were looking forward to peace, to a period in which mankind would rejoice in the treasures which science can spread to all classes if the conditions of peace and justice prevail. Five years ago to talk of war would have been regarded not only as a folly and a crime but almost as a sign of lunacy. The difference in our position now!

Getting down to the specific issue under discussion he pointed out that the German leader had gained an enormous triumph which would enable him to consolidate his nation behind him. Fortifications would be erected in the Rhineland making it a 'barrier across Germany's front door, which will leave her free to sally out eastwards and southwards by the back door'. But the overriding problem was not so much the reoccupation or remilitarization of the Rhineland as the rapid rearmament of Germany: 'the great wheels revolving and the great hammers descending day and night in Germany, making the whole industry of the country an arsenal, making the whole of that gifted and valiant population into one great disciplined war machine'. Dismissing the policy of letting the German explosion blast itself east and south while Britain and France stood together in the west, Churchill called for an alliance of all peace-loving countries to resist any further aggression collectively and within the framework of the League:

I desire to see the collective forces of the world invested with overwhelming power. If you are going to run this thing on a very slight margin, one way or the other, you are going to have war. But if you get five or ten to one on one side, all bound rigorously by the Covenant and the conventions which they own, then, in my opinion, you have an opportunity of making a settlement which will heal the wounds of the world.[26]

Evidently the contradiction between wrecking the League by calling for an end to sanctions and building it up as an instrument to contain Germany did not occur to Churchill at the time or when writing his memoirs later.

26 26 Mar. 1936. 310 H.C. Deb. 5s., cols. 1523–30.

Less forceful and more cautious than Churchill, Sir Austen Chamberlain was unsure about his response to Hitler's action. Writing to his sister on the day of the invasion he described the news as 'grave' but added that he had not yet committed himself on the matter.[27] A week later he had come to the conclusion that the reoccupation was a serious affair and gloomily forecast a complete triumph for Germany and ruin for Britain from a succession of such moves.[28] And in the debate he warned the House of Commons not to think that the issue was simply 'one of those internal squabbles between France and Germany which disturb the peace of the world'. The real issue was 'whether in future the law of force shall prevail or whether there shall be substituted for it the force of law'. If the force of law was to prevail Germany must offer more than verbal assurances that she was willing to submit to it: 'All the acts are forceful; only the words are reassuring.' Above all, Britain should not allow itself to be lulled into an acquiescent mood by Hitler's conciliatory proposals. But this is not to say that Chamberlain was advocating a bellicose course:

> If there be any division among us, it is not between those who want peace and those who want war; it is between those who take a short view of what lies in front of us and those who, looking further ahead, cannot feel it in their consciences to accept an easy settlement to-day if they know that it will bring disaster to their children a few years ahead.

A firm believer in regional pacts, as became an author of the Locarno treaties, Sir Austen did not support Churchill's vigorous plea for collective security to contain Germany, but he did point out that when the present troubles were over the country would have to do some hard thinking about the meaning of collective security and decide if it was to be anything more than 'a pretty phrase to adorn a meaningless speech'.[29]

With the exception of one member who was making his maiden speech all the back-benchers who spoke from the Government side of the House voiced the same concern as Chamberlain and Churchill. Harold Nicolson advocated an immediate, precise guarantee of the Dutch, Belgian, and French frontiers until the

[27] Sir Austen Chamberlain to Ida Chamberlain, 7 Mar. 1936. A.C. Letters.
[28] Id. to Hilda Chamberlain, 15 Mar. 1936, ibid.
[29] 26 Mar. 1936. 310 H.C. Deb. 5s., cols. 1482–7.

League could be strengthened and this temporary barrier rendered redundant.[30] In a letter to his wife a couple of weeks later he argued that the British public would probably only go to war for France and Belgium against Germany: 'We must therefore make that a definite geographical basis for our policy. It is not a question of liking or not liking the French; it is a question of the defence of London.'[31]

Robert Boothby told the House of Commons that Germany's foreign policy was more intelligible when it was related to the nature of the Nazi regime. He pointed out that the methods by which the German leaders had come to power and maintained themselves there were now being applied to foreign affairs: 'They are following the method of the *coup*, of the *fait accompli*. They give us the greatest assurances, and smooth everybody down, and when everybody is feeling happy and nobody is looking, they pounce.' In one of the earliest references to *Mein Kampf* in the House of Commons Boothby referred to Hitler's dictum that the really big bluff was the acme of statesmanship in foreign affairs. The way to call Hitler's bluff was by resolute action on the part of other countries. Some people, however, advocated unlimited concessions to Germany in the hope that

> a day will come when we shall get the Germans and the Russians fighting each other and everybody else can stand back; and then, somehow or other, these two great menaces will 'do in' each other and we shall be free from Communism and Socialism and everything of that kind. That is at the back of the minds of a number of people, and on the face of it it is a simple and alluring proposition, but that sort of thing does not happen and is not going to happen.

Boothby argued that Germany would take the easier road to the south, leaving Britain to decide at what point it was going to say 'Enough'. And in the long run, he concluded, Britain could never 'tolerate a Nazi Germany astride of the whole of Europe omnipotent right across the Continent'. The touchstone was the Rhineland, because if Britain did not stand by France and the League at this time the smaller countries would hasten to make what terms they could with Germany.[32]

[30] 26 Mar. 1936. 310 H.C. Deb. 5s., cols. 1471–2.

[31] Harold Nicolson to Victoria Sackville-West, 8 April 1936. Nicolson, *Diaries and letters 1930–1939*, p. 257.

[32] 26 Mar. 1936. 310 H.C. Deb. 5s., cols. 1493–1501.

Brigadier-General E. L. Spears and Paul Emrys-Evans also tried to call the attention of the House to the seriousness of the situation and the significance of what had happened in the Rhineland. Both pointed out that unless the League of Nations could be made into an effective instrument for collective security Britain would have to fall back on a policy of alliances as the best form of security. And neither of them put much faith in Hitler's promises. 'I have heard the argument advanced on the Continent', said General Spears,

> that at any rate, having invaded the Rhineland this year and having offered a treaty of 25 years' duration, next year they will take Austria and offer a treaty of 50 years; that after that it will be the turn of Memel and the Corridor, when they will offer a treaty of 75 years, and we can look forward to eternal peace once France and England have disappeared.[33]

But the feeling of the House of Commons was not with them. As Lieutenant-Commander Fletcher of the Labour party said:

> We have heard a number of speeches to-day on the necessity for upholding the sanctity of treaties.... In spite of all that may be said on that head, I feel that a very large section of public opinion regards the present crisis as part of the eternal wrangle between France and Germany, and the force of the argument that the whole basis of international law is at stake is, I think, weakened in this country by the feeling that Germany has some valid grievances arising out of the Treaty and of other incidents that have taken place since that Treaty was concluded.[34]

Neville Chamberlain was more in tune with the House's mood when he stated, in winding up the debate, that the Government would not join France in any move to force German troops out of the Rhineland.[35] The interjection of an unidentified member at this point was indicative of the general feeling: 'What is all the fuss, then?'

It was not until a couple of years later that the invasion of the Rhineland came to be regarded as a major turning-point in relations between Germany and other European powers. The great arguments and recriminations did not come until long after the event. At the time it caused remarkably little stir. Few

[33] 26 Mar. 1936. Ibid., col. 1509.
[34] Ibid., col. 1511.
[35] Ibid., col. 1547.

8214871 I

people recognized that the failure to make Germany respect its treaties, or at least submit its claims for revision to Geneva to be dealt with in an orderly diplomatic fashion, meant another serious blow to the League and the collective system at the very moment that sanctions were breaking down. Few even suspected that Hitler's method of redressing his country's grievances might provide a clue to his future conduct. With almost insignificant exceptions everyone in England grasped the larger hope that this was the last blow that Hitler would administer to the peace and stability of Europe.

6. The Spanish Distraction

THE Spanish Civil War, which broke out in July 1936 and lasted for three years, was the most important event between the wars for socialists, liberals, intellectuals, and perhaps even the workers. Many of those who had been pacifists since the end of the First World War saw the Spanish conflict as a confrontation of democracy and Fascism and their hatred of the latter was great enough to overcome their previous conviction that war was the greatest of all evils. Within the Labour party the war provoked a lively debate and was of crucial importance in the development of the Labour party's foreign policy, strengthening the conviction which originated in Mussolini's invasion of Abyssinia, that there were issues in the international sphere which justified a resort to arms. After the ignominious failure of sanctions against Italy socialists and liberals threw themselves on to the Loyalist side of the new struggle, resolved that Fascism should not gain yet another easy victory. But the socialist recognition of the threat to democracy posed by the dictators did not mean that they were converted to the idea that peace must be defended by force, much less that they saw the need for British rearmament so that the country, or the League, would be in a stronger position to deal with Hitler and Mussolini. Quite the contrary. As one writer put it in the *New Statesman*: 'I see no intellectual difficulty in at once working for the victory of the Spanish people and in being glad of the growing pacifist movement in England.'[1]

At the very moment that some observers could discern the possibility of another major war in Europe the Spanish Civil War served to split the country into two distinct camps. K. W. Watkins concluded from his study of British opinion towards the war: 'Probably not since the French Revolution had a "foreign event" so bitterly divided the British people, and this at a time when national unity was essential for our very survival.'[2] The National Government's attitude and conduct towards the contending factions did nothing to resolve these difficulties but

[1] Critic, 'A London Diary', *New Statesman*, 22 Aug. 1936.

[2] K. W. Watkins, *Britain Divided: The Effects of the Spanish Civil War on British Political Opinion* (London, 1963), p. vii.

rather sharpened the Opposition's criticism of its foreign policy. But, while left-wingers became engrossed in the long-drawn-out war and their own Government's approach to it, their attention was diverted from events in the rest of Europe. To ignore the invasion of the Rhineland while preoccupied with sanctions was serious enough; but during the three years that attention was fixed on Spain it was hard to see clearly the significance of the *Anschluss*, the absorption of half of Czechoslovakia in two stages, and the Italian seizure of Albania. While the dictators were making these gains the British Government received no strong pressure from the Labour and Liberal parties to pursue a different course. Even the stubborn Neville Chamberlain might have been forced to stiffen his attitude towards Hitler and Mussolini under the combined and sustained criticism of the Opposition parties and his own back-benchers. But these two groups were fatally divided on their attitude towards the Spanish Civil War.

If the Spanish troubles divided the British political community as a whole they did much to unite the supporters of the National Government and smooth over many of their former disagreements over foreign policy. The conflict was never the burning issue for National M.P.s that it was for the Opposition; indeed the Spanish Civil War provoked less dissent among them than any other international problem that arose in the decade. It did not even produce much comment from Conservatives, who found it difficult to understand why their opponents were so exercised over the war. Almost to a man the back-benchers supported the official policy of non-intervention, some because they were indifferent to the issues being fought over in Spain, more because they soon realized that non-intervention was working to the advantage of the insurgents, who would rescue the country from Communism and anarchy. And as the ideological issues in Spain became sharper and more extreme, Conservatives became more anti-Government and more pro-Franco.

One result of the relatively detached Conservative attitude towards Spain was that those who feared German expansion were able to keep their eyes more firmly fixed on Hitler's actions and to continue pressing the Cabinet to see that the danger to European peace came not from Spain but from Germany. In so far as they argued that no vital British interests were at stake in Spain they were preaching to the converted, but the National Government went one step further in maintaining that Germany did not present a threat that could not be resolved.

When the fighting began in Spain everyone in Britain agreed that the correct policy was one of strict non-intervention in conjunction with France. The Spanish borders would be sealed and the Spaniards left to fight out their differences among themselves. This policy was perfectly acceptable to the Labour party so long as it was effective, because under such conditions the Spanish Government would almost certainly succeed in putting down the revolt. But when it became clear that non-intervention was working against the Government and that first the Italians and then the Germans were aiding Franco, the Liberal and Labour parties began to oppose the policy, advocating instead the sale of arms to Spain in the same manner as they would be supplied to any other legitimate Government facing an insurrection. This was an effective argument to support the Spanish loyalists but it contradicted the Labour party's charge that armaments manufacturers were merchants of death, whose activities were among the chief causes of war, to say nothing of its earlier principle that war does not really solve any issues. Furthermore, the National Government and its supporters could always embarrass members of the Opposition by challenging them to declare that they would be willing to supply arms to Germany in the event of a revolt against the Nazi government. An affirmation could be as damaging as evasion. Philip Noel-Baker, for example, when asked the question in December 1936, found himself saying:

> I will reply at once to the hon. Member with the utmost candour. I believe in the mutual respect of differing regimes, in favour of which the Foreign Secretary pronounced in answer to a question the other day. That is embodied in Article X of the Covenant. Unless we stand on international law I believe there is no hope for world peace.[3]

But, as Brigadier-General Spears pointed out, this argument really amounted to a denial of any revolt, whether against a good government or against oppression: 'Some of the greatest movements in the world have been due to revolutionary movements. According to the arguments of the party opposite all revolution under any conditions would become impossible, and if only for

[3] 1 Dec. 1936. 318 H.C. Debs. 5s., col. 1067.

that reason I beg hon. Gentlemen not to be too partisan in this case.'[4]

Thoughtful and moderate supporters of the National Government were less certain of the attitude they should adopt towards the Spanish Civil War than members of the Opposition. Harold Nicolson illustrated their dilemma in August 1936 when he described the loyalist Administration as 'a mere Kerensky Government at the mercy of an armed proletariat', but he also concluded that 'Franco and his Moors are no better'. In addition 'the Germans are fussing outside Barcelona with their pocket-battleships "making themselves felt". It is serious in that it emphasises the division of Europe between left and right. Which way do we go?' Gloomily he predicted: 'The pro-German and anti-Russian tendencies of the Tories will be fortified and increased.'[5] Most back-benchers agreed with their leaders that the chief danger lay in the possibility that the war in Spain would spread and escalate into a general European conflagration. As Stanley Baldwin put it, with the 'two electric currents' of Communism and Fascism 'beating across Europe', the best course lay in trying to contain the conflict lest it 'set the whole of Western Europe on fire. When Western Europe is on fire chaos comes.'[6] Few Conservatives, whether in the Government or on the back benches, seem to have thought that the struggle was connected with Fascist expansion, which might prove a threat to Britain in Gibraltar and the western Mediterranean. Nor was this a matter in which people could call enthusiastically for the intervention of the League of Nations: the organization might offer its services as a mediator but sanctions and collective security were not applicable to a civil war. Even thoughtful and uncommitted back-benchers had to conclude that under the circumstances even an imperfect non-intervention policy was preferable to taking sides and converting the domestic Spanish problem into an international one. As Sir Robert Horne, a senior Conservative back-bencher, put it: 'For my part, simply facing the real practical issue, I am prepared, even though non-intervention proves more ineffective than it is to-day, to support that policy in order to prevent the spread of a conflict which would be disastrous to

[4] 1 Dec. 1936. 318 H.C. Deb. 5s., col. 1088.

[5] Diary entry, 8 Aug. 1936. Nicolson, *Diaries and Letters*, p. 270.

[6] 29 Oct. 1936. 316 H.C. Deb. 5s., cols. 151–2.

the whole civilisation of Europe.'[7] Right-wing Conservatives, of course, cheerfully supported Franco. Sir Henry Page Croft announced: 'I recognize General Franco to be a gallant Christian gentleman, and I believe his word.' And in June of the same year Sir Arnold Wilson declared: 'I hope to God Franco wins in Spain and the sooner the better.'[8] But it is worth noticing that even Franco's most ardent supporters in the Conservative party did not suggest that British aid be given to him. Perhaps they did not need to: the insurgents were the obvious beneficiaries of the partial nature of non-intervention.

One after another those Conservatives who had pressed for an effective sanctions policy against Italy or who had worried about the invasion of the Rhineland either stood up to declare their support of the National Government's non-intervention policy or acquiesced in it by their silence. And they believed that the Opposition's strong views on the war marked a triumph of sympathy over reason. Brigadier-General Spears charged that

> in the matter of Spain the Opposition have shown themselves completely incapable of showing any impartiality, and even unwilling to do it. They see only a distorted picture. We had an example of it this afternoon. We heard a great deal about Italian and German volunteers, but we had to jog the memory of the right hon. Gentleman to remind him that there had been such a thing as an international brigade. We hear a great deal about German and Italian plots before the rebellion broke out, but we do not hear anything about the Russian intervention before the rebellion broke out.

He also pointed to the danger of espousing one side of the case and rejecting the other so fiercely:

> The more bitterly hon. Gentlemen opposite attack their opponents, the more violently they take sides, the more violent becomes the opposition to themselves. Out of the line taken by hon. Gentlemen opposite, Fascism is born, and I beg them to deal with this question objectively and in the interests of this country and of Europe.[9]

Although few Conservative consciences were stirred by the fate of Spain, there were two conspicuous defenders of the Spanish government within the party, Vyvyan Adams and the Duchess of Atholl, both of whom shared the Opposition's attitude

7 29 Oct. 1936. Ibid., cols. 72–3.
8 Quoted in Watkins, *Britain Divided*, p. 118.
9 19 July 1937. 326 H.C. Deb. 5s., cols. 1895–6.

towards the Civil War. This was hardly surprising in Adams's case as his views on foreign policy had always followed closely those of the Labour party. As the champion of generous causes, too, he had no sympathy with Franco and his followers, even when he had to admit that the British Government had little alternative but to adopt a policy of non-intervention:

It seems to me safely predictable that military success in Spain is going to that type of patriot who rebels against his own Government. . . . The ruthless and resolute armed minority is going in yet another country to gain the victory. From the first to the last in this dispute the dice have not been evenly loaded. They have been heavily loaded against the Government. Equipment and organization—both those vital factors in any military dispute—have been upon the side of the rebels, and whatever may be the inevitable course of our policy, the Spanish Government has not even enjoyed the elementary right in international law of purchasing arms from abroad.[10]

The emergence of the Duchess of Atholl as a defender of the Spanish Government was little less than incredible. Formerly a leading Conservative die-hard, she had been an outstanding opponent of the Government of India Bill and the use of sanctions against Italy. It came as something of a surprise when she announced, on 5 November 1936, that she welcomed the Foreign Secretary's pledge to revive the League: 'Most of us regard as an absolutely essential principle of the League the principle of collective security through a system of mutual assistance for the victims of unprovoked aggression.' After expounding the case for collective security, at the very least in Europe, the Duchess turned to Spain and declared: 'I think it is possible that there has been some exaggeration of the extent of Communist intrigue in Spain. It is only fair to say that I have it on good authority that there was a great deal of Nazi propaganda in Spain before the outbreak of the insurrection.' This sudden change in her attitude was due, she revealed, to reading *Mein Kampf*: 'It is true', she conceded, 'that it was written before Hitler got into power, and if he had allowed the book to get dusty on his shelves I should not thing of referring to it.' But in fact the book's circulation was enormous: 'As long as that continues, it is impossible to ignore the possibility that this may still be the policy of Herr Hitler's government, and I submit that this policy, if it were carried out,

[10] 29 Oct. 1936. 316 H.C. Deb. 5s., col. 94.

is one of such all-round aggression that Europe as a whole has a common interest in doing everything possible to prevent it being carried into effect.'[11] Few of the Duchess's colleagues, it would seem, took the same course and read Hitler's book; or if they did they came to a more comfortable conclusion. Even those who were acutely aware of the German danger regarded the war in Spain as an irrelevant distraction from the central issue.

On 1 December 1936 the Duchess of Atholl made a much stronger speech on Spain. She observed that 'as the weeks have gone on, I think it has become ever clearer that the Government can count on the support of a much larger part of the Spanish people than the insurgents.' But it was obvious that, 'owing to the peculiar circumstances of the insurrection, the non-intervention policy was perhaps bound to tell rather against the constitutional government.' The Duchess also charged that the British Government had made a great mistake in putting an embargo on the export of arms before being assured that other governments would do the same. As for the breaches of non-intervention she was convinced that the Russian ones had taken place much later than those of the Fascist powers. Furthermore: I think we must not forget the fight which the Spanish government is waging has attracted to itself not merely help from Soviet Russia, but help from exiles from Fascist countries.' She concluded that Britain had less to fear from a governmental victory than a triumph of the rebels: 'The fear that, if the existing Spanish government won, we should be faced with a State which might be subject to the dictation of Soviet Russia seems to be a remote contingency. I probably would not like the form of government that might emerge, but I do not believe it would be a government that would be subservient to Russia.' If, on the other hand, the insurgents won: 'they have had the most valuable assistance from Fascist powers which could not well be repaid in money, and would therefore have to be repaid by some transfer of territory or the use of ports, air bases, and so on.'[12] Far more perceptive than her fellow right-wingers the Duchess of Atholl realized that the British Empire would be threatened by Fascist control of the eastern Mediterranean; but her standing in the party was not enhanced by Sir Stafford Cripps's congratulations for saying

[11] 317 H.C. Deb. 5s., cols. 337–42.
[12] 318 H.C. Deb. 5s., cols. 1130–4.

things 'which, I am sure, will be more convincing to the public coming from her, than they would be coming from these benches'.[13] Indeed the Duchess's ardent championing of the Spanish cause soon earned her the title 'Red Kitty'.

In the period between the outbreak of the Spanish Civil War and his death in March 1937 Sir Austen Chamberlain, the leading Conservative back-bencher, made no speech on the topic. Presumably he saw the war as a distraction from the main German challenge, but perhaps also he was puzzled as to what course to advocate.

Winston Churchill's attitude towards the conflict underwent a characteristic evolution. By the time the war had ended he had reversed the view he held of it when it began. Writing about the period later he said: 'In this quarrel I was neutral.'[14] But this comment hardly does justice to his approach to the problem at the time. Shortly after the outbreak of war he wrote to the French ambassador in London advocating a policy of 'absolutely rigid neutrality with the strongest protest against any breach of it'. If this broke down he feared that the natural sympathies of the British Government would assert themselves and the country would find itself supporting the Fascist powers and opposing France. 'I do not like to hear people talking of England, Germany and Italy forming up against European Communism,' he added. 'It is too easy to be good.'[15] Despite the lofty impartiality of this letter, however, when Churchill was introduced to the Spanish Republican Ambassador in October he allegedly turned red with anger and refused his hand, muttering 'Blood, blood, blood'.[16] And in August 1936 he wrote:

Here on the one hand the passions of a poverty-stricken and backward proletariat demand the overthrow of Church, State and property, and the inauguration of a Communist regime. On other other hand the patriotic, religious and bourgeois forces, under the leadership of the army, and sustained by the countryside in many provinces, are marching to re-establish order by setting up a military dictatorship.[17]

[13] 318 H.C. Deb. 5s., col. 1134.

[14] Churchill, *The Gathering Storm*, p. 214.

[15] Winston Churchill to M. Corbin, 31 July 1936. Quoted in Churchill, *The Gathering Storm*, p. 215.

[16] Hugh Thomas, *The Spanish Civil War* (New York, [1961] 1963), p. 220n.

[17] 10 Aug. 1936. Churchill, *Step by Step*, p. 50.

By April 1937 Churchill's preference for the insurgents had given way to puzzlement about the relative virtues of the two sides. Contemplating the quarrel he could not detect 'in either of these two Spanish factions which are at war any satisfactory guarantee that the ideas which I personally care about, and to which I have been brought up in this House to attach some importance, would be preserved'. And he declared that he was unwilling to be thrown 'in this headlong fashion into the risk of having to fire cannon immediately on one side or another of this trouble'.[18] But by July he was alarmed at the large cannon being built near Gibraltar by the insurgents; and he urged the immediate recognition of Franco's government in order to placate the Spanish leader who might be induced to remove the threat to Gibraltar.[19] A few months later he claimed that it was 'foolish in the last degree for the neutral Powers like Britain and France to deny that measure of recognition to the *de facto* Government of the greater part of Spain which is necessary to safeguard their commercial and political interests'.[20] He argued that accredited agents to both sides would ensure the British Government accurate information and earn goodwill so that whichever faction won it would be favourably disposed to Britain. The National Government, however, had no intention of recognizing both sides and exposing itself to more charges of being pro-Franco and pro-Fascist.

At the end of 1938, when Germany had seized Austria and part of Czechoslovakia, Churchill was anxious to enlist the aid of Russia in restraining Hitler. In the light of this objective his views on Spain underwent another adjustment. 'It would seem to-day the British Empire would run far less risk from the victory of the Spanish Government than from that of General Franco', he observed.

If at this moment the Spanish Government were victorious they would be so anxious to live on friendly terms with Great Britain, they would find so much sympathy among the British people for them, that we should probably be able to dissuade them from the vengeance which would have attended their triumph earlier in the struggle. On the other hand, if Franco won, his Nazi backers would

18 14 Apr. 1937. 322 H.C. Deb. 5s., col. 1063.
19 19 July 1937. 326 H.C. Deb. 5s., cols. 1830–6.
20 26 Nov. 1937. Churchill, *Step by Step*, p. 189.

drive him to the same kind of brutal suppressions as are practised in the Totalitarian States.[21]

But these comfortable words to the hard-pressed Loyalists came rather late in the day: the war was entering it last stages and Franco's victory was virtually assured. The only real difference between Churchill's attitude to the conflict and the Government's was that ultimately he realized the threat to France and Gibraltar which might result from Fascist control of Spain while the Administration and most of its followers persisted in regarding Communism as the chief threat in Spain and in Europe generally.

The main effect of the Spanish Civil War on the Conservative party was to produce that hardening of attitudes towards Communism and the Soviet Union that Harold Nicolson had predicted. Those who had always suspected Russia of wanting to spread her doctrine and rule to the rest of Europe found new evidence for their belief in the conflict. Even those who had earlier imagined that Russia was preoccupied with her internal problems and a force for stability on the Continent now regarded her intervention in West European affairs with apprehension. This intensification of anti-Rusian feeling came, moreover, at a very crucial time for checking Hitler. Even Winston Churchill, who was more willing than most to put aside ideological prejudices in order to secure the Soviet Union's support against Germany, was prevented from pressing his views too far by Russia's role in the Spanish troubles. 'There never was any question so baffling as the attitude which the liberal democracies should adopt towards Soviet Russia', he announced in November 1936. While he agreed that Britain and France were not going to be lured into a Nazi crusade against Communism he also believed that 'but for Russia and for the Russian Communist propaganda and intrigues which for more than six months racked Spain before the outbreak, the Spanish horror need never have occurred'. With everything 'so obscure, so double-faced, so transitional in that enormous country', he felt that the Foreign Secretary, Anthony Eden, was quite right to exclude Russia from his diplomatic calculations.[22] Only as the European scene darkened further did Churchill look once more to the Soviet

[21] 30 Dec. 1938. Churchill, *Step by Step*, p. 313.
[22] 5 Nov. 1936. 317 H.C. Deb. 5s., cols. 318–19.

Union as a useful ally for containing Nazism. Much less agile, the National Government, supported and encouraged by its back-benchers, continued to leave Russia out of its diplomatic calculations even when the need for every possible ally was absolutely essential. Germany and Italy, of course, did everything in their power to encourage this anti-Russian attitude, meanwhile observing once more from the Spanish Civil War that the British Government would go to the greatest lengths to avoid involvement in foreign troubles which did not affect the narrowest British interests.

7. A Popular Front?

FOLLOWING the invasion of the Rhineland, which clarified Germany's intentions in his mind, while finishing his chances of office for the time being, Winston Churchill embarked on a vigorous campaign for collective security within the framework of the League of Nations. It is true that he had made speeches in favour of the League from time to time during the last two years but he had not held to this theme with much consistency. People continued to see him as the bellicose advocate of rearmament for its own sake, the opponent of disarmament conferences and the leader of the die-hard resistance to the Government of India Bill. Now, in the second half of 1936, he underwent a brief metamorphosis and appeared for a time as the champion of freedom and democracy and the possible leader of a new anti-Nazi political alliance.

Before Churchill could appear as the leader of the League forces, however, he had to play his part in urging the suspension of sanctions against Italy in the hope of luring that country into an anti-German alliance. Once sanctions had been lifted, in the summer of 1936, he began advocating really effective sanctions to be used against German expansion. In order to reconcile his opposition to sanctions against Italy and his support of them against Germany he claimed to draw two lessons from the Italian experiment: 'First, do not deal in shams. Second, if it is known that you do not intend to fight, and will do nothing which forces the other side to attack you, it is better not to take a leading part in fierce quarrels. Leadership cannot exist upon the principle of limited liability.' Sanctions had failed in this case, he claimed, because the Government—Churchill did not mention himself or its other supporters—had not been sufficiently resolute about making them work. But this did not mean that sanctions need fail in future: 'There is no reason to despair of collective security against the Aggressor. If sufficient a number of powerfully armed nations were ready to enforce economic sanctions, the Aggressor would in many cases have to submit or attack the combination.'[1]

[1] 'Why Sanctions Failed', 26 June 1936. Churchill, *Step by Step*, pp. 43–4.

The event which drew attention to Churchill's new role was ıis acceptance of the presidency of the New Commonwealth, a ociety which urged armed collective security through an interıational force which would be controlled by the League. Churchill's association with this organization attracted coniderable comment from the press. The *New Statesman* was loud n its praise of the new convert:

t is usually said that only his lack of judgement prevented him rom reaching the top of the tree. But I think his brains have been n even more severe handicap. He is intellectual and logical—a evere handicap in a party that prides itself on instinct and a conempt for general principles. But from smiling at Mr. Churchill, I ear that leading members of the National Government are now urious with him. He is their most effective opponent. He has no use or their pretence about collective security as an excuse for rermament, even while they give Hitler the tip that we do not mind vhat he does so long as he does not come West or ask for colonies.[2]

The *Saturday Review*, on the other hand, was more suspicious of Churchill's motives. Noting that he had 'accepted the leadership f a nebulous body which advocates an International Force, that mpractical and dangerous addendum to the League of Nations, nd he is rumoured to be about to join the Executive Committee f the League of Nations Union', the writer could not understand ow he could 'reconcile his plea for a strong Britain while he oquettes with these disarmament fanatics'. The only explanaion was that his new stand was a devious attempt to get into the abinet:

Can it be a condition of Mr. Churchill's return to office that he hould publicly show his adherence to the Baldwin–Eden creed of Geneva first—and Britain nowhere? After consistently attacking Mr. Baldwin over the betrayal of India, Mr. Churchill, before the elecon, stood on a public platform and paid him some sickening comliments. Is his new infatuation for Leagues of Nations and nternational Forces another way of making his political peace with nen who so recently earned his righteous vituperation?[3]

Churchill's presidential address to the New Commonwealth vas a major political and social event. The luncheon at the Dorchester Hotel on 25 November 1936 was attended by about

[2] Critic, 'A London Diary', 13 June 1936.
[3] Historicus, 'Winston to the Left of Us?', 15 Aug. 1936.

450 people, including M.P.s from all parties, diplomats from forty countries, and prominent figures in industry, the armed forces, the law, the Church, and the press. The new president paid generous tribute to the organization's aim:

Nothing is easier to mock at than the plan of an international force to carry out the decisions of a European or, if possible, of a worlc council. Nothing is easier than to marshal and magnify the obviou difficulties which stand in the way. But no one can dispute that th achievement of such an ideal and its acceptance simultaneously b many countries would be the greatest blessing that could come t mankind.

But the central theme of his speech was that, since such an idea could not be realized at present,

peoples and governments should not be invited to lay aside thei own means of defence, unless and until new, real and superio guarantees are in fact provided. All true members of the League o Nations in Europe must play their part and each must do his shar and it must be proved quite plainly that there are enough whe added together to restrain, to overawe, and in the last to overcom the aggressor, from within the League or from without.[4]

Although he did not mention the country by name it was clea that Churchill was calling for an armed alliance agains Germany. And if that could be achieved within the framewor of the League of Nations it would have the added virtue o enlisting the support of those who pinned their hopes for worl peace, and even world government, on that institution.

The other group with which Churchill was associated, Focu for the Defence of Freedom and Peace, attracted less attention a the time; indeed very few people had heard of it until 1963 whe Eugen Spier, its chief financier, published his account of its activ ties. Spier had originally planned to publish his book at the en of the Second World War but at Churchill's urging he put aside. After repeated requests from Spier Churchill finally replie that he would prefer publication after his death but would n insist on this.[5] Perhaps Churchill was afraid that Spier migh embarrass him by publishing some private remark; more likel he felt that the book would detract from the picture he ha

[4] 'Mr. Winston Churchill and the New Commonwealth', *New Commonwealt* Dec. 1936.

[5] Eugen Spier, *Focus: A Footnote to the History of the Thirties* (Londo 1963), pp. 13–14.

drawn of himself as the lone dedicated struggler against appeasement. Certainly he made no reference to this group or the New Commonwealth in *The Gathering Storm*.

'Focus' was made up of members of all political parties as well as those who had no political affiliations.[6] It had the sympathy of Sir Robert Vansittart, the Permanent Under-Secretary at the Foreign Office;[7] and in December 1937 Anthony Eden came to address the group while he was still Foreign Secretary.[8] Wickham Steed, one of its prominent members, went on a tour of North America to publicize the group's activities and even had an interview with President Roosevelt. But Focus's chief function was to provide Winston Churchill with an organization and a platform in his campaign for arms and the Covenant. It arranged many of the large meetings which he addressed around the country in the late 1930s, including the great Albert Hall meeting in December 1936, although they were usually attributed to the League of Nations Union.

Although Focus had impressive connections it could never provide Churchill with the facilities of a political party and he at least realized this. While he accepted the group's help in promoting his views he knew that the only way of putting them into effect lay in capturing the party machine. 'In the sphere of politics', he told Spier, 'one of the most important things is to have behind one the party machine, of which I am now deprived. You perhaps do not realize the power of the party machine.'[9] Not only was Churchill aware of this power but he was also careful not to provoke it by publicizing his activities in Focus. Other members were just as hesitant. While they were quite willing to meet privately to discuss the problems of collective security most of them were reluctant to voice their support openly or have it known that they were associating with members of other political

[6] Prominent Conservatives in addition to Churchill were Sir Austen Chamberlain, Ronald Cartland, Commander Oliver Locker-Lampson, Duncan Sandys, Paul Emrys-Evans, the Duchess of Atholl, and John McEwen. Labour M.P.s included Seymour Cocks, Philip Noel-Baker, Lt.-Commander Reginald Fletcher, and Arthur Henderson. Sir Archibald Sinclair, the Liberal leader, belonged to the group and so did two of his followers, James de Rothschild and Dingle Foot. Sir Arthur Salter and Eleanor Rathbone, two independent M.P.s, also attended the Group's meetings.

[7] Spier, *Focus*, p. 43.

[8] Ibid., pp. 128–9.

[9] Ibid., p. 108.

8214871 K

parties. Hugh Dalton, who did not attend the meetings but who was well aware of the group's existence, wrote later: 'Leaders of the Parliamentary Labour Party took no overt part in this organization, though a number, including myself, were in sympathy with it. We should have lessened our influence inside our own Party if, on this controversial question, we had publicly associated with members of other parties.'[10] The last sentence is particularly revealing considering that the Labour party's apologists maintain that armed collective security was orthodox doctrine by the end of 1936.

Focus's most important meeting was that held at the Albert Hall on 3 December 1936. The gathering attracted considerable attention. Two weeks before it was held the *Spectator* predicted: 'Mr. Churchill will be the most talked-of politician in this country in the next fortnight. . . . If he bids for the role of democratic leader there may be considerable stirring in the square half mile south of Trafalgar Square.'[11] 'But where is all this leading to?' inquired the *New Statesman.*

> The logic of present politics is surely the formation of a Centre Front with Winston Churchill as the effective leader, if not as the potential Prime Minister. Such a Front would include the more progressive Tories, the Liberal Party and some Labour leaders. It would leave the extreme Right Conservative Party on the one hand, and a Socialist Labour Party on the other. I am not suggesting that this will happen, but I regard it as a possibility. It would at least have the merit of clarifying issues.[12]

These hopes and predictions seemed amply justified when the meeting was held. Sir Walter Citrine, the chairman of the Trades Union Council, presided, and twenty M.P.s were among those on the platform. The list of speakers included Lady Violet Bonham Carter of the Liberal party, A. M. Wall, the secretary of the London Trades Council, Lord Lytton who spoke for the League of Nations Union, and Winston Churchill.

Citrine began proceedings by denying that there was any intention of 'forming a popular front or a centre party, or some new political combination. There is not a vestige of truth in any of these statements. None of us would be associated with such a

[10] Hugh Dalton, *Fateful Years* (London, 1957), p. 111.
[11] Janus, 'A Spectator's Notebook', 20 Nov. 1936.
[12] Critic, 'A London Diary', 21 Nov. 1936.

manœuvre.' The various speakers, he maintained, were there in their private capacities, not as representatives of groups, parties, or organizations. This disclaimer was certainly necessary in view of the means by which Citrine proposed to stop the dictators:

It seems to me that we have to choose between relative risks. If I have to choose between trusting a Hitler or a Mussolini, heavily armed, aggressive in intention, and scornful of all moral considerations, with a people powerless to restrain his will; or a British Prime Minister, pledged to the hilt in support of the system of collective security, with a Parliament and a people vigilantly watching, common sense impels me to prefer the government over which I, as a citizen, can exercise some control.[13]

Wall went further: 'We belong to different parties, but we all speak freely and without fear. We will not have our consciences dictated to by anybody, not even by the bosses in our own party.'[14] Winston Churchill, for whom the occasion had been designed as the champion of 'Law and Peace under Law', presented a good case for collective security, but many of his colleagues felt that he was not in his best form.[15] This was not surprising: on the same day the British press had broken its silence to tell the country about the King and Mrs. Simpson. Churchill wanted to make a statement on the matter at the Albert Hall but Citrine forbade it.[16]

The abdication crisis brought to an abrupt end the moves to put Churchill at the head of a popular front. His warm-hearted support of the King cost him the support of the other anti-Nazi politicians and revived the familiar charges that he was unstable and lacked judgement. The leaders of all parties endorsed Baldwin's view that the monarch must abdicate if he insisted on marrying a divorced woman; and when Churchill tried to protest against this in the House of Commons he was howled down. Harold Nicolson wrote to his wife: 'Winston collapsed utterly in the House yesterday [8 December] . . . He has undone in five minutes the patient reconstruction work of two years.'[17] His misjudgement of the political mood and the suspicion that

[13] Quoted in Spier, *Focus*, pp. 62–6.
[14] Ibid., p. 69.
[15] Ibid., p. 70.
[16] Lord Citrine, *Men and Work: An Autobiography* (London, 1964), p. 357.
[17] Harold Nicolson to Victoria Sackville-West, 9 Dec. 1936. Nicolson, *Diaries and Letters*, p. 284.

he was trying to create a King's Party out of the troubles alienated those who had looked to him as the great democratic leader the day before. A columnist in the *New Statesman* wrote: 'If he held an Albert Hall meeting now Sir Walter Citrine would hesitate to take the chair for him and . . . people who were rallying around him are beginning to mutter again about his notorious lack of judgement.'[18] The *Spectator* concluded sadly:

Mr. Churchill has hopelessly compromised not only himself but the cause for which he has been working by his persistent intervention in the constitutional crisis. . . . No one will deny Mr. Churchill's gifts, but a flair for doing the right thing at the right moment—or not doing the wrong thing at the wrong moment—is no part of them. He has utterly misjudged the temper of the country and the temper of the House, and the reputation which he was beginning to shake off of a wayward genius unserviceable in counsel has settled firmly on his shoulders again.[19]

Not until the crises of 1938–9 got under way did Churchill's reputation, now as low as it had ever been while he was fighting the Government over India, begin to revive.

Apart from the Spanish Civil War 1937 was, on the surface at least, a relatively quiet interlude between the storms of 1935–6 and those of 1938–9. Most Conservatives stopped worrying about foreign affairs. Even the *Spectator* believed that the peace which lay over much of the world was

stable and deep-rooted. It is going very little too far to say that war has been banished from the whole of the Western Hemisphere. Even in Europe, where the embers of potential conflict smoulder unextinguished, the peaceful States are increasingly determined to deter aggression in advance, even though it involves them in disastrous expenditure on armaments for which there might be no need and no excuse.[20]

Against such depressing optimism, which reigned among intelligent and well-informed people, Churchill and those who shared his fears of Germany could not hope to make much of an impression—at least not until a major crisis arose to give their case a semblance of validity.

18 Critic, 'A London Diary', 12 Dec. 1936.
19 Janus, 'A Spectator's Notebook', 11 Dec. 1936.
20 'As 1936 Ends', 25 Dec. 1936.

Even if Churchill's part in the abdication crisis had not brought to a premature end the idea of a popular front, it would almost certainly have been killed by other serious differences among those who hoped to bring it about. The Spanish Civil War created an impassable gulf between Conservative and Opposition M.P.s; and members of all parties would have hesitated for a long time before breaking with their own political organizations to embark on an uncharted course. Perhaps too, the end of 1936 was too late for any such move: popular ardour for the League had cooled sufficiently for the Government to end sanctions six months before without provoking an outcry. But the threat from Churchill and his allies looked real enough at the time; and no doubt the Administration was grateful for the abdication crisis which restored the prestige their leader had lost a year before while discrediting Churchill and removing the possibility that another political combination would secure the backing of moderate, pragmatic opinion which was the National Government's chief strength.

As for Winston Churchill, having failed to achieve office as the leader of the collective security forces, or at least to gather a significant political group around him, he now turned to winning office by ingratiating himself with the new Prime Minister.

8. Chamberlain versus Eden

WHEN Stanley Baldwin finally retired, immediately after George VI's coronation, he stood high in the esteem of his countrymen; and when he took his leave of the House of Commons (to become Earl Baldwin of Bewdley) Harold Nicolson, no great admirer, wrote: 'No man has ever left in such a blaze of affection.'[1] More than any other Conservative leader since Disraeli, Baldwin could claim to have educated his party to accept the demands of modern society. The symbol of cautious reform, he was able to appeal to the large body of unadventurous but well-disposed liberal opinion in the country and to ignore the wishes of his right-wing supporters after 1931. To the exasperation of many of his followers he seemed more interested in conciliating his political opponents than the members of his own party. His concern that socialism should realize its aims through parliament rather than by direct action drew a remarkable tribute from David Kirkwood, the Independent Labour M.P. In 1940, when everyone was blaming the war and the state of British defences on Baldwin, Kirkwood wrote to him saying that his plea for industrial peace in 1925 'made flesh the feelings of us all, that the antagonisms, the bitterness, the class rivalry, were unworthy and that understanding and amity were possible'.[2]

Although Baldwin, by superb tactics, had survived every challenge to his position since 1923, he had always had powerful critics within the party. Strong Conservatives were not enthusiastic about his conciliatory approach to politics and his insistence on basing his policies on a broad consensus of public opinion; but the electoral appeal of 'the greatest party manager the Conservatives ever had'[3] was such that the die-hards had no alternative—especially at election time—but to swallow their

[1] Harold Nicolson, diary entry 27 May 1937. Nicolson, Diaries and Letters, p. 301. Part of the reason that Baldwin departed with such goodwill was that his last act as Prime Minister was to announce a raise of £200 a year for members of the House of Commons. This news was especially welcome to the Labour party.

[2] Quoted in Robert Keith Middlemas, *The Clydesiders: A Left Wing Struggle for Parliamentary Power* (London, 1965), pp. 281–2.

[3] Churchill, *The Gathering Storm*, p. 33.

dislike in order to gain as much benefit as they could from their leader's popularity. During his last few months in office, however, Baldwin's followers were more restless than usual under his easy yoke. Ever since the Hoare–Laval fiasco they had been concerned about the old man's indolence and lack of grip in dealing with foreign affairs. Only the knowledge that the more precise and energetic Neville Chamberlain—who was only two years younger than Baldwin—would soon take over, restrained them from showing more irritation. As it was, their criticism was severe enough. Winston Churchill expressed the exasperation of the back-benchers just before the abdication crisis raised Baldwin's prestige to new heights and plunged his own to a new low:

> Anyone can see what the position is. The Government simply cannot make up their minds, or they cannot get the Prime Minister to make up his mind. So they go on in strange paradox, decided only to be undecided, resolved only to be irresolute, adamant for drift, solid for fluidity, all-powerful to be impotent. So we go on preparing more months and years—precious, perhaps vital to the greatness of Britain—for the locusts to eat.[4]

The very looseness of Baldwin's leadership, his constant search for compromises, and even his personal charm were regarded as faults by the younger M.P.s who yearned for a sense of direction and a firm lead. Captain J. R. J. Macnamara, a Conservative back-bencher, wrote after the Prime Minister's retirement:

> Lord Baldwin, the defender of democracy, was in reality a dictator. His personality was very strong and almost irresistible. It permeated into every cranny of the building [the palace of Westminster] and oozed out into the whole land. He built up around him a camarilla that did not disturb the atmosphere; to some fog, to others restful dream clouds. . . . When his monument comes to be erected . . . it should stand at the narrow entrance of a great harbour helping to make it yet narrower for the shelter of the ships within. It should look seawards, heeding not the frothing billows behind but facing squarely the storms without, doing absolutely nothing whatsoever about them, except just being there.[5]

Conservatives of every stripe were happy to see their leader step down, but the editor of the *New Statesman* shrewdly predicted

[4] 12 Nov. 1936. 317 H.C. Deb. 5s., col. 1107.

[5] Major J. R. J. Macnamara, *The Whistle Blows* (London, 1938), pp. 152–3.

that 'in six months time many of Mr. Baldwin's severest critics will be regretting his departure'.[6]

By the spring of 1937 it was clear that Baldwin's successor would be Neville Chamberlain. Sir Samuel Hoare had ruined his chances by his agreement with Laval over Abyssinia and Winston Churchill presented no threat after failing to become Minister of Defence. 'It has come to me without raising a finger to obtain it,' wrote Chamberlain rather unctiously, 'because there is no one else, and perhaps because I have not made enemies by looking after myself rather than the common cause.'[7]

The new leader certainly received a warm welcome from all sections of the party when he took up his duties. Writing about the change of administration later Churchill said: 'In those closing years before the war, I should have found it easier to work with Baldwin as I knew him, than with Chamberlain.'[8] Perhaps Churchill was thinking of the happy days when he had dominated the Cabinet between 1924 and 1929, because this was hardly his opinion in the 1930s. Having failed to break the National Government or oust Baldwin from his position since the beginning of the decade, Churchill now hailed Chamberlain's accession to the prime ministership, perhaps hoping that his chances of office would improve. As the senior Conservative back-bencher since Sir Austen Chamberlain's death, he seconded Lord Derby's nomination of the new leader. In a generous speech, not mentioned in *The Gathering Storm*, he paid fulsome tribute to Chamberlain's qualities. Carefully avoiding any reference to the controversial topics of defence and foreign policy he stressed that the principal task facing the Conservative party was to beat the socialists. This was a theme which all the faithful could applaud and Churchill's speech might have been designed to draw attention to his usefulness in such an undertaking. Grasping the larger hope he expressed his confidence that the new leader would pay more attention to the views of those outside the Cabinet than had been the custom under his predecessor: 'His great experience of the party and all its branches, and all its organization, would make it certain that party opinion would not be denied; that, if subordinate, it would have its rightful

[6] Critic, 'A London Diary', 15 May 1937.

[7] Quoted in Feiling, *Life of Neville Chamberlain*, p. 294.

[8] Churchill, *The Gathering Storm*, p. 222.

place in the mind of the leader. They had to combat Socialism and they would be able to do it far more effectively as a pack of hounds than as a flock of sheep.'[9]

The following day Churchill wittily defended the new Prime Minister in the House of Commons, enabling Chamberlain to get off to a good start by withdrawing gracefully from an unpopular position he had adopted in his last budget as Chancellor of the Exchequer. In the course of his remarks Churchill told the House that he took 'a friendly interest in the new Government. I do not quite know why I do. I cannot go so far as to call it a paternal interest, because, speaking candidly, it is not quite the sort of Government I should have bred myself. If it is not a paternal, at any rate I think I may call it an avuncular interest.'[10] But although Churchill adopted a benevolent attitude towards the Administration and refrained from criticism until Anthony Eden's resignation nine months later, he was no more successful in obtaining office than he had been in Baldwin's day.[11]

Chamberlain, who was less tolerant and more partisan than Baldwin, preferred taunting the Opposition to conciliation. Ten years earlier Baldwin had urged him to remember that his opponents were gentlemen: 'I always gave him the impression, he said, when I spoke in the House of Commons, that I looked on the Labour party as dirt.'[12] Chamberlain's attitude had not altered significantly in the intervening years and he took the line that with his enormous majority he need not take the views of the Liberal and Labour parties into consideration. But if he disappointed those who had become accustomed to Baldwin's courteous approach to party politics those who expected him to form a 'real' Conservative government were also soon disenchanted. The *National Review*, which recommended such stern and unbending Tories as Lord Lloyd and Sir Henry Page Croft for Cabinet office, was annoyed that he did not fortify his

[9] Reported in *The Times*, 1 June 1937.

[10] 1 June 1937. 324 H.C. Deb. 5s., col. 882.

[11] Churchill told Leslie Hore-Belisha of his desire to get into the Cabinet and the Secretary for War discussed the matter with the Prime Minister. But Chamberlain was firm in his refusal: 'If I take him into the Cabinet . . . he will dominate it. He won't give others a chance of even talking.' When Hore-Belisha brought up the subject again the Prime Minister replied: 'I won't have anyone who will rock the boat.' R. J. Minney, *The Private Papers of Hore-Belisha* (London, 1960), p. 130.

[12] Diary entry 19 June 1927. Quoted in Feiling, op. cit., p. 142.

Ministry with such recruits.[13] But once his policies became clear no one supported him more fervently than the right-wing Conservatives.

In his own fashion Neville Chamberlain was trying to get away from party politics as much as Stanley Baldwin. But while Baldwin had tried to base his policies on what he sensed the public wanted, Chamberlain sought the solution to each problem in an objective, commonsense appraisal of all the factors in each case as it arose. He believed that a decision arrived at in this way could hardly fail to elicit the support of sensible people in Parliament and in the country. To assist him in this task Chamberlain preferred Cabinet Ministers whose detached, unemotional and empirical approach to problems made them resemble good civil servants rather than politicians in touch with the mood of the electorate. Sir Samuel Hoare, Sir John Simon, Lord Halifax, and Sir Kingsley Wood were his idea of what a Cabinet Minister should be, not the emotional and temperamental Anthony Eden and Duff Cooper whose rash and unconsidered policies might lead the country into dangerous adventures.

Because Chamberlain's administration was simply a reshuffle of the previous one this change in tone was not immediately apparent.[14] But until the outbreak of war arrested the process it looked as though the Prime Minister were trying to create a Cabinet of professional administrators rather than party politicians. Lord Maugham, a Lord of Appeal (and brother of the writer, Somerset Maugham), was appointed Lord Chancellor in March 1938—a post usually reserved for a senior lawyer politician of the party in power. Seven months later Sir John Anderson, formerly Permanent Under-Secretary at the Home Office and more recently Governor of Bengal, became Lord Privy Seal. Anderson, who did not belong to any party, simply sat in the House of Commons as a 'National' M.P. And in January 1939 Lord Chatfield, the recently retired First Sea Lord, joined the Administration as Minister for the Co-ordination of Defence. In addition to these appointments Chamberlain removed many of

13 'Episodes of the Month', Apr. and July 1937.

14 Ramsay MacDonald retired at the same time as Baldwin; Sir John Simon succeeded Chamberlain at the Exchequer; Sir Samuel Hoare moved from the Admiralty to the Home Office and was succeeded by Duff Cooper.

his department heads from the heat and dust of the House of Commons by appointing peers to important Ministries. Not since Bonar Law's time had there been so many members of the House of Lords in the Cabinet. All this fitted in with Chamberlain's idea that he should be the chief policy maker and his colleagues primarily departmental administrators. 'Where Baldwin, as Prime Minister, was content to assume that his colleagues were competently discharging their duties', wrote Leopold Amery,

> Chamberlain soon showed that he was not merely chairman of the Cabinet, but a general manager who wished to know what his departmental managers were doing, to discuss their problems with them and keep them up to the mark. What is more, he knew his own mind and saw to it that he had his way. An autocrat with all the courage of his convictions, right or wrong.[15]

Chamberlain's conception of how a government ought to function naturally extended to foreign affairs. He had long felt that the Foreign Office was not devising clear, firm solutions to diplomatic problems; and he was determined that it would either become as efficient as the other departments over which he had charge or he would turn to other sources for advice. But it is going too far to assert that

> As early as the spring of 1936, he seems to have reached a decision to secure for himself a dominant position in the formulation of British policy. Through a combination of chance and fanatical determination, his goal was achieved and was dramatically signalized two years later by the resignation of his Foreign Secretary, Anthony Eden, on February 20, 1938.[16]

In fact Eden himself recalled: 'Before Chamberlain became Prime Minister, I would think it true to say that he and I were closer to each other than to any other member of the Government, exchanging opinions on many Cabinet matters without any disagreement.'[17] This in spite of their differences over sanctions. Indeed Eden was at first delighted at the prospect of receiving support from an energetic leader and not at all apprehensive

[15] Amery, *Unforgiving Years*, p. 225.

[16] Marion L. Kenny, 'The Role of the House of Commons in British Foreign Policy During the 1937–8 Session', in Norton Downs, ed., *Essays in Honor of Conyers Read* (Chicago, 1953), p. 138. The view that Chamberlain was bent on removing Eden is repeated in, among other places, George, *The Warped Vision*, p. 176, and Rock, *Appeasement on Trial* (Hamden, Conn., 1966), p. 20.

[17] Eden, *Facing the Dictators*, p. 501.

when Chamberlain said: 'I know you won't mind if I take more interest in foreign policy than S.B.'[18] He could hardly have taken less.

There was nothing inevitable about Eden's resignation, and the new Prime Minister was well enough aware of his younger colleague's prestige in the country not to drive him out of the Government on any trivial issue. It is true that Chamberlain distrusted the Foreign Office, feeling that its machinery put obstacles in the way of understanding between nations, while Eden, who had never served in any other department, was more impressed by the value of traditional diplomacy, less willing to trust the dictators' word, and more conscious of the necessity of maintaining a certain standard in international affairs. But the difference between the two men can be overstated: just two months before he left the Cabinet Eden told the Foreign Affairs Committee that 'there is no imminent likelihood of war and a far better prospect of appeasement than ever before'.[19] Still, after a year and a half of almost perfect freedom under Baldwin it would not be easy for anyone to accommodate himself to a Chief who wanted to exercise firm control over his Ministers. No doubt there was tension between the two men from the beginning, but it need not have led to Eden's resignation. The fatal split can better be understood as being forced on both sides than as the culmination of Chamberlain's 'master plan' to seize total control of the country's foreign policy machinery.

Those who think that Chamberlain was determined to remove Eden from the outset see the 'promotion' of Sir Robert Vansittart from Under-Secretary at the Foreign Office to the honorific post of Chief Diplomatic Adviser to the Government on 1 January 1938 as the step which paved the way to dismissing the Foreign Secretary. But in fact Vansittart's removal was Eden's doing. A new appointment, he thought, would strengthen his staff and make a greater impact on the Government.[20] Eden probably resented Cabinet Ministers murmuring 'his master's voice' whenever he advocated a firmer line against Germany, the implication being that it was Vansittart rather than Eden who made foreign

[18] Loc. cit.

[19] Harold Nicolson, diary entry, 9 Dec. 1937. Nicolson, *Diaries and Letters*, p. 314.

[20] Eden, op. cit., p. 521.

policy.[21] In any event the two had long disagreed over Italy, which Vansittart was eager to conciliate, while Eden felt that Mussolini had humiliated him over sanctions. Neville Chamberlain was not reluctant to get rid of this self-willed and autocratic civil servant who bombarded the cabinet with long rhetorical memoranda on the German menace and who did not scruple to supply Winston Churchill and other back-bench critics with information from the Foreign Office.[22] But it was Eden who took the decision to relegate Vansittart to a position of no importance. And in spite of Vansittart's parting words to Eden—'If I go, you won't last long'—there was no connection between this event and Eden's resignation.[23]

Eden's triumph in freeing himself from Vansittart was short-lived. Even before the transfer Chamberlain was trying to bring Eden around to a more 'realistic' foreign policy. He also circumvented the Foreign Secretary to some extent by taking into his confidence two former—and previously discredited—Foreign Secretaries, Sir John Simon and Sir Samuel Hoare, as well as Lord Halifax who also shared the Prime Minister's outlook on foreign affairs. Later on these men made up the 'Big Four' or Inner Cabinet on foreign policy.

Meanwhile a more sinister attempt was afoot to put the Foreign Secretary in leading strings. J. P. L. Thomas, who became Eden's Parliamentary Private Secretary in May 1937, soon discovered that he had been recommended for the job by Sir Horace Wilson, who knew him well. Wilson, Chamberlain's *éminence grise*, and Sir Warren Fisher, the head of the Civil Service, were as dissatisfied with the Foreign Office as the Prime Minister. They told Thomas that Vansittart was an alarmist, hampering all the Government's attempts to contact the dictators and that his influence over Eden was very great. They also told him that he had been recommended for his job in order to help 'build a bridge between 10 Downing Street and the Foreign Office, and to create a better understanding between the two Departments. This might lessen the damage which had been done by the Foreign Office in general and by Vansittart in particular.' Unfortunately for the civil servants Thomas refused to co-operate.[24]

[21] Colvin, *Vansittart*, p. 148.

[22] Ibid., p. 171. [23] Ibid., p. 172.

[24] Thomas's record of these events is quoted in Eden, op. cit., pp. 504–5.

The attempt to place an informer in the Foreign Office failed and there is no evidence to suppose that Chamberlain even knew what Wilson was doing, though his advisers must have thought that they were acting in the Prime Minister's interests.

The divergence in attitude between Chamberlain and Eden first came to the surface in January 1938, when President Roosevelt sounded out the British Prime Minister as to the possibility of an international conference to lay down a standard of conduct among nations for redressing grievances. Eden, who was on holiday on the French Riviera at the time, was informed of this communication by his officials and hurried back to London. But by the time he arrived Chamberlain had rebuffed the President's offer. The Prime Minister and those who agreed with him on foreign policy, were sceptical of Roosevelt's ability to offer any practical aid, especially in light of the recent American record in foreign affairs, and they also felt that any line-up of the democratic powers against the dictators would jeopardize Chamberlain's attempts to improve relations with Germany and Italy.[25] Eden, on the other hand, was 'outraged and uneasy' at the way in which the American initiative had been handled, partly because the 'growing tendency for confidential Anglo-American discussion on a deteriorating world scene which I had been doing my best to encourage, was clumsily nipped', partly because he resented Chamberlain's abrupt reply without consulting his Foreign Secretary, when he knew that he could be back in London in twenty-four hours.[26]

For the first time since they started working together Chamberlain and Eden now found themselves seriously at odds. After arguing about the matter for several days they discovered that there was a great gulf between them and Eden concluded that they could not work together much longer. He was determined to resign if the Cabinet's Foreign Affairs Committee did not sustain his view.[27] But it was almost impossible to leave the Government on this issue as Roosevelt's overture to Chamberlain had been confidential. J. P. L. Thomas intimated to Sir Horace Wilson that if Eden resigned at this moment 'the whole of this

[25] Neville Chamberlain, diary entries, 19–27 Feb. 1938. Quoted in Macleod, *Neville Chamberlain*, p. 212; Eden, op. cit., pp. 560–1.
[26] Eden, op. cit., pp. 552 and 554.
[27] Eden, op. cit., p. 560.

American business might leak out from the American end and . . . the country would then know that the Prime Minister preferred to turn down the help of a democracy in order that he might pursue his flirtations with the dictators untrammelled'. Wilson, who dismissed Roosevelt's plan as 'woolly rubbish', did not take this veiled threat passively. In a 'towering rage' he warned that 'if America produced the facts he would use the full power of the Government machine in an attack upon A.E.'s past record with regard to the dictators and the shameful obstruction by the F.O. of the P.M.'s attempts to save the peace of the world'.[28] Finally a compromise was patched up between the Prime Minister and his Foreign Secretary whereby Roosevelt was asked to postpone his plan for the time being while Chamberlain continued his efforts to approach the dictators unilaterally. In his memoirs Eden maintains that he would have resigned immediately had the matter not been secret.[29]

A political crisis had been averted for the time being, but with sore feelings on both sides it was only a matter of time until some further issue arose to divide Chamberlain and Eden even more. The next confrontation came a few weeks later, as a result of Chamberlain's eagerness to start talks with Italy in the hope of detaching that country from Germany. The Prime Minister was willing to overlook the fact that the Italian government had not fulfilled its promise to withdraw its troops from Spain and was ready to offer *de jure* recognition of the Italian conquest of Abyssinia. Eden, on the other hand, remembering the sanctions fiasco and being more imbued with Foreign Office caution, insisted that formal talks should be preceded by some indication of Mussolini's good faith. On 18 February Chamberlain and Eden actually argued out their differences in front of the Italian ambassador, Count Grandi, with the Prime Minister calling on him to support his case against the Foreign Secretary.[30] The following day they took their differences to the Cabinet, each threatening to resign if his position were not endorsed.

At the Cabinet meeting Chamberlain told his colleagues of his conviction that

[28] Thomas's record. Quoted in Eden, op. cit., p. 563.

[29] Eden, op. cit., p. 565.

[30] Neville Chamberlain, diary entries, 19–27 Feb. 1938. Quoted in Macleod, op. cit., pp. 215–16; Eden, op. cit., pp. 580–3 and Appendices C and D.

the present occasion provided one of the opportunities that came at rare intervals and did not recur. It was an opportunity to show Signor Mussolini that he might have other friends besides Herr Hitler. . . . If we rejected the present approach [from Italy] it would be taken as a final rebuff and as a confirmation of the suspicions the Italians had long harboured that we were postponing them until we were strong enough to impose our own conditions. In that event the relations between the two countries would be seriously embittered.

Eden conceded that talks with the Italians might be profitable but he disagreed with the Prime Minister's method of inaugurating them. In Eden's view Mussolini had given Hitler a free hand in Austria in return for a *quid pro quo* in the Mediterranean and now needed talks with the British to compensate for the loss of prestige over Austria. If the Italian dictator were as eager to change camps as the Prime Minister thought, he would surely be willing to give some proof of his changed attitude. But without such an assurance the only result of the talks would be 'a panic among our friends and a rush to make a composition with Italy and Germany'. Meanwhile the British Government should not go beyond the informal talks which had already begun with Count Grandi.[31] After listening to both cases most Cabinet members, seeing the dispute as a squabble over minor detail, supported the Prime Minister's decision to begin talks immediately. Eden then announced that he would have to resign as he could not support such a decision in the House of Commons or in the country.

No doubt Eden's hand and nerve were strengthened in these trials by his permanent officials and by the meeting of the Conservative party's Foreign Affairs Committee on 17 February, which had been called to demonstrate their support of the Foreign Secretary in what they felt was his testing time. Harold Nicolson spoke against trying to secure Italian friendship at the price of recognizing the conquest of Abyssinia while Winston Churchill urged support of Eden in even stronger terms. This uncompromising expression of back-bench opinion aroused the Chief Whip, who prevailed on Paul Emrys-Evans, the Chairman of the Committee, to modify the terms of the communiqué, thereby provoking an 'indignant response' from Winston Churchill. The next morning, the day of the meeting with Count

[31] Cab. 23/92.

Grandi, Eden read the record of the discussion which must have been given to him by one of the officers as the meetings were private.[32]

After discussing the matter with Malcolm MacDonald following the Cabinet meeting Eden decided to resign the following day, Sunday, 20 February. Chamberlain had already concluded that Eden should resign and there was relief on both sides when the two men met shortly after noon. When the Cabinet met later in the day, however, there was considerable dismay. Only yesterday the Cabinet members had been led to believe that the difference between Chamberlain and Eden amounted to nothing more than a detail of timing for talks with Italy. Now they learned that the issue was of such fundamental importance that the Foreign Secretary had resigned and the Prime Minister had done nothing to stop him. No wonder they were perplexed and concerned about the political crisis that would be produced by Eden's departure. No wonder, too, that the discussion turned on devising some formula whereby Eden could be kept in the Cabinet. As for the foreign policy issue which had produced the resignation, Viscount Hailsham, the Lord Chancellor, was speaking for most of his colleagues when he wrote to his son: 'I can't tell you why Anthony resigned because I couldn't make out myself.'[33]

Lord Halifax, who had made his reputation by conciliating Gandhi, was particularly eager to reach a compromise for the peculiar reason that 'it was precisely the difference of viewpoint of the Prime Minister and the Foreign Secretary that was of value to the Cabinet, as giving them the best of both minds'.[34] Sir John Simon, who had a less enviable reputation for resolving contradictions, had already suggested to J. P. L. Thomas the previous evening that Eden was unwell and should take a six months' holiday: 'During this period he [Simon] and his Cabinet colleagues would keep his seat for him and look after foreign affairs.'[35] But neither of the principles, having taken a firm stand, was prepared to back down. The Prime Minister maintained his customary calm stubborness while the excitement of the last few days was beginning to tell on Eden. Lord Halifax recorded

[32] Eden, op. cit., pp. 579–80.

[33] 21 Feb. 1938. Quoted in R. F. V. Heuston, *Lives of the Lord Chancellors 1885–1940* (Oxford, 1964), p. 488.

[34] Birkenhead, *Halifax*, p. 379.

[35] Thomas's record. Quoted in Eden, op. cit., pp. 584–5.

privately: 'I think myself, although should never say this in public, that Anthony's judgement was not at its best; he was overstrained and tired; the thing had got out of proportion. And once everybody begins to feel they are being a martyr for high principle it becomes very difficult to avoid this conviction having melancholy issue.'[36] Nevertheless, Eden could probably count on great support from his permanent officials, back-bench M.P.s, and the press. As Duff Cooper wrote in his diary: 'If he goes it will certainly be a body-blow for the National Government. There were crowds in Downing Street last night and tonight, and when he drove off there were loud cheers. This I am afraid will stiffen his attitude, he will feel that he has popular opinion behind him, which he has.'[37] On the other hand, the Prime Minister had behind him most of the Cabinet, who supported him when it became clear that no compromise was possible. The only people who resigned with Eden were his immediate followers: Lord Cranborne, his Under-Secretary; Cranborne and Eden's Parliamentary Private Secretaries, Mark Patrick and J. P. L. Thomas; and Ronald Tree, Parliamentary Private Secretary to the Overseas Trade Department. No other Cabinet member left with Eden; and on the following day Lord Halifax was appointed to the Foreign Office, joining the Prime Minister in his talks with the Italian ambassador.

Neville Chamberlain now had complete control of foreign policy but at the price of losing the National Government's most popular figure. At one stroke, Winston Churchill argued, the Prime Minister had destroyed the vital consensus which permitted the Government to represent itself as 'national':

The Liberal, Labour and non-party voters whom Mr. Baldwin had painstakingly gathered, have been summarily dismissed and will not be easy to recall. In Mr. Eden the National Government have lost their only popular figure. A fortnight ago they could have appealed to the electors with confidence. No friend would recommend them to do so now.[38]

The *Spectator* also observed that Eden's resignation had split the country into two political camps:

When the House rose on Friday of last week [18 February] it would

[36] Quoted in Birkenhead, *Halifax*, p. 380.
[37] Duff Cooper, *Old Men Forget* (London, 1953), p. 213.
[38] 4 Mar. 1938. Churchill, *Step by Step*, p. 219.

have been true to say that the demarcation between parties was becoming more and more blurred. Now the whole scene is transformed. The drama of the week-end has given new and vigorous life to political controversy both inside and outside the walls of Parliament.[39]

Those who put their trust in the League of Nations were particularly distressed, recalling how Eden had been appointed to the Foreign Office in December 1935 as a kind of symbolic gesture of the Government's intention to base its foreign policy on the League. Now that assurance was gone. The day after Eden's departure the executive of the League of Nations Union met to record its

dismay at the loss by H.M. Government of that Minister who more than any other commands the admiration and confidence of supporters of the League of Nations and, indeed, of the great mass of the British People; and its regret that H.M. Government should have rejected Mr. Eden's policy in circumstances which have created a widespread impression that Mr. Eden and Lord Cranborne were sacrificed to the hostility of certain Governments, a hostility largely due to the support by these Ministers of the League of Nations and all it stands for.[40]

Right-wing Conservatives, on the other hand, were overjoyed. With Eden, they hoped, went the policy of the League and collective security. The *National Review* articulated this attitude:

The horizon will be the clearer for his departure—he was not the man for difficult times. He had nourished himself on dreams of being the British Foreign Secretary who would lead the tribes of Europe into the promised land of Geneva. He had founded his policy on this belief, and is now sitting among the ruins of his hopes. . . . The Government will be the stronger for having let Mr. Eden go.[41]

The immediate concern of the party managers after Eden's resignation was the response which the Government's supporters would make to it. Duff Cooper's Parliamentary Private Secretary, Hamilton Kerr, told him that if Eden went 'the situation in the House would be hopeless, that more than a hundred of our supporters would vote against us. I gathered that he would be

[39] 'News of the Week', 25 Feb. 1938.
[40] *Headway*, Mar. 1938.
[41] 'Episodes of the Month', Mar. 1938.

inclined to do so himself.'[42] Much depended, of course, on what Eden would do and the kind of case he would make for leaving the Government. Journals as opposed as the *New Statesman* and the *National Review* expected him to cross the floor of the House or at least make some bid for power based on his popularity in the country.[43] Winston Churchill, who had not been conspicuously successful in his own political tactics during the last few years, wrote to Eden encouraging him not to spare his former colleagues in making his resignation speech to the House of Commons. Churchill was naturally eager to associate with this latest dissenter who brought an air of respectability to Conservative criticism and he advised Eden not to say anything 'that fetters your action in the future. You owe this not only to yourself—which you no doubt feel the least part of the event—but to your cause, which is also the cause of England.'[44] Such advice fell on deaf ears: Eden had no intention of making an appeal to Parliament or the country, much less of leading a revolt against the National Government.

In his memoirs Eden recalled that he considered the idea of forming a new political party but rejected it as impractical: 'Within the Conservative Party, I, and those who shared my views, were in a minority of about thirty members of Parliament out of nearly four hundred. Our number might be expected to grow if events proved us right, but the more complete the break, the more reluctant would the newly converted be to join us.'[45] It is easy to see in this political cowardice and to criticize Eden for not trying to break the Government and defeat the policy of appeasement. But perhaps the former Foreign Secretary was playing a subtler game, expecting the Administration to collapse and the country to rally behind him as the great national leader. Randolph Churchill, in his hostile and frequently unreliable study, maintains that Eden sought the advice of Stanley Baldwin who said that 'if his resignation should create a political crisis involving Chamberlain's position and were he consulted by the King as to whom he should invite to form a Government, he would recommend Eden. Baldwin and Eden saw each other

[42] Duff Cooper, diary entry. Cooper, *Old Men Forget*, p. 212.

[43] 'Current Comments', *New Statesman*, 26 Feb. 1938; 'Episodes of the Month', *National Review*, Mar. 1938.

[44] Quoted in Eden, *Facing the Dictators*, p. 598.

[45] Anthony Eden, Earl of Avon, *The Reckoning* (London, 1965), p. 4.

frequently at this period and went so far as to draw up a list of names for an alternative Government.'[46] And when Vansittart advised Eden to wait and resign on a bigger issue—perhaps the *Anschluss* which was already looming up—Eden defended his decision by saying: 'They will not be able to stand it.'[47]

The calculation that the Government would collapse as a result of his resignation and that he would soon be called upon to become Prime Minister, may account for the mildness of Eden's resignation speech, which was certainly a disappointment to the House of Commons. Instead of the full-blooded attack on the Administration and its policies which everyone expected Eden quietly explained that he and the Prime Minister had disagreed about talks with Italy and he had decided to resign. Harold Nicolson felt that the speech failed because it was 'too restrained in parts and then too unrestrained. Either he should have confined himself to the distressed-colleague point of view or launched out into an appeal for decency in foreign policy. He fell between the two stools.'[48] Another factor which prevented Eden from making a better case was that the previous dispute over President Roosevelt's offer could not be mentioned publicly. Only once did he allude to this earlier clash when he said: 'I should not be frank with the House if I were to pretend that it is an isolated issue between my right hon. Friend the Prime Minister and myself. It is not. Within the last few weeks upon one most important decision of foreign policy which did not concern Italy at all, the difference was fundamental.'[49] The significance of this remark, however, could not be appreciated by anyone outside the Cabinet and no one asked him to elaborate on it. For the most part Eden based his case on the diplomatic propriety of dealing with Mussolini while Italian propaganda against England was so strong. The country could not afford another capitulation to the Fascist leader, and unless Italy gave some real demonstration of good faith the British Government should stand firm in any dealings with it.

In his defence Neville Chamberlain naturally tried to

[46] Randolph S. Churchill, *The Rise and Fall of Sir Anthony Eden* (London, 1959), p. 149.

[47] Colvin, *Vansittart*, p. 193.

[48] Harold Nicolson to Victoria Sackville-West, 22 Feb. 1938. Nicolson, *Diaries and Letters*, pp. 324–5.

[49] 21 Feb. 1938. 332 H.C. Deb. 5s., cols. 48–9.

minimize the differences between himself and the former Foreign Secretary—no difficult task in view of Eden's speech. He emphasized that they were agreed on goals and differed only on the means by which they could best be achieved: 'To the rest of the Government, including myself, it did not seem that such differences of opinion as have arisen upon the imediate question at issue were of sufficient importance to make it necessary for my right hon. Friend to leave us. My right hon. Friend took a different view. He has said, and said truly, that each man must be the keeper of his own conscience.'[50] To most of the National Government's supporters, listening to both sides of the case, it must have seemd that Eden had resigned over some minor diplomatic nicety; perhaps because of his well-known dislike of Mussolini. The actual timing and conditions for talks with Italy were surely too insignificant to stand in the way of the Prime Minister's magnificent scheme of negotiating with the dictators to save 'the peace of Europe for a generation'.[51] As one back-bencher put it:

I believe that I owe it to those whom I represent to say that in my opinion the one thing that matters to the British people is that although principles must of course be observed, nothing should be done, simply from a desire to stick too meticulously to forms of procedure, which might hinder a satisfactory solution of the difficulties with which we, and the Italian government, no less than ourselves, are at present faced.[52]

Since Eden had failed to present a strong case for his resignation, too, back-benchers were receptive to the story put about by the party managers that the Foreign Secretary had become rattled by the strains of office. One Conservative M.P. told the House:

In the incident we are considering I think the mental balance of the Foreign Secretary was wrong. I do not think he ought to have resigned. . . . Looking at the fact that we have had in two or three years two Foreign Ministers, who, to my mind, failed because they were overworked, I think it is very important that the Government should remember the great strain which is now thrown on a Foreign Secretary.[53]

[50] 21 Feb. 1938. 332 H.C. Deb. 5s., col. 53.

[51] Neville Chamberlain, 21 Feb. 1938. Ibid., col. 64.

[52] Commander Sir Archibald Southby, 21 Feb. 1938. Ibid., col. 109.

[53] Sir Alan Anderson, 22 Feb. 1938. Ibid., col. 274.

The Opposition parties were not slow to see the advantage given them by Eden's resignation. Although they had bitterly attacked his non-intervention policy in the Spanish Civil War they now hailed him as the champion of the League of Nations sacrificed by a pro-Fascist Prime Minister in his eagerness to do a deal with Hitler and Mussolini. Charging that the Government had once again abandoned its 1935 election platform, the Labour party challenged the Prime Minister to dissolve Parliament and seek a new mandate for this 'new, contradictory policy. . . . Where you get a complete reversal of Government policy affecting world affairs, it is the duty of the Government to meet the people. We make this challenge; it is for the Government to accept it.'[54] Chamberlain had no intention of putting his head in that noose, but he had given the Opposition a gift of great price by declaring that the League of Nations was no longer capable of providing collective security. As the opposition Liberal, Kinsley Griffith, pointed out, this amounted to abandoning the official policy of every Government since the end of the First World War:

> There is a traditional League policy in this country, built up, not only by the League of Nations alone, not only by the churches and the chapels of this country, although they have played their part, but by the successive speeches of Prime Ministers, including Conservative Prime Ministers. That policy has had a great volume of public opinion behind it. Now, from what has been indicated this afternoon it appears that the Front Bench opposite are going to tie that policy neatly up in a parcel and deliver it on the doorstep of the right hon. Gentleman the Leader of the Opposition, so that he can claim it for his own, as if he alone were concerned.[55]

From that day forward, right through the Second World War, the Liberal and Labour parties could claim that they had been the League's defenders and the National Government its destroyer.

In spite of the rumblings of revolt which arose when the news of Eden's resignation became public, the former Foreign Secretary had hardly given the signal for rebellion when he defended his action in the House of Commons. After he had finished

[54] Arthur Greenwood, 22 Feb. 1938. Ibid., col. 220.
[55] 22 Feb. 1938. Ibid., col. 235.

speaking most Conservative back-benchers must have been relieved to discover that he was not about to embark on a campaign to destroy the National Government. The situation closely resembled the Hoare–Laval crisis: so long as their seats were not in danger the average Conservative M.P.s were not concerned about the principles at stake—if indeed they understood the principle in this latest case—and only too happy to obey the instructions to rally behind the Government. Once more the Whips office, and apathy, had triumphed. But there were a few back-benchers who were perturbed about the differences between Eden and Chamberlain and who rose to take Eden's part.

Winston Churchill, who had supported the Administration since Chamberlain became Prime Minister, now declared his disagreement with the Government's foreign policy. In a careful and restrained speech Churchill paid tribute to Eden as 'the one fresh figure of first magnitude arising out of the generation which was ravaged by the War'. The whole speech was devoted to supporting Eden's view of foreign affairs and condemning the Government's; and Churchill warned the Cabinet that 'the day will come when at some point or other on some issue or other you will have to make a stand, and I pray God that when that day comes we may not find that through an unwise policy we are left to make that stand alone'. But even here he hedged his position by asserting that 'if it were possible for Italy to discharge her duty in aiding Great Britain and France in defending the integrity and independence of Austria; for the sake of that I would go as far as any man in making concessions.' He did add, however, that he thought such a development unlikely.[56]

Other back-benchers who voiced their support for Eden included Harold Nicolson, Major J. W. Hills, Paul Emrys-Evans, Brigadier-General E. L. Spears, Ronald Cartland, A. C. Crossley, and Vyvyan Adams. Harold Nicolson, the champion of the new diplomacy, made an angry speech condemning Italy's record in international affairs and praising Eden's struggle for the rule of law between nations: 'The late Foreign Secretary stood for a certain measure of behaviour and conduct in foreign affairs and . . . his repudiation means that the present Government, unconsciously perhaps, feel we must not permit highbrowism, or ethics,

[56] 22 Feb. 1938. 332 H.C. Deb. 5s., cols. 235–47.

or uplift to stand in our way. That, I think, is the issue.'[57] Cartland felt that the difference between Eden and Chamberlain was one which ran through the whole country:

Perhaps those who can scan the horizon and have many years ahead of them look with rather different eyes at all the problems of to-day from those who have not so many years ahead. I know that there are many people who sincerely say that to maintain a certain conduct in international relations at the present time is foolhardy, in face of the existing dangers, but expediency in foreign politics has never been a tenet of the Tory faith.[58]

Adams believed that 'what happened yesterday and the day before will thrill every pro-Fascist and elate every pro-Nazi in the country and throughout the world'. And he told the House that he intended to support the Labour party's vote of censure, 'not because I wish to support His Majesty's Opposition, but because it is the only way in which I can show my loyalty to my right hon. Friend'.[59] No one else followed Adams into the Opposition lobby when the vote was taken but at least twenty-one others abstained.[60] According to the *New Statesman* many others who would have liked to abstain were induced to record a purely party vote by the threat of an immediate general election.[61]

The attitudes of two other M.P.s also deserve notice. Robert Boothby, who had previously supported Winston Churchill's position on foreign policy, now diverged from the elder statesman by refusing to support Eden's resignation. Arguing that the rest of the Cabinet must have been in favour of Chamberlain's policy since no one else had resigned, he expressed his relief that the period of vacillation was over and that there would be direction from the top at last:

For my part, I would only say that any positive policy is better than no policy at all. . . . My right hon. Friend the Prime Minister is

[57] 21 Feb. 1938. Ibid., cols. 99–100; Harold Nicolson to Victoria Sackville-West, 22 Feb. 1938. Nicolson, *Diaries and Letters*, pp. 324–5.

[58] 22 Feb. 1938. 332 H.C. Deb. 5s., col. 279.

[59] 22 Feb. 1938. Ibid., col. 298.

[60] These were: Anthony Eden, J. P. L. Thomas, Lord Cranborne, Mark Patrick, Winston Churchill, E. L. Spears, Harold Nicolson, Anthony Crossley, Major J. W. Hills, J. R. J. Macnamara, R. H. Turton, R. A. Cary, H. J. Duggan, R. Pilkington, Paul Emrys-Evans, Harold Macmillan, Col. L. Ropner, Ronald Cartland, Captain R. L. Briscoe, Hamilton Kerr, and Brendan Bracken. *The Times*, 24 Feb. 1938.

[61] 'Current Comments', 26

playing for high stakes. He would not do so if he did not believe in the policy which he has undertaken. He is playing with very great courage. I think my right hon. Friend the Member for Warwick and Leamington [Eden] and my noble Friend the Member for South Dorset [Cranborne] were quite right to resign, because they could not play the game with those stakes, if they did not believe in it. And they did not. The only chance of success is that the game shall be played by a man who does believe in it to such a point that he considers that any other policy would be fatal.[62]

Boothby continued to support the Prime Minister's conduct of foreign affairs until Munich, when he and Churchill found themselves in agreement once more.

Leopold Amery, who was soon to be working closely with Eden, also welcomed the resignation. Upholding Italy's case as usual, he told the House of Commons: 'As a spectator from outside I say that it redounds greatly to the Prime Minister's credit that as soon as he came to office he determined to end the senseless quarrel between this country and Italy, and to extricate us from the rut into which we were getting more and more deeply involved.'[63] And speaking to his constituents at the end of the week Amery claimed that Eden should have resigned two years earlier when sanctions against Italy were abandoned. The Foreign Secretary had been in a false position ever since and his decision to resign at last did him credit, Amery maintained, because it was better to stick to principles than to office.[64]

If Eden's resignation was not the signal for a back-bench revolt it did mark the renewal of the back-benchers' criticism of foreign policy after nine months of agreement; and this time the criticism did not cease until Chamberlain himself resigned two years later. But this did not mean that the critics worked together in attacking the Government. Winston Churchill, for his part, was well aware of Eden's prestige in Parliament and in the country; but Eden showed no desire to link his fortunes with Churchill's. Perhaps he was advised in this, as Randolph Churchill states, by Baldwin.[65] Avoiding Churchill may have been astute but Eden's conduct as a dissenter was certainly peculiar. Perhaps he lacked the confidence to launch an all-out

62 22 Feb. 1938. 332 H.C. Deb. 5s., cols. 252–3.
63 21 Feb. 1938. Ibid., col. 83.
64 Reported in *The Times*, 26 Feb. 1938.
65 R. Churchill, *Rise and Fall of Sir Anthony Eden*, p. 154.

attack on an administration which had so easily survived his resignation and the *Anschluss*; or perhaps, like his mentor Sir Austen Chamberlain, he was constitutionally incapable of leading a revolt. Whatever the reason until war broke out he assumed Sir Austen's role of moderate and cautious, if highly respected, critic. His one theme, as every crisis arose in international affairs, was that old differences should be forgotten and a real national government formed to include Conservative backbenchers and members of the Opposition. Many people, watching Eden's attempts to get back into office in this fashion, must have wondered why he left it in the first place. But if Eden missed being in office in the short run his resignation laid the foundation of his later political career. As A. J. P. Taylor put it: 'Eden, the man of strong words, acquired retrospectively a mythical reputation as the man who favoured strong acts and became a symbol of resistance to Chamberlain's policy.'[66]

[66] A. J. P. Taylor, *English History 1914–1945* (Oxford, 1965), p. 423.

9. *Anschluss:* The Lull before the Storm

THE arguments over Anthony Eden's resignation had scarcely ceased before the British Government was faced with a major international crisis. On 12 March Hitler marched his troops into Austria and incorporated it into his Empire. Such a move had been expected for over a month and the Cabinet had been discussing it at the time of Eden's resignation. Indeed it was Germany's interference in Austrian affairs without any Italian resistance which convinced Eden that Mussolini was firmly committed to Hitler and that Chamberlain was wasting his time trying to woo him away. But it is interesting to notice that Eden did not recommend any strong action to the Cabinet when the Austrian problem was reviewed on 16 February. He merely said that he 'would have to watch the situation very carefully and he would have to keep in close contact with the Prime Minister. . . . He did not want to put himself in the position of suggesting a resistance which we could not, in fact, furnish.'[1] The Conservative party's Foreign Affairs Committee, which met the following day to support the Foreign Secretary, was evidently in a more vigorous mood. A majority of the 100 M.P.s present indicated that they were in favour of stopping Hitler's expansion, by force if necessary; and in their communiqué to the Prime Minister they called for 'a more positive attitude by this country in Europe'.[2] But when Hitler actually seized Austria there was remarkably little stir in England—certainly nothing to compare with the outcry touched off by Eden's resignation. Perhaps that event had exhausted political passions for the time being.[3]

[1] Cab. 23/92.

[2] Gordon Brook-Sheperd, *Anschluss: The Rape of Austria* (London, 1963), pp. 87–8.

[3] Even in the memoirs of this period there is little discussion of the submergence of Austria. Lord Halifax, the Foreign Secretary at the time, dismissed it in half a sentence as 'an unpleasant reminder of the way the Nazi Government of Germany was likely to handle other European affairs'. Earl of Halifax, *Fulness of Days* (London, 1957), pp. 195–6. Hugh Dalton did not even mention it in his autobiography, which at least saved him the embarrassment of discussing the socialist frame of mind which produced the following statement from Kingsley Martin, the editor of the *New Statesman*: 'Today, if Mr. Chamberlain would come forward and tell us that his policy was really one

To Neville Chamberlain Hitler's latest move was an irritation and a distraction from the vital task of securing the appeasement of Europe. But far from inducing him to abandon his policy or even pause seriously to reconsider it, the take-over of Austria only confirmed Chamberlain in his belief that he must try harder to get on good terms with Italy. 'It is tragic to think', he wrote, 'that very possibly this might have been prevented if I had had Halifax at the Foreign Office instead of Anthony Eden at the time I wrote my letter to Mussolini.'[4] On the day of the seizure Chamberlain called a Cabinet meeting because, 'although there was probably not very much that could be done, he thought it right that the Cabinet should meet'. While sharing his thoughts with his colleagues he made it clear that he had no intention of taking any action:

> The manner in which the German action in Austria had been brought about was most distressing and shocking to the world and was a typical illustration of power politics. This made international appeasement much more difficult. . . . In spite of all, however, he felt that this thing had to come. Nothing short of an overwhelming display of force would have stopped it.

It was almost with a sigh of relief that he concluded: 'At any rate the question was now out of the way.' More ominously he announced that the next problem was 'to prevent an occurrence of similar events in Czecho-Slovakia and he hoped that the Secretary of State for Foreign Affairs [Halifax] would consider this question with the French, who had a treaty with Czecho-Slovakia and had announced their intention to fulfil it'.[5]

Others were at least as complacent about the latest *fait accompli*. Lord Lothian, who had provided a soothing comment on the invasion of the Rhineland, rose to the occasion once more in a letter to the editor of *The Times*:

not only of isolation, but also of Little Englandism in which the Empire was to be given up because it could not be defended, and in which military defence was to be abandoned because war would totally end civilization, we for our part would wholeheartedly support him.' 'The Inescapable Facts', *New Statesman*, 19 Mar. 1938. It is only fair to add that the article went on to say that since such a policy was unlikely to be adopted, considering the Tory tradition, the best chance of preventing war lay in Churchill's idea of an immediate alliance against Germany. Still it is significant that the *New Statesman* ranked collective security after a policy of total non-involvement in foreign affairs.

[4] Letter dated 13 Mar. 1938. Quoted in Feiling, *Life of Neville Chamberlain*, p. 342.

[5] Cab. 23/92.

The most important single aspect is that at long last it ends the disastrous period when the League of Nations Powers attempted, in the name of the Covenant, to deny to the Germans, who were certainly not solely responsible for the Great War, their national unity and so drove them to accept a totalitarian regime as the one method by which they could secure their national unity and their natural rights, at a fearful price in the destruction of individual freedom at home and in the return to power politics in international affairs.[6]

For most people the disappearance of independent Austria did not appear to be a matter of vital concern to Britain. If two German-speaking countries wished to unite—despite the prohibition of the treaty of St. Germain—that was certainly not the concern of any third party. Hitler had not conquered Austria by force and to all outward appearances his arrival was welcomed by the Austrians. Winston Churchill was correct in predicting that the situation would be accepted in the same placid fashion as the reoccupation of the Rhineland:

My right hon. Friend the Prime Minister will perhaps repeat what he said a few weeks ago that the tension in Europe is greatly relaxed. *The Times* will write a leading article to say how silly those people look who on the morrow of the Austrian incorporation raised a clamour for exceptional action in foreign policy and home defence, and how wise the Government were not to let themselves be carried away by this passing incident.[7]

Not every observer, of course, took such a calm view of the *Anschuluss*. The xenophobic *National Review* was true to form in announcing that the annexation marked the point at which the German nation, 'at one time apparently civilised, reverted to the practice of its most savage ancestors. . . . The ruthlessness of the persecution which the German Austrians are undergoing at the hands of the Third Reich is evidence of how absolute is the abandonment of morality and religion in the satrapy of Herr Hitler.' This, the magazine maintained, was a direct result of sanctions which had driven Italy into Germany's arms and made her lose interest in preserving an independent Austria.[8] The liberal Conservative *Spectator* condemned the blow 'dealt by a Government that knows no morality but force and recognizes no

[6] *The Times*, 14 Mar. 1938.

[7] 24 Mar. 1938. 333 H.C. Deb. 5s., col. 1453.

[8] 'Episodes of the Month', Apr. 1938; 'Austria has Paid for Abyssinia!' Apr. 1938.

judgement but what it passes itself on its own course. It was a violation of repeated pledges and it makes every future undertaking given by Germany worthless and irrelevant.' The only way to prevent a recurrence of this type of *coup* in the future lay in adopting a real system of collective security.[9] Rather more optimistically the *Economist* claimed that Hitler's triumph had been achieved at the cost of revealing 'the mailed fist under the velvet glove' and asserted: 'Even the British ostrich has at last been compelled to lift his head out of the sand and open his eyes to the gravest crisis that has confronted him since 1914.'[10] It soon resumed its customary posture.

Like his march into the Rhineland Hitler's seizure of Austria took place on a Saturday. When the House of Commons reassembled on the Monday the Government agreed to the Opposition's request for an immediate debate on the international situation. In his opening speech the Prime Minister maintained that his Government bore no responsibility for Hitler's latest outrage and repeated what he had already told the Cabinet: 'The fact is—and of its truth every hon. Member can judge for himself—that nothing could have arrested this action by Germany unless we and others with us had been prepared to use force to prevent it.' The Prime Minister admitted that he had not demanded that Hitler remove his troops from Austria but his Government had followed the diplomatically correct course of consulting the French and the Italians. As a result of this prompt move: 'His Majesty's Government and the French Government addressed similar protests to the German Government on the action that has been taken.' But in spite of this discouraging pronouncement there were indications in Chamberlain's speech that the latest *coup* would call forth a stiffer attitude towards Germany in the future:

> It seems to us that the methods adopted throughout these events call for the severest condemnation, and have administered a profound shock to all who are interested in the preservation of European peace. It follows that what has passed cannot fail to have prejudiced the hope of His Majesty's Government of removing misunderstandings between nations and promoting international co-operation.

Indeed he announced that the seizure of Austria might lead to

[9] 'After Austria—?', 18 Mar. 1938.
[10] 'The Shadow of the Sword', 19 Mar. 1938.

accelerated rearmament and a review of the country's foreign policy.[11] Perhaps Chamberlain's critics were reassured by the firm tone of this speech, but the Prime Minister, accepting Hitler's statement that he had no designs on Czechoslovakia, soon retreated from this advanced position. Once more Hitler was able to carry off a *fait accompli* without any appreciable hardening of the British Government's attitude towards him.

In the debate which followed, both the Leader of the Opposition, Clement Attlee, and the Liberal leader, Sir Archibald Sinclair, deplored the way in which Austria had been annexed to the German Reich but they had to admit that the union would have been justified on the grounds of self-determination in happier days. Both of them, however, called on the National Government to take a firm stand to avoid similar surprises in the future and to re-dedicate itself to the doctrine of collective security. But soon the discussion degenerated into a futile argument about the responsibility for the general situation in Europe and the value of courting Italy as an ally to restrain Germany. The Spanish Civil War was still in the forefront of most Labour M.P.s' minds and much of the debate consisted of a rehearsal of familiar attitudes towards that struggle. Few speakers concentrated directly on the Austrian problem which had occasioned the debate.

The attitude of the average Conservative back-bencher was expressed by an undistinguished M.P., Thomas Moore, in a letter to *The Times*. Praising Hitler's new technique of 'bloodless revolution' he declared that the German leader's lightning moves were possible only because he was doing what the people who were affected wanted: 'If the Austrian people had not welcomed this union, physical opposition and bloodshed must have occurred. That so far there has been none proves, I submit, the inherent desire of the two nations to secure the *Anschluss* of which they have been so long deprived by the determined interference of the leading European Powers.' The union would mean that henceforth Austria would be a vital economic community once more: 'Let us therefore consider and assess the benefits with which Austria and Europe are confronted before allotting blame for a development which in the end may prove a decisive factor in European appeasement.'[12] Lord Tweedsmuir, the former

[11] 14 Mar. 1938. 333 H.C. Deb. 5s., cols. 45–52. [12] *The Times*, 17 Mar. 1938.

Conservative M.P. and novelist John Buchan, kept in close touch with British politics while serving as Governor-General in Canada. He wrote to his sister in a vein similar to Moore's:

> I do not myself quite see what there is to fuss about. Austria will be much more comfortable, economically, under Germany's wing. That should have been done long ago in the Versailles Treaty. The chief trouble will be if there is any real threat to Czechoslovakia; but there again, I think, the frontier should be rectified. Surely the Versailles agreement was the most half-witted thing ever perpetrated.[13]

In so far as they were concerned about Central and Eastern Europe at all the majority of the Government's supporters wanted a quiet solution to the economic and social problems of that area in order to reduce the chance of war. They were certainly not disposed to blame Chamberlain for the latest crisis. Although some of them had had their confidence shaken by Eden's resignation, many more believed that the Prime Minister knew what he was doing in the realm of foreign policy and that he would manage to find some commonsense solution to international problems once he had the opportunity of establishing his control of foreign policy and given more careful consideration to the European situation. Robert Boothby defended his leader in these terms: 'The least one can say about the Prime Minister is that no Minister has ever made more crystal clear at any stage, or voiced so frankly to the House of Commons what he was trying to do.'[14]

Anthony Eden, who knew of the impending German seizure of Austria before he resigned, might have been expected to make political capital of this development. He could have used the *Anschluss* to demonstrate that Chamberlain's policy was a failure, to urge the Cabinet to take a stronger line with the dictators, and to rally those back-benchers whose confidence in the Administration had been shaken when he resigned. But Eden, who was once more on the Riviera, did not hurry back to England as he had when he heard of President Roosevelt's message. Rather: 'While the clouds were gathering over Austria, I remained in the South of France, reading the French newspapers and listening to the Vienna radio.'[15] Later on he pontificated in

[13] John Buchan to Anna Buchan, 14 Mar. 1938. Quoted in Janet Adam Smith, *John Buchan* (London, 1965), p. 443.

[14] 14 Mar. 1938. 333 H.C. Deb. 5s., col. 63.

[15] Eden, *The Reckoning*, p. 7.

his memoirs: 'In March 1938, the successful invasion of Austria should have pointed the danger for Czechoslovakia, even to the obtuse.'[16] But despite his enormous prestige Eden did nothing to help the obtuse in their task at the time. In fact he did not even return to the House of Commons for another two months.[17] Perhaps he stayed abroad in the expectation that the Government would fall over the *Anschluss* and he would be called upon to form a new one.

Winston Churchill, the other prominent Conservative outside the Government, saw a further confirmation of his suspicions about Nazi Germany in this latest blow, and his doubts about the conduct of foreign affairs since Eden's departure were strengthened. Although he did not advocate the use of force to remove German troops from Austria he did insist that

> this Nazi conquest of Austria cannot remain where it is, and . . . a patient, determined, persevering discussion of it ought to take place and to be pushed forward, first of all, no doubt, through the Chancelleries and by the diplomatic channels but also and ultimately it should be pushed forward in the natural place for such discussions to take place—under the League of Nations at Geneva.

In what Harold Nicolson called 'the speech of his life'[18] Churchill warned that the only hope of averting war at this late date lay in forming a 'grand alliance' of states around Britain and France, all co-ordinating their staff arrangements and basing their co-operation on the Covenant of the League of Nations. 'If that were sustained, as it would be, by the moral sense of the world; and if it were done in the year 1938—and, believe me, it may be the last chance there will be for doing it—then I say you might even now arrest this approaching war.'[19]

The most unexpected speech of the debate came from Leopold Amery, hitherto one of the leading isolationist-imperialists who had urged the Government to strengthen the bonds of Empire and avoid Continental entanglements. Now the *Anschlus* came as a bitter warning that the British Empire could not go its own way unmolested while benevolently encouraging the Continental countries to form some economic and political union of their

[16] Eden, *The Reckoning*, p. 8.

[17] Ibid., p. 16.

[18] Diary entry, 14 Mar. 1938. Nicolson, *Diaries and Letters*, p. 331.

[19] 333 H.C. Deb. 5s., cols. 93–100.

own. 'A small nation, standing for something rather unique in the world, the last remnant of that old tradition of a united western Christendom, a super-national State . . . has been trampled down by brute force.' Amery advised the Government to tell the Germans 'in language as plain and simple as we can make it that the first German soldier or aeroplane to cross the Czech border will bring the whole might of this country against Germany'.[20] On the day of the invasion he recorded his shock in his diary:

> The news of Austria's collapse came to me as a terrible blow. . . . But what is the value of an ideal if you are not prepared to defend it, and so Austria has fallen and with it, for a long while I fear, any idea of European unity on free co-operative lines. . . . For us it means facing realities and much as I dislike, from the Empire point of view, a policy of Continental entanglements. . . .[21]

But Austria's submergence did not convert Amery to collective security to resist any similar moves in the future. On the contrary, like the *National Review*, he blamed the whole tragedy on collective security and sanctions: 'Looking back it has all fulfilled exactly what I feared when Eden was allowed by Baldwin's ineptitude and vote-catching to launch the Abyssinian folly at Geneva. Now events have gone so far that it looks as if we may be irretrievably committed to the policy of two camps in Europe.'[22] Nor was he really convinced that anything could be done to protect Czechoslovakia. A few days after his speech Amery wrote in his diary that Britain might have to resign itself to 'falling back with Italian support, on holding Yugoslavia and the Balkans and letting Germany find her elbow room in the rest of the Danubian area and in Eastern Europe'.[23] Italy was now more than ever the key to the situation and in April, when he was in Italy to study the workings of the corporative industrial system, Amery added his personal efforts to those of the Government in the attempt to win over Mussolini. But even from Amery's record of their talk it is obvious who was flattering whom.[24]

The fact that the German annexation of Austria did not have much effect on Conservative M.P.s at the time can be seen in the

[20] Ibid., cols. 84–7.
[21] Leopold Amery, diary entry, 12 Mar. 1938. L. S. Amery Papers.
[22] Diary entry. Amery, *Unforgiving Years*, p. 238.
[23] Ibid., p. 239. [24] Ibid., p. 240.

cold treatment given to the Soviet proposals for a four-power conference between Britain, France, the United States, and the U.S.S.R. This offer, which was announced on 19 March, was considered by the British Cabinet and rejected three days later—even faster than President Roosevelt's January proposals. Neville Chamberlain was convinced that the Russians were 'steadily and cunningly pulling all the strings behind the scenes to get us involved with Germany (our Secret Service doesn't spend all its time looking out the window)'.[25] In his defence of this rejection in the House of Commons the Prime Minister revealed that he had no intention of confronting Germany with any overwhelming combination of nations that could be assembled to resist further aggression—especially if such a combination included the Soviet Union. 'Their proposals', he told the House,

> would appear to involve less a consultation with a view to settlement than a concerting of action against an eventuality that has not yet arisen. . . . His Majesty's Government are of the opinion that the indirect, but none the less inevitable, consequence of such action as is proposed by the Soviet Government would be to aggravate the tendency towards the establishment of exclusive groups of nations, which must, in the view of His Majesty's Government, be inimical to the prospects of European peace.[26]

His supporters, who shared Chamberlain's fear and distrust of Russia, were quite satisfied with the rejection of Litvinov's plan. 'There must be something wrong with Russia,' as one of them said with compelling logic, 'otherwise there would not be so many people shot.'[27] Even Winston Churchill, who was soon to be advocating some kind of overture to the U.S.S.R., did not refer to that country or even discuss the offer when he spoke in the debate.

[25] Diary entry, 20 Mar. 1938. Feiling, *Life of Neville Chamberlain*, p. 347.
[26] 333 H.C. Deb. 5s., col. 1406.
[27] George Lambert. Ibid., col. 1435.

10. Munich: The Crisis of Conservative Conscience

EVERYONE recognized that the incorporation of Austria into Germany raised the problem of the German-speaking minority in the western part of Czechoslovakia. After the *Anschluss* the area was surrounded on two of three sides by Germany and it was only a matter of time until Hitler demanded that the predominantly German parts be allowed to join the Reich on the same principle of self-determination which had justified the annexation of Austria. The question facing the British Government was whether it was prepared to let Hitler take the territory by intimidation or force, thereby effectively destroying Czechoslovakia as a country and removing the chief barrier to his eastward and southern expansion if, as he stated in *Mein Kampf*, this was his aim; or whether it would support the French guarantee of Czechoslovakia and deny the principle of self-determination in order to prevent the German domination of Europe. If the British Government decided to stand by Czechoslovakia there was the further problem of the means that would have to be used to stop the German dictator. This was the issue which divided the Conservative party more than any other save India in the decade before the Second World War. This later division involved a smaller and less confident group of M.P.s and at no point, as it turned out, did it threaten the survival of the party or its leaders; but its future significance was far greater than the earlier dispute. Reputations were made and destroyed in the debates on Czechoslovakia which affected political careers for the next quarter-century.

No one who had observed the National Government's conduct of foreign affairs in the last few years could have been in much doubt about the way it would lean, but only a prophet with a taste for black humour would have foretold that Hitler would get what he wanted and the British Government, grappling for some kind of control of the situation, would emerge looking like his accomplice.

Before the National Government had made a statement on the latest crisis to appear on the horizon, a good indication of its attitude was given in March 1938 by Alan Lennox-Boyd, the Parliamentary Secretary to the Ministry of Labour. Lennox-Boyd's position was a minor one—and he had only held that for three weeks—but his speech attracted considerable attention because he was regarded as one of the most promising young men in the Conservative party. In his remarks the junior minister declared that

> he could countenance nothing more ridiculous than a guarantee that the frontiers of Czechoslovakia should not be violated when the people of the country could not be relied on to be loyal to the Government of the day; and from what he knew of Mr. Chamberlain, he did not think he would make a move to give a guarantee of that kind.
>
> Germany, he said, could absorb Czechoslovakia and Great Britain would remain secure; but Germany could not invade France without threatening us. We should therefore reaffirm our understandings to France to defend her if she should be invaded.[1]

This speech, which the Opposition claimed was broadcast to Czechoslovakia in German by the Germans, caused such an uproar that the House of Commons held a short debate on it on 21 March. Denying that the statement had been intended as a stalking-horse for the Government the Prime Minister tried to defend his colleague by claiming that the speech had been incorrectly reported. Lennox-Boyd himself merely apologized for his conduct, claiming that he had not spoken for the Administration.[2] Technically this was correct but his remarks were an accurate reflection of the last Cabinet discussion of Czechoslovakia. No doubt Lennox-Boyd had picked up the tone of the meeting from those Ministers who attended.

At the Cabinet meeting on 16 March the Prime Minister and his Foreign Secretary, Lord Halifax, were primarily concerned to ensure that Britain did not find itself in a position of having to fight for Czechoslovakia. The Chiefs of Staff had produced a report which painted a gloomy picture of British and French air power and which claimed that the countries of South-East Europe (Russia was excluded from the survey) would be of

1 Reported in *The Times*, 19 Mar. 1938.

2 333 H.C. Deb. 5s., cols. 950–66.

limited value and might even be a liability, as Britain would then incur a moral obligation to defend them against German invasion. Given this situation the first task was to persuade the French to abandon their guarantee of Czechoslovakia lest a German attack lead to a Franco-German war. In that case Britain would almost certainly have to rescue France, and the other countries of Europe would take advantage of the situation to increase their own territory. The other half of this policy was that the British Government would induce the Czech Government to remedy the grievances of the Sudeten Germans. The British and French Governments would then concentrate their efforts on getting Hitler to accept this solution to the Czechoslovakian problem. Although some Cabinet Ministers questioned this lucid and simple plan the general consensus at the end of the discussion was that 'the policy proposed by the Foreign Secretary and supported by the Prime Minister was the best available in the circumstances.'[3]

Outside the Government most back-benchers were willing to support such a scheme for avoiding disaster in Eastern Europe but there were some who were becoming increasingly apprehensive about the direction of the Government's foreign policy. Anthony Eden's resignation had been the major turning-point which had led people to question Chamberlain's foreign policy; but in view of the threat to Czechoslovakia the *Anschluss* also took on a greater retrospective significance.

In the spring and summer of 1938 a group of Conservative back-benchers, known simply as 'The Group', began to meet informally to discuss foreign affairs. Unfortunately it is impossible to tell precisely when this group came into existence[4] or exactly who were those M.P.s sneeringly referred to by the Whips as 'the Glamour Boys'.[5] As it was only an informal discussion group with no fixed membership, organization, or officers, even those who attended its meetings cannot remember all the names of those who belonged to it. No doubt its size differed from time to

[3] Cab. 23/93.

[4] Randolph Churchill implies that it existed before Eden's resignation. *Rise and Fall of Sir Anthony Eden*, p. 154. According to Sir John Wheeler-Bennett the group came into being after Eden left the Government. *Munich, Prologue to Tragedy* (London, 1948), p. 183. Eden himself vaguely states that it began in the summer of 1938. *The Reckoning*, p. 31.

[5] Eden, op. cit., p. 31.

time, depending on the seriousness of the foreign situation, but it seems to have consisted of about twenty members. In addition to Eden and his followers, Lord Cranborne, J. P. L. Thomas, and Mark Patrick, it contained at least the following M.P.s: Leopold Amery, Robert Bower, Ronald Cartland, Anthony Crossley, H. J. Duggan, Paul Emrys-Evans, Sir Derrick Gunston, Sir Sidney Herbert, Dudley Joel, C. G. Lancaster, Richard Law, Harold Macmillan, Harold Nicolson, Duncan Sandys, E. L. Spears, Ronald Tree, and Viscount Wolmer.[6] Anthony Eden characterized their discussions as 'entirely free-for-all and not bounded by either the prolix or the tedious'.[7] Nor were those who attended in any way bound by a decision of the group. In addition to their concern about foreign affairs this group of predominantly young Conservatives was undoubtedly excited by Eden's plans to 'make a few big speeches on such general topics as Democracy and Young England, in which (while avoiding current topics in Foreign Affairs) he will clearly indicate that he stands for postwar England against the old men'.[8]

Here was a group which should have had considerable influence on the House of Commons in the months before Munich. Its central figure was one of the most popular politicians in the country and other M.P.s had automatically gravitated to him because they shared his views on foreign policy and saw him as a symbol of resistance to the dictators. This group, which saw more merit in traditional diplomacy and the balance of power than the Cabinet, was opposed to any further concessions to Germany, at least without substantial guarantees as to its future conduct. After the *Anschluss* this meant supporting the territorial integrity of Czechoslovakia, whether concessions were made to the Sudeten Germans or not. Brigadier-General Spears, who had been in Prague when the Germans marched into Austria, argued that the two Western Democracies had a duty to stand by Czechoslovakia, not simply in defence of a nation but of a vital principle, 'that of freedom and democracy'. This, he maintained, was the best if not the only way of averting a general war and he went on to predict: 'If the Czechs are annihilated the last rampart of

[6] Eden, op. cit., pp. 31–2; Wheeler-Bennett, *Munich*, p. 183; Amery, *Unforgiving Years*, p. 298; R. Churchill, *Rise and Fall of Sir Anthony Eden*, p. 154.

[7] Eden, op. cit., p. 32.

[8] Harold Nicolson, diary entry, 11 Apr. 1938. Nicolson, *Diaries and Letters*, p. 334.

political freedom in Central Europe will disappear and Nazi Germany will predominate, annihilating liberty as it goes, as far as the Bosphorus, absorbing on its way immense resources, from the wheat of Hungary to the oil of Roumania.'[9]

But although this group's views differed significantly from those of the Government it did not cause much stir in Parliament. Anthony Eden continued to follow a prudent course, meeting the group in private but saying nothing in public that would give offence to the Government. Perhaps he felt that this tactic, which did not pit him against the party machine with the risk of being discredited like Winston Churchill, made him appear to be above party intrigue and preserved his reputation as the great national figure who could form a government when Neville Chamberlain's policies brought him to disaster. Certainly there was much reserved judgement about Chamberlain in the spring of 1938. Harold Nicolson wrote: 'Nobody understands anything. There is a real impression that the whole show is going to crack up. This view is held, not only by the protagonists like Winston, but by the silent useful members of whom nobody ever hears. They think that a new Government will emerge on a wider basis, possibly a Coalition Government.'[10] When politicians were thinking this way it was not surprising that Eden kept his powder dry: had a new coalition been formed no one would have had a better claim to lead it than he.

Neville Chamberlain, who was no mean party tactician, was well aware of the potential danger from Eden. When the former Foreign Secretary turned up in the House of Commons, after a three-month absence following his resignation, Chamberlain offered him a post in the Administration, though not the Foreign Office. But Eden refused this transparent offer to buy him off. He had everything to lose and nothing to gain by giving the National Government the benefit of his prestige on these easy terms.[11]

Winston Churchill stood somewhat apart from this group of dissenters. Following Eden's resignation he resumed his familiar role as the Government's scourge and by the middle of the

[9] *Daily Telegraph*, 19 Mar. 1938.

[10] Harold Nicolson to Victoria Sackville-West, 17 May 1938. Nicolson, *Diaries and Letters*, pp. 341–2.

[11] Eden, op. cit., pp. 16–17.

summer the *Spectator* noted that his shafts were 'barbed, almost as they were in the days of the Baldwin régime'.[12] But even though his line of attack was much the same as the Eden group's the latter were not interested in any close association with a man whose reputation was that of an unstable political gangster and a failure to boot. 'Don't be worried, my darling,' Harold Nicolson assured his wife. 'I am not going to become one of the Winston brigade.'[13] Nor was Churchill himself, while he recognized Eden's prestige, interested in leading a small group of back-benchers against the National Government's overwhelming majority. He had tried that once before and suffered humiliating defeat. Moreover the young M.P.s gathered around Anthony Eden were not of the same calibre as the well-established figures he had led on the Indian issue. At this juncture Churchill preferred to work alone, representing himself as the national saviour. His only follower in Parliament was Brendan Bracken; even Robert Boothby had been following his own course since Eden's resignation.

Although Churchill had virtually no following in the party his stock was rising in the country. In the spring of 1938 his son published *Arms and the Covenant,* a collection of Churchill's speeches and foreign policy over the last five years. In the introduction Randolph Churchill told his readers:

> Nowhere had I omitted any argument or statement on the grounds that its re-publication today in vastly different circumstances might prove a source of political inconvenience to its author. That there should have been no temptation to do so may perhaps be thought a testimony to the integrity of the double theme—a strong Britain based upon the Covenant of the League—which emerges as the author's plan for the defence of freedom and peace.

The book provided an impressive historical foundation for Churchill's current speeches on foreign policy and only the most pedantic reader would have been prepared to show that Churchill's course had been a good deal less consistent and that his activities had involved much more than this volume revealed.

In the spring of 1938 Churchill also embarked on a speaking tour organized by Focus and the League of Nations Union.

[12] 'News of the Week', 5 Aug. 1938.

[13] Harold Nicolson to Victoria Sackville-West, 2 Mar. 1938. Nicolson, *Diaries and Letters*, p. 328.

Following a meeting in Birmingham—Neville Chamberlain's city—he visited the Austen aeroplane factory with Ronald Cartland. 'The men were thrilled to see him,' Cartland told his sister. 'I've never seen such enthusiasm. It's not surprising—he has such presence—such personality—also the man in the street realizes that he has been right in everything he has said since 1933. Those in high places say he's finished—I don't believe it. He has a following in the country far bigger than those in Westminster think.'[14] Even in the House of Commons Churchill's prestige was rising—at least among the Opposition parties—for the first time since the abdication crisis. During a defence debate the right-wing Conservative, Victor Raikes, observed:

> My right hon. Friend the Member for Epping has found strange bedfellows in these critical times among hon. and right hon. Members opposite, who have applauded him again and again to-day. I could not help but wonder whether that applause was due entirely to their new-found desire for rearmament, or whether the Opposition realise first and foremost that they have had to go outside their own ranks to find anybody who could put up any argument against the Government Front Bench.[15]

These signs of Churchill's popularity did him no good inside his own party. Even Lord Derby, an old friend in spite of their differences over India, refused to act as chairman of Churchill's Manchester meeting at the last moment. 'If, being head of the Conservative party here,' he wrote, 'I intervened now, I would give the matter more prominence and more publicity than it would otherwise get.' Churchill was deeply shocked by Derby's message, which came as a nasty reminder of the lengths to which party members would go to avoid association with him. It was only with great difficulty that he could be persuaded to continue with the meeting and he was certainly not mollified by Eugen Spier's comment: 'Derby's refusal was a blessing in disguise; that nobleman's appearance in the chair would have given the impression that this was a Conservative party affair, wheras we wanted it to be, and be seen to be, strictly non-party.'[16]

Even though Churchill's views differed from the Government's he was careful to voice them in a moderate way. And he was

[14] Cartland, *Cartland*, p. 111.
[15] 25 May 1938. 336 H.C. Deb. 5s., col. 1294.
[16] Spier, *Focus*, pp. 139–40.

particularly careful not to say anything that could be construed as disloyal to Chamberlain, who was notoriously touchy about dissent. Speaking in Sheffield on his tour he said that the Prime Minister

> had made clear his abhorrence of totalitarian tyranny in all its forms. He had declared his resolve to defend free, democratic parliamentary Government, and he had affirmed his loyalty to the Covenant of the League of Nations.
>
> Upon these assurances . . . organized labour, and especially the skilled unions, ought to throw their whole energies into the task of national defence. These are not the times when we can afford to have anything less than the full tide of national effort.

In the same speech he also went a long way towards supporting the Administration's approach to the Czechoslovakian problem and he claimed:

> The fact that several of the greatest nations had given their support to Czechoslovakia against a violent incursion should make the Government of that country all the more earnest to meet the legitimate grievances to the German people in their country. There were all the elements of a friendly and lasting settlement in Czechoslovakia if only there was no violent outside interference.[17]

Whatever Churchill's private misgivings about the conduct of foreign affairs his public speeches were not in the same fire-breathing category as those he had delivered on India. The activities of Anthony Eden and his followers were even more innocuous. This was due partly to the fact that neither Churchill nor Eden had any real alternative to the Government's Czechoslovakian policy and partly to the fact that Chamberlain kept a firmer grip on the party than Baldwin. Indeed his position in the party had been strengthened after weathering the storm of Eden's resignation, even though this was largely owing to Eden's refusal to become an active rebel. Summing up the situation at the time of the summer adjournment the *Manchester Guardian* concluded that Chamberlain's position in the House of Commons was almost as strong as it had been at the beginning of the session in November. The most important reason for this was that no one 'knows in the least where to turn for a successor—that is a

[17] Reported in *The Times*, 1 June 1938.

Tory successor, for the Tory party is not likely to accept a Simonite or National Labour successor'.[18]

As soon as Parliament had adjourned for the summer the British Government dispatched a mission, headed by Lord Runciman, a retired Cabinet Minister, to mediate in the differences between the Sudeten Germans and the Czech Government. Runciman's task was to find a solution which would de-fuse a potentially explosive situation and at the same time one which would avoid British commitments to Central Europe.

Apart from his German sympathies it was inevitable that Runciman would favour some kind of special status or local autonomy for the German minority, as it was their dissatisfaction with the political arrangements in Czechoslovakia which had produced the mission. And so long as it could get the British Government to guarantee the results the Czech Government was willing to make very far-reaching concessions to the Sudeten Germans. But once the talk turned to autonomy and then to the *Anschluss* of the German-speaking areas into Hitler's Reich the Czech Government became alarmed. So did some of the National Government's supporters in England.

As the Czechoslovakian question moved into the crisis stage in September those M.P.s who feared that the Administration intended to force the Czechs to make territorial concessions to Germany, found that they were without their usual facilities for expressing their views, as Parliament was not in session. The two most prominent back-benchers, Churchill and Eden, of course had enough prestige to approach Cabinet Ministers directly and try to influence official policy that way. 'As on similar occasions', Churchill wrote, 'my contacts with His Majesty's Government became more frequent and intimate with the mounting of the crisis.'[19] By the end of August he was bombarding Lord Halifax with advice, stressing the necessity of a peaceful solution to Czechoslovakia's problems but also proposing that Britain, France, and the U.S.S.R. issue a joint warning to Hitler that the use of force would raise a 'capital issue' for the three Powers.[20]

On 8 September Anthony Eden suddenly cut short a holiday in Ireland to return to England. The previous day *The Times*, in the leading editorial, had aired the idea that the Czech

[18] *Manchester Guardian*, 1 Aug. 1938.
[19] Churchill, *The Gathering Storm*, p. 308. [20] Ibid., p. 293.

Government should cede the frontier, 'Sudeten' areas to Germany. On 9 September Eden hurried around to the Foreign Office, where he urged Halifax to impress on the German Government that war in Central Europe would not be localized and that any European war involving the French would be bound to include Britain. He also pressed for some kind of mobilization as a sign to Hitler that the British Government was serious about forbidding German armed intervention in Czechoslovakia. Lord Halifax, a past master at pleasing everyone, soothed his visitor by replying: 'Great minds are thinking alike, for my mind is moving on just such a project and indeed I was going to speak to Neville about a draft today.'[21]

These efforts by Churchill and Eden to sway the Cabinet had some short, temporary success. When the 'Big Four' (Chamberlain, Halifax, Hoare, and Simon) emerged from the Cabinet room after hearing the Prime Minister's dramatic plan of flying to Germany to seek a direct settlement of the Czechoslovakian problem with Hitler, they found Winston Churchill waiting for them in the hall. According to Hoare: 'He had come to demand an immediate ultimatum to Hitler. He was convinced that it was our last chance of stopping a landslide, and according to his information, which was directly contrary to our own, both the French and the Russians were ready for an offensive against Germany.'[22] The following day, after consulting Churchill, Eden, and the leaders of the Opposition parties,[23] the Prime Minister did issue a warning that 'Germany cannot with impunity carry out a rapid and successful military campaign against Czechoslovakia without fear of intervention by France and Great Britain'.[24] But this hardening of the Government's heart against Germany proved to be only a brief triumph for the critics. Chamberlain's attitude soon softened and there is no indication that the dissenters had the slightest effect on his course once he had embarked on direct talks with Hitler. Indeed the Prime Minister did not even recall Parliament until his second flight to Germany had ended in apparent failure.

[21] Eden, *The Reckoning*, pp. 21–2.

[22] Templewood, *Nine Troubled Years*, pp. 301–2.

[23] There is no mention of any consultation in Eden's memoirs; however, he did see Halifax again on 11 September and perhaps the Foreign Secretary conveyed his views to the Prime Minister. Eden, *The Reckoning*, p. 22.

[24] Quoted in Wheeler-Bennett, *Munich*, p. 97.

The Czechoslovakian crisis of September and October 1938 produced a great deal of running to and fro, meeting and arguments, between the various Conservative back-benchers who disagreed with Chamberlain's handling of the matter. Robert Boothby, who had by this time lost confidence in the Prime Minister, recalled the chaos of those exciting days in his memoirs:

> The days and nights of the 'Munich crisis' now seem like a confused and interminable nightmare. I vaguely remember a series of meetings on the part of various political groups, punctuated by 'set' debates in the House of Commons. There was a Churchill group, an Eden group, and an Amery group. I belonged to the last and we met pretty frequently. . . . On at least one occasion all three groups met together, when it was decided that each of us should take our own line in the event of a division in the House of Commons.[25]

But even at this critical juncture the various dissenters were unable to work together, formulate a common policy, or decide on a clear line of action. They never attempted to draw up a statement of their views and present it to the Government or bring pressure to bear on their leaders by stating what they would do if their views were not accepted or at least considered. Apart from working off their frustration in all this feverish activity and airing their ideas to one another, it is hard to see what influence they had on foreign policy before the Munich Agreement was signed. Leopold Amery hurried around, encouraging wavering Cabinet Ministers to resist the Prime Minister's policy, but his task would have been easier if he could have assured them of the support of a considerable number of M.P.s when he was asked the natural and inevitable question about the likely reaction of the House of Commons.[26] Only after Chamberlain had signed his agreement with Hitler did the critics' policy become clear, for then they had something to react against. Before that it is hard to avoid the conclusion that they were far less certain than the Prime Minister about what should be done.

One point which distinguished most of the Conservative critics from the Government was their insistence on getting the U.S.S.R., a possible ally in the event of war with Germany, involved in the discussions on Czechoslovakia. This idea certainly ran contrary to all Conservative prejudices, but by September 1938 it seemed

[25] Boothby, *I Fight to Live* (London, 1947), p. 164.
[26] Amery, *Unforgiving Years*, p. 275.

to some of them that Nazi Germany presented a greater threat to Europe than Communist Russia and that the Soviet Union, while hardly a friendly power or an ideal ally, at least had a vital interest in restraining Germany. In the spring of 1938 Winston Churchill reminded a public gathering:

To the east of Europe lies the enormous power of Russia, a country whose form of government I detest, but which at any rate seeks no military aggression upon its neighbours, a country whose interests are peace, a country profoundly menaced by Nazi hostility, a country which lies as a great background and counterpoise at this moment to all those states of Middle Europe I have mentioned.

In a mixture of caution and urgency he advised the Government not to go

cap in hand to Soviet Russia, or count in any definite manner upon Russian action. But how improvidently foolish we should be when dangers are so great, to put needless barriers in the way of the general association of the great Russian mass with resistance to an act of Nazi aggression.[27]

Early in September Ivan Maisky, the Soviet Ambassador, told Churchill that the U.S.S.R. was prepared to use force if Germany attacked Czechoslovakia. Churchill conveyed this news to the Foreign Secretary, but the Government was not impressed. They had heard this story before and as far as they were concerned it was a Soviet trick to get Britain and France embroiled in a war with Germany while Russia took advantage of the opportunity to expand to the west. Perhaps this analysis was correct but the British Government might have put it to the test by making some overtures to the Soviet Government. When Lord Halifax had to justify Russia's absence from the Munich conference he did so by shifting the ultimate responsibility to Germany and Italy:

Five days ago it seemed vital if war was to be averted, somehow or other to get matters on to a basis of negotiation; but if we were to face the facts—and nothing was to be gained by not facing them—we were obliged to recognise that in present circumstances the heads of the German and Italian Governments would almost certainly—at least without much preliminary discussion for which there was no time—be reluctant to sit in conference with a Soviet representative.

[27] Speech in the Manchester Free Trade Hall, 9 May 1938. Churchill, *Blood, Sweat, and Tears*, pp. 27–8.

Halifax also claimed that this

> in no way signified any weakening of the desire on our part, any more no doubt than on that of the French Government, to preserve our understanding and relations with the Soviet Government.[28]

This smooth and plausible reasoning allowed the National Government to turn the tables on its critics and claim that consultations with the Soviet Government—which would probably have been lengthy—would have endangered peace rather than contributed to its preservation. The obvious answer to this was that the British Government should have made overtures to Russia in March when it started thinking seriously about the Czechoslovakian problem. But it was quite clear that the Government in fact was horrified at the prospect of lining up with the U.S.S.R. against Germany.

Only momentarily did Chamberlain relent in his fear and hatred of Russia and that was on 26 September after he had had two meetings with the German dictator and rejected Hitler's ultimatum for the cession of the Sudeten areas by 1 October. On that day Churchill was able to persuade the Prime Minister and the Foreign Secretary to issue a communiqué declaring the unity of Britain, France, and the Soviet Union against German agression.[29] But this mood was short-lived: three days later Chamberlain was back in Germany discussing the fate of Czechoslovakia with Hitler at Munich.

26 September was a day of much pro-Soviet feeling in the Conservative party. That morning Leopold Amery went to Brigadier-General Spear's office in St. Stephen's House (across the road from the Parliament buildings) where he found half a dozen conspirators, unfortunately not named, 'all desperately keen about pressing the Government to make it clear that we were in direct touch with Russia in order to impress the Germans, who have taken our non-contact with Russia as a clear proof that we do not mean to go in—nothing will even induce them to understand us.' They also told Amery that they wanted to issue a public declaration, as Conservatives, stating that they stood for co-operation with Russia. Amery objected strongly to this proposal: 'At the moment it would only put off many of our people, while once war is declared they will only too readily welcome help

[28] 3 Oct. 1938. 110 H.L. Deb. 5s., col. 1302.
[29] Churchill, *The Gathering Storm*, p. 309.

from the Devil himself, and as for the effect on Germany I didn't think much of it, though I had no objection to the request going forward to Halifax without my name added.'[30] That evening there was another meeting in Churchill's flat at which about fifteen people agreed that Russia must become involved in stopping Hitler. In addition to Churchill's close associates, Brendan Bracken and Professor Lindemann, the group included such strong Conservatives as Lord Lloyd and Sir Edward Grigg as well as Robert Boothby, Richard Law, and Harold Nicolson. Archibald Sinclair, the Liberal leader, was there and so were Lord Robert Cecil and Lord Lytton, prominent League of Nations figures.[31] Leopold Amery, who also attended, described these individuals as a 'queer collection'.[32] Once again he warned that 'putting Russia in the forefront would not help with wavering Conservatives'.[33] Amery's sense of proportion on both occasions was probably better than his colleagues'. Such stern and unbending Tories as Lloyd and Grigg may have been swept away with enthusiasm for co-operation with Russia in the heat of the moment, but it is unlikely that they were real converts. If the Government had made any kind of agreement with the U.S.S.R. these were the very people who would soon have been regrētting it. As for the young men, Amery found them the next day in Spears's office once more, 'particularly Harold Macmillan, very wild, clamouring for an immediate pogrom to get rid of Neville and make Winston Prime Minister before the House met [on the following day]. I poured cold water on that sort of talk.'[34] Still it would be interesting to know how they intended to carry out this plan.

Within the Government itself there were some who were apprehensive about the Prime Minister's reckless brand of personal diplomacy: dashing off to see Hitler, granting him concessions without taking into consideration the wishes of the Czechs, apparently unaware that this might simply whet Hitler's appetite for more territory, blithely disregarding what this would

30 Leopold Amery, diary entry, 26 Sept. 1938. L. S. Amery Papers.

31 Churchill, *The Gathering Storm*, p. 309; Amery, *Unforgiving Years*, p. 278; Nicolson, *Diaries and Letters*, pp. 366–7. The company was not, as Churchill states, all Conservative.

32 Amery, *Unforgiving Years*, p. 278.

33 loc. cit.

34 Leopold Amery, diary entry, 27 Sept. 1938. L. S. Amery Papers.

do to the balance of power in Europe and apparently callously indifferent to the morality of carving up a small country in such a way that it could not carry on an independent existence—even in the interests of peace. Among those who were uneasy about the Prime Minister's activities were Duff Cooper, the First Lord of the Admiralty, Oliver Stanley, President of the Board of Trade, Walter Elliot, Minister of Health, Earl Winterton, Chancellor of the Duchy of Lancaster, and Earl de la Warr, Lord Privy Seal. Even the Foreign Secretary had his characteristic moment of doubt following the Prime Minister's second meeting with Hitler at Godesberg, at which the German dictator, adopting a more menacing tone than at the first meeting at Berchtesgaden, demanded the occupation of the German-speaking areas of Czechoslovakia by 1 October. At first Halifax was prepared to accept this ultimatum to the Czechs like the rest of the inner Cabinet, but overnight he accepted the advice of his Permanent Under-Secretary, Sir Alexander Cadogan, and recommended that the Cabinet reject the terms. Chamberlain's comment on this change was: 'Night conclusions are seldom taken in the right perspective.'[35] In any event the Foreign Secretary was soon an enthusiastic supporter of the Prime Minister's third visit to Hitler at Munich.

Despite these waverings the members of the Government were as relieved as the rest of the country when the threat of war was removed. This could be hailed as a triumph for Chamberlain's efforts and the Munich settlement, which provided for the occupation of the Sudetenland over ten days, instead of the one which Hitler had demanded, could be represented as a genuine compromise rather than a capitulation to Nazi Germany. But Hitler had gone even further and signed an agreement with the British Prime Minister renouncing the use of force in favour of negotiation in the event of future grievances. The only Cabinet member who was unable to accept the Munich agreement was Duff Cooper and even he felt that 'the differences between the Munich and the Godesberg terms . . . are really considerably greater than I had understood.'[36] But he felt obliged to resign because even these terms were not good enough and he feared what they might mean for the future. Had British defences been in better condition,

[35] Birkenhead, *Halifax*, pp. 399–401.
[36] Duff Cooper, diary entry, 30 Sept. 1938. Cooper, *Old Men Forget*, p. 242.

he argued, the Government would not have had to concede so much to Germany and representing the Munich agreement as meaning 'peace in our time' could only impede rearmament and expose the country to more humiliating retreats. The Prime Minister was not sorry to lose this temperamental colleague; but in spite of Cooper's well-known apoplectic disposition his departure was even less disruptive than Eden's. When Walter Elliot suggested that he also should resign, the First Lord of the Admiralty disagreed: 'It would be easier for me to go alone, as I had no wish to injure the Government, which I should not do if my resignation were the only one.'[37]

Cooper's thesis that the surrender at Munich could have been avoided if the Prime Minister had been able to negotiate from a position of strength, is credible and attractive but it misses the central point: Chamberlain was prepared to make great sacrifices, especially if they were not at the expense of what he considered vital British interests, to secure a lasting settlement in Europe. It is at best debatable whether a higher level of armaments would have affected his conduct significantly, though it might have increased the resistance to his policy both within the Cabinet and outside; and perhaps this opposition would have been sufficient to produce a different response to Hitler's demands. But this is about all that can be said for the most popular criticism of Munich and the whole of British foreign policy in the 1930s. Its most basic weakness lies in the assumption that foreign policy can be seen almost entirely in geographical and military terms and that ideology, individual or class presuppositions, and the framework of domestic politics are only of peripheral importance.

The only time that Parliament met during the Czechoslovakinan crisis was on 28 September following Chamberlain's discouraging discussion with Hitler at Godesberg. Most M.P.s believed that they had been summoned to learn that the country would soon be at war. But the House of Commons never began its debate. Just as the Prime Minister was coming to the end of his long opening narrative about the negotiations with Hitler he received a message stating that Hitler had agreed to a four-power conference (Britain, France, Germany, and Italy) at Munich the following day. When Chamberlain announced that he would accept the invitation the whole House broke out into

[37] Loc. cit.

what Harold Nicolson—who alone remained seated—described as 'one of the most lamentable exhibitions of mass hysteria that that great institution has ever witnessed'.[38] One member summed up the collective relief of all the M.P.s when he shouted: 'Thank God for the Prime Minister!' Leaders of all parties wished Chamberlain well on his mission. Even Winston Churchill drew a large cheer as he cordially shook the Prime Minister's hand;[39] but what he said was: 'I congratulate you on your good fortune. You were very lucky.'[40] The only vocal protester amid this general rejoicing was William Gallagher, the Communist M.P.

In the smoking-room Leopold Amery found that the general feeling was that 'Hitler having once consented to confer could be persuaded by Mussolini to be reasonable, especially if Mussolini joined in the guarantee for the fulfilment of the terms'. The Italian dictator still appeared in Conservative fantasy as the strong key man in European affairs. Amery himself was not sure whether to think that Chamberlain

> did really well or only that he has managed to see through a very unsatisfactory surrender to German force. It may be that the best thing for us is to accept German hegemony and preoccupation with Central Europe, and if so what has happened, however lacking in chivalry or fairness, may have been the best way of liquidating the Czech problem. We shall see.

Later Amery walked home with Godfrey Nicholson and Hugh Dalton, who was 'very pessimistic both about the betrayal of the Czechs and about Russia being left out of the picture'. Amery revealed all his anti-Communist, isolationist, and imperial preconceptions as he reflected:

> If this were the prelude to a real European settlement [the exclusion of Russia] would certainly not weigh with me, for I have always looked before this issue became acute, to Germany, France and Italy working together with our co-operation as forming the only basis of a satisfactory European system excluding Russia.[41]

[38] Speech in Manchester, 1 Oct. 1938. Reported in *The Times*, 3 Oct. 1938. In the same speech Nicolson accused Chamberlain of 'short circuiting' the House of Commons by an emotional appeal for support in his next meeting with Hitler.

[39] *The Times*, 29 Sept. 1938.

[40] Harold Nicolson, diary entry, 28 Sept. 1938. Nicolson, *Diaries and Letters*, p. 371.

[41] Leopold Amery, diary entry, 28 Sept. 1938. L. S. Amery Papers.

Lady Asquith (Lady Violet Bonham Carter) and Harold Nicolson recalled an interesting episode that took place on 29 September while Chamberlain was at Munich. The members of Focus had assembled for luncheon and to draft a telegram to the Prime Minister threatening to fight him in the House of Commons if he betrayed the Czechs at the conference. Winston Churchill suggested that it be signed by himself, Eden, Lord Lloyd, Lord Robert Cecil, Clement Attlee, and Sir Archibald Sinclair. Cecil, Lloyd, and Sinclair agreed but Eden predictably declined on the grounds that it would be 'interpreted as a vendetta against Chamberlain'. Attlee too, despite the urgings of Philip Noel-Baker, refused to sign without the approval of his party, 'who were meeting at some watering-place a fortnight hence'. In these circumstances it was decided not to send a telegram at all. Lady Asquith recollected: 'Leaden despair descended on us as we realized our helplessness; and when we parted there were tears in Winston Churchill's eyes.'[42]

Following the Munich conference Parliament was recalled for a four-day debate starting on 3 October. As the Prime Minister entered the Chamber he was greeted by a standing ovation, only Churchill, Duncan Sandys, Harold Nicolson, Commander Robert Bower, and Ronald Cartland remaining seated.[43] The *Manchester Guardian* analysed the rather pathetic Conservative opposition in a perceptive, if pessimistic, editorial: 'It is the old Churchillian group (plus Mr. Nicolson) and they have been routed on so many Parliamentary fields. There may be a few more to add to them. Sir Roger Keyes, for instance. But it would take a revolt of 200, not 20, Tories to disturb this Government.' Apart from the dissenters there were others within the party who disliked the Munich settlement,

> but they will swallow a lot of unpleasantness before voting against the Government. There remains the great bulk of the party, and it shares the more general view that Mr. Chamberlain saved us from war last week, and on better terms than those of the Godesberg ultimatum—in short, through wringing some concessions from Hitler.
>
> To them, as to so many of the general public, Mr. Chamberlain

[42] Lady Violet Bonham Carter, Introduction to Spier, *Focus*, pp. 11–12; Harold Nicolson, diary entry, 29 Sept. 1938. Nicolson, *Diaries and Letters*, pp. 371–2.

[43] *Manchester Guardian*, 4 Oct. 1938.

has become the deliverer, and they will vote for him to a man. Mr. Chamberlain will have a huge majority in the division.[44]

The Prime Minister got the majority predicted by the *Manchester Guardian* but not before running the gamut of criticism from his own followers and the official Opposition. Even those who voted for the Government were not so enthusiastic about the settlement as to support it in the House of Commons. When Harold Nicolson inquired about the chances of airing his views the Speaker told him that he was 'trying to spread things out; there are four days of bread and none to much butter'.[45]

The *motif* of Conservative criticism was announced in Duff Cooper's explanation of his resignation. If war had come in the last few days, he maintained, it would not have been over Czechoslovakia but to prevent the brutal domination of Europe by one great power. In indignant tones he declared his disagreement with Chamberlain's assumption that Hitler could be trusted as a gentleman: dictators did not understand, or respect, polite language; but Hitler had understood quite clearly when the Royal Navy had been mobilized. Faced with that kind of language he had agreed to the Munich conference. 'That is the deep difference between the Prime Minister and myself throughout these days,' Cooper summed up. 'The Prime Minister has believed in addressing Herr Hitler through the language of sweet reasonableness. I have believed that he was more open to the language of the mailed fist.' The former First Lord also objected to the indecent way in which the Sudeten area was transferred without allowing the Czechs to remove their property and military installations: 'After all, when Naboth agreed to give up his vineyard he should have been allowed to pack up his goods in peace and depart, but the German Government, having got their man down were not to be deprived of the pleasure of kicking him.' As befitted a former member of the Foreign Office he also criticized the way in which Chamberlain and Hitler had signed a casual declaration to substitute negotiation for war:

I would suggest that for the Prime Minister of England to sign, without consulting his colleagues and without, so far as I am aware, any reference to his Allies, obviously without any communication with

[44] *Manchester Guardian*, 4 Oct. 1938.

[45] Harold Nicolson, diary entry, 4 Oct. 1938. Nicolson, *Diaries and Letters*, p. 375.

the Dominions and without the assistance of any expert diplomatic advisers, such a declaration with the dictator of a great State is not the way in which the foreign affairs of the British Empire should be conducted.[46]

Winston Churchill sent Duff Cooper a note after he sat down: 'Your speech was one of the finest Parliamentary performances I have ever heard. It was admirable in form, massive in argument and shone with courage and public spirit.'[47] No doubt this speech encouraged and heartened other dissenters, but the solid mass of the Government's supporters were not stirred by Cooper's carping in the Prime Minister's hour of triumph, even though he was addressing them in ringing Conservative rhetoric.

It was only natural that the Opposition parties should seek to make political capital of the Munich agreement,[48] although they had to be careful not to provoke the Prime Minister into calling a general election while his popularity was so great. Both the Liberals and the Labourites condemned Chamberlain for abjectly surrendering to the threat of force. Clement Attlee, the Leader of the Opposition, delivered an uncharacteristically rousing speech that might have come from Duff Cooper or Winston Churchill:

The events of the last few days constitute one of the greatest diplomatic defeats this country and France have ever sustained. There can be no doubt that it is a tremendous victory for Herr Hitler. Without firing a shot, by the mere display of military force, he has achieved a dominating position in Europe which Germany failed to win after four years of war. He has overturned the balance of power in Europe. He has destroyed the last fortress of democracy in Eastern Europe which stood in the way of his ambition. He has opened the way to the food, the oil and the resources which he requires in order to consolidate his military power, and he has successfully defeated and reduced to impotence the forces that might have stood against the rule of violence.[49]

It was a different matter for the Government, however, when the same charges were levelled from their own back benches. In one of the most powerful speeches in the whole debate Richard Law,

[46] 3 Oct. 1938. 339 H.C. Deb. 5s., cols. 29–40.

[47] Quoted in Cooper, *Old Men Forget*, p. 249.

[48] The pacifist M.P.s, such as George Lansbury, and the Independent Labour party supported Chamberlain for having saved the peace.

[49] 3 Oct. 1938. 339 H.C. Deb. 5s., col. 52.

son of the former Conservative leader, declared his agreement with Duff Cooper's position and echoed Attlee's sentiments: 'I believe that we have now obtained, by peaceful means, what we fought four wars to prevent happening, namely the domination of Europe by a single Power.' This was a strange kind of triumph for the Government to celebrate. Nor was it an ordinary regime which was now assuming the hegemony of Europe:

There are, I believe, enormous numbers of people who regard the Nazi Government in Germany as being the most ruthless, the most cruel, the most inhuman tyranny that the world has ever known, and that is the firm that this country has joined, and, as the Leader of the Opposition pointed out this afternoon, that is the firm we have joined as a junior partner.[50]

Anthony Eden, who spoke on the same day, delivered a weaker speech along the same lines, but his remarks were overshadowed by the impassioned and telling denunciations of his younger colleagues.

As the attacks mounted from their own supporters the Conservative leaders resorted to threats of a general election to restore some discipline to the ranks. Later in the evening of the first day of the debate Harold Macmillan told Hugh Dalton:

Kingsley Wood was very eager for an immediate General Election, in which it was hoped that Chamberlain, as Saviour of Peace, would sweep the country. It was being put about, Macmillan said, that the vote on the Government's motion approving their policy would be treated as a test of loyalty . . . Those who abstained this week, as well as those who voted against the Government, would be marked down for destruction and official Tory candidates run against them.[51]

At this critical juncture the dissident Conservatives were eager to co-operate with the Labour party to save their political skins. On the same night Churchill, Eden, Macmillan, Bracken and J. P. L. Thomas met with Dalton and urged him not to make the Labour amendment to the Government's motion approving the Munich agreement too obviously one of censure. In this way, they reasoned, the maximum number of Conservatives abstentions could be organized, both on the Labour amendment and on the main motion. They also told Dalton that 'twenty or thirty' Conservative M.P.s might be victimized by the Whips and

[50] 3 Oct. 1938. Ibid., cols. 110–14.
[51] Dalton, *Fateful Years*, pp. 198–9.

inquired about the possibility of some agreement for mutual support in the event of an election. Dalton put off this question until the situation became clearer.[52] Also on the same night, though whether before or after they talked to Dalton is impossible to determine, Churchill and his fellow conspirators told Amery that they were in favour of creating their own distinctive political group if Chamberlain decided to call an election. But once again Amery was for 'caution and not committing ourselves too far for the moment. I am convinced that the more the situation can be kept open, the more events are allowed to shape themselves, the more the present enthusiasm will evaporate.'[53]

The chief factor which saved the dissenters from this agonizing decision was the furious speech delivered by Sir Sidney Herbert, a highly respected back-bencher whose loyalty to the Government was beyond question and whose intervention was all the more effective because he was rarely provoked to speak in the House. Anthony Eden recalled him 'leaning heavily on his stick and in evident physical difficulty' as the Chamber filled up for what proved to be his last speech there.[54] He had no difficulty in finding effective phrases for what he had to say. In blunt terms he told the Cabinet that there were many M.P.s who could not in good conscience give their vote of confidence for an agreement which they considered a grave and desperate humiliation. Speaking for the rank and file he said:

> We can be led but we cannot be bullied. I am not talking so much about what appears in the Press, but if it is a case of going into the Lobbies, and if we are to be told that only those who vote straight are to get the coupon, then I say, quite honestly, that there will be a great many people in the Conservative party who will not vote straight.[55]

The effect of Herbert's speech was tremendous, but there was still a possibility of a general election in which Conservatives would fight Conservatives. The Prime Minister, presumably watching the situation from hour to hour, did not show his hand until the House was getting ready to divide at the end of the debate. In his closing speech he gave the appearance of mag-

[52] Dalton, *Fateful Years*, p. 199.
[53] Leopold Amery, diary entry, 3 Oct. 1938. L. S. Amery Papers.
[54] Eden, *The Reckoning*, p. 33. Herbert died on 22 Mar. 1939 at the age of 48.
[55] 4 Oct. 1938. 339 H.C. Deb. 5s., col. 243.

nanimity, but kept his opinions open by announcing that he would not call an election unless a new issue arose or unless he lost the confidence of his supporters—a plain warning to those back-benchers who were considering whether to abstain from the division or even vote against the Government.

In spite of Herbert's speech then, the National Government's supporters were aware that they were taking great risks in criticizing their leader. But the attacks continued. Harold Nicolson described the 'Munich capitulation' as 'one of the most disastrous episodes that have ever occurred in our history'.[56] Viscount Cranborne maintained that peace had been preserved in Europe only by 'throwing to the wolves a little country whose courage and dignity in face of almost intolerable provocation has been a revelation and an inspiration to us all'.[57] And Leopold Amery denounced the cession of the Sudetenland as a 'triumph of sheer, naked force, exercised in the most blatant and brutal fashion'.[58] In his diary a few days later, however, he qualified this condemnation:

We may be giving Germany much greater power in Central Europe, but on the other hand our own position becomes psychologically and strategically much simpler. Fundamentally it is a policy which I have always favoured; my difference on this occasion has been, not with the policy itself, but for adopting a very different policy up to the last moment and then abandoning it under panic conditions which are only likely to increase Hitler's annoyance.[59]

The strongest denunciation in this debate came from Winston Churchill who, 'having fortified [himself] by the example of others', proceeded to emulate them by upbraiding the Administration. He began his oratorical *tour de force* by saying, 'what everybody would like to ignore or forget but which must nevertheless be stated, namely, that we have sustained a total and unmitigated defeat, and that France has suffered even more than we have'. 'Nonsense', said Lady Astor, but Churchill continued his indictment, claiming that the Czechs, 'left to themselves and told they were going to get no help from the Western Powers, would have been able to make better terms than they have got—

[56] 5 Oct. 1938. Ibid., col. 431.
[57] 4 Oct. 1938. Ibid., col. 233.
[58] 4 Oct. 1938. Ibid., col. 199.
[59] Leopold Amery, diary entry, 8 Oct. 1938. L. S. Amery Papers.

they could hardly have had worse—after all this perturbation'. It was obvious that the Munich agreement had ruined Czechoslovakia economically, financially, and politically and that the rump state would not survive much longer: 'All is over. Silent, mournful, abandoned, broken Czechoslovakia recedes into the darkness. She has suffered in every respect by her association with the Western democracies and the League of Nations, of which she has always been an obedient servant.' Churchill understandably took the opportunity to impress on his audience that this was a result of ignoring his good advice of the last five years—'five years of futile good intentions, five years of eager search for the line of least resistance, five years of uninterrupted retreat of British power, five years of neglect of our air defences'. And he urged the House not to think that Munich was the end: 'This is only the beginning of the reckoning. This is only the first sip, the first foretaste of a bitter cup which will be proffered to us year by year unless by a supreme recovery of moral health and martial vigour, we arise again and take our stand for freedom as in the olden time.'

Turning to the rumours of a general election Churchill tried to dissuade the Prime Minister by flattery. Surely Chamberlain, with his huge majority, would not 'be capable of such an act of constitutional indecency.' But if there were a dissolution on 'the Munich Agreement, on Anglo-Nazi friendship, on the state of our defences and so forth', he tried to intimidate the Government by claiming that 'everyone will have to fight according to his own convictions, and only a prophet could forecast the ultimate result'.[60] This was one of the most impressive speeches in a debate characterized by a high level of oratory; indeed it was one of the greatest speeches of Churchill's parliamentary career; but it had less effect on the House of Commons than Sir Sidney Herbert's short, simple statement. Richard Law was undoubtedly thinking of the Munich debate when he wrote, some years later, that in times of stress the average back-bencher tends to be impressed less by the argument of a prominent M.P. whose views are well known than by the intervention of 'some obscure back-bencher . . . some individual, little known, perhaps, to the public at large,

[60] 5 Oct. 1938. 339 H.C. Deb. 5s., cols. 359–73. In the event of an election Churchill and Eden had apparently decided to stand as independent Conservatives. Eden, *The Reckoning*, p. 33.

whose experience, character, and freedom from personal ambition have given him an unusual degree of influence with his fellow members'.[61]

In the division which concluded the four-day debate, twenty-two of the Administration's supporters abstained from the vote on the Government motion and the Labour amendment.[62] Others may have chosen to abstain less ostentatiously than those who sat in the Chamber to be counted by newspaper reporters while M.P.s trooped through the lobbies. Robert Boothby split his vote, siding with the Government against the Labour amendment but refraining from expressing his confidence in the Munich Agreement. After a seven-month estrangment his views were coming back into line with Churchill's, but it is worth noticing that on 1 November he claimed: 'Munich was something to be profoundly thankful for, and I agree with the Prime Minister that it is nothing to be ashamed of.' He did add, however: 'It is nothing to cheer; and if something far worse than Munich is to be avoided, we must negotiate, in the future, not from weakness but from strength.'[63]

Among those who obeyed the party whip in the division were two members of the Eden group, C. M. Patrick and Ronald Tree, both of whom had resigned their junior posts at the same time as Eden. Commander Oliver Locker-Lampson, a founder and active member of Focus, also voted with the Administration. As none of these M.P.s spoke in the debate it is impossible to say with any certainty why they did not abstain; but no doubt part of the reason was their calculation that discretion was the better part of valour. Certainly their prudence saved them from the displeasure of the party managers which was about to be visited on their more venturesome colleagues. Those who dissented may have been few but the fact that they included all those on the Government benches who took a particular interest in foreign affairs impressed the House of Commons and rattled the

[61] Richard Law, 'The Individual and the Community', in Ernest Barker, ed., *The Character of England* (Oxford, 1947), p. 45.

[62] They were: Vyvyan Adams, Leopold Amery, Robert Bower, Brendan Bracken, Ronald Cartland, Winston Churchill, Duff Cooper, Lord Cranborne, A. C. Crossley, H. J. Duggan, Anthony Eden, Paul Emrys-Evans, Sir Derrick Gunston, Sir Sidney Herbert, Sir Roger Keyes, Richard Law, Harold Macmillan, Duncan Sandys, E. L. Spears, J. P. L. Thomas, Harold Nicolson, and Lord Wolmer.

[63] 340 H.C. Deb. 5s., col. 123.

Cabinet.[64] The intriguing question on the morrow of the debate was what action the Conservative party would take against the rebels and what the latter would do to protect themselves.

[64] Harold Nicolson, diary entry, 6 Oct. 1938. Nicolson, *Diaries and Letters*, p. 376.

11. A Conservative Split?

ALTHOUGH only about two dozen M.P.s had refused to support Chamberlain's policy at Munich the Conservative party, indeed the whole country, was badly shaken by the arguments and recriminations of September and October 1938. A decade later Winston Churchill recalled: 'Among Conservatives families and friends in intimate contact were divided to a degree the like of which I have never seen . . . Men and women, long bound together by party ties, social amenities and family connections, glared upon one another in scorn and anger.'[1]

The Prime Minister was determined to remedy this situation by stamping out dissent and restoring order to the ranks of his party. On 1 November he told the House of Commons in petulent tones: 'It is not one of the characteristics of totalitarian States, at any rate, that they are accustomed to foul their own nests. I do strongly deprecate all the statements made by persons in responsible or even irresponsible positions, who take opportunities of broadcasting to the world or in other countries in particular that their own country is in a state of decadence.' Clement Attlee, the Leader of the Opposition jumped up to object to this remark, but the Prime Minister assured him that he was not the person he had in mind: 'Others have gone a great deal further than the right hon. Gentleman, but the observation which he has made gave me an opportunity of expressing an opinion which I think is very widely held.'[2] It was clear that the charge was really directed against Chamberlain's own followers, Winston Churchill in particular. On 16 October Churchill had broadcast his appraisal of the Munich Agreement to the United States and called for the 'swift gathering of forces to confront not only military but moral aggression'. But the Prime Minister must have been annoyed less by this appeal than by the opening sentences of Churchill's speech:

I avail myself with relief of the opportunity of speaking to the people of the United States. I do not know how long such liberties

[1] Churchill, *The Gathering Storm*, p. 324.
[2] 340 H.C. Deb. 5s., cols. 73–4.

will be allowed. The stations of uncensored expression are closing down; the lights are going out; but there is still time for those to whom freedom and Parliamentary government mean something, to consult together. Let me, then, speak in truth and earnestness while time remains.[3]

In spite of this provocation and his understandable edginess after Munich, however, Chamberlain's remarks had a particularly sinister ring. Just three weeks before, on 9 October, Hitler had declared: 'It only needs in England instead of Chamberlain, Mr. Duff Cooper or Mr. Eden or Mr. Churchill should come to power, and then we know quite well that it would be the aim of these men immediately to begin a new World War. They make no secret of the fact: they admit it openly.'[4] The Prime Minister's outburst against the dissenters in his own party gave the impression that he was trying to supress criticism in order to allay Hitler's supposed fears and suspicions.

Chamberlain also had other, less public means of curbing his critics. As soon as the debate on Munich was over all those who had deserted their leader found themselves in trouble in their constituencies. A certain amount of friction was only to be expected, as the local officials usually supported the party leader with dog-like loyalty; but in this case the natural tension was increased by pressure from the Conservative Central Office on the constituency chairmen to get rid of the dissenters.[5] Given these efforts it was rather surprising that only one member lost her seat and that was due more to her own actions than to the party machine. In the spring of 1938 the Duchess of Atholl learned that her constituency executive, having tired of her support of the Spanish government, was seeking a new candidate for the next general election. At the time of Munich she was in the United States, where she defended Chamberlain, but rumours that she had 'blackened' her country were accepted by the execu-

[3] Churchill, *Blood, Sweat, and Tears*, pp. 69–74.

[4] Quoted in Churchill, *The Gathering Storm*, p. 329. 'When the news was broadcast on the evening of Sunday, October 9, the whole nation was moved to wrath. Of the depth of its wrath hardly a hint was given next morning in the leading British newspapers, some of which were almost apologetic . . . Certain large advertising agents had warned journals for which they provide much revenue that advertisements would be withheld from them should they "play up" the international crisis which was "bad for trade".' Wickham Steed, Introduction to *The Press* (Penguin Books, 1939).

[5] Private information.

tive. Facing the issue boldly the Duchess decided, against the advice of Churchill and other friends, to resign and fight for her seat as an independent. In the ensuing election she was supported by the Liberal and Labour parties in a straight fight against the official Conservative candidate; and in her campaign she denounced the Munich settlement and the Government's Spanish policy, calling for collective security and rearmament. Severe weather, which cut the size of the poll, in her Scottish constituency, may have been the chief factor in her narrow defeat but the elimination of one rebel strengthened the party managers' hands and dismayed the other dissenters.[6]

Most of the other critics were called upon by their constituency associations to justify their disloyalty to the Prime Minister. Lord Cranborne, who came from the most staunchly Conservative family in the country, wrote to his uncle that he was in trouble with

> my local Blimps, but have extorted from them, after a very long wrangle, a free hand to say what I like about the Gov't's foreign policy. They think all the same, that I am (*a*) a Socialist, (*b*) a war monger & (*c*) a poison pen against the Prime Minister. I don't know what has happened to the Conservative Party. They seem to me insanely shortsighted and wrongheaded. One can only hope that the question of Colonies will open their eyes.[7]

Others had a harder time than Cranborne. The executive committee of Duff Cooper's division, for example, questioned him for over an hour on the Government's policy and his own personal views. At the end of this ordeal they passed a unanimous resolution, to which Cooper assented, recognizing that 'no other course was open to him than to tender his resignation from the Cabinet to the Prime Minister, and respect his action in so doing'. But they went on to declare that they were

> in complete agreement with the actions of the Prime Minister and with the policy of the Government, and are satisfied that Mr. Duff Cooper, as long as he remains Member of Parliament for the St. George Division, will direct his efforts and ability to the preservation of unity in the party and will support the Government, especially in the strengthening of the defences of the country.

[6] The election was held on 21 Dec. 1938. The Duchess received 10,495 votes, her opponent 11,808. *The Times*, 23 Dec. 1938; Katharine, Duchess of Atholl, *Working Partnership* (London, 1958), pp. 220–30.

[7] Lord Cranborne to Lord Robert Cecil, 16 Oct. 1938. British Museum, Add. MS. 51087.

To make sure that Duff Cooper adhered to these conditions they also left themselves free to adopt another candidate at the next election.[8] This obviously put severe limitations on Cooper's freedom to attack the Administration.

Other dissenters, convinced that time would justify their prophecies and reveal the shortcomings of Chamberlain's policy, tried to put off meeting their local association as long as possible. Winston Churchill was particularly fortunate in this as his meeting did not occur until 14 March 1939—the day before Hitler seized Prague. It was clear by then that Czechoslovakia was falling apart and Germany was making overt preparations for the take-over. Churchill could afford to take a high line with his constituents and he addressed them in his best Burkean fashion. What, he demanded, was all this complaint made 'in some of the outlying parts of the Constituency' about his speech on the Munich agreement?

Never did I make a truer statement to Parliament. Practically everything I said has already proved true. And who are those people who go about saying that even if it were true, why state the facts? I reply, why mislead the nation? What is the use of Parliament if it is not the place where true statements can be brought before the people? What is the use of sending Members to the House of Commons who say just the popular things of the moment, and merely endeavour to give satisfaction to the Government Whips by cheering loudly every Ministerial platitude, and by walking through the Lobbies oblivious of the criticisms they hear? People talk about our Parliamentary institutions and Parliamentary democracy; but if these are to survive it will not be because the Constituencies return tame, docile, subservient Members and try to stamp out every form of independent judgement.

Here was no searching examination and no humiliating resolution to curtail the member's actions. 'I don't mind busybody individuals attacking me', said Churchill. 'I shall not accept any restriction upon my free independence . . . and I shall call upon you to give me at the next election the largest possible majority in order that I may carry out my work effectively.'[9] Churchill was lucky in his timing. Had the meeting been called earlier he would have hesitated to address his constituents in such confident and trenchant terms. And if a general election had been called before

[8] *The Times*, 12 Oct. 1938.

[9] Reported in *The Times*, 15 Mar. 1939. Parts of the speech appear in *Blood, Sweat and Tears*.

March 1939 he and the other critics might have shared the Duchess of Atholl's fate. It may be virtually impossible to dislodge an M.P. but it is not very difficult for a constituency association to adopt a new candidate if they fail to agree with the sitting member.

In the months after Munich then, it was clear that the dissenters had to tread carefully if they wanted to stay in the party, keep their seats in the House of Commons and thereby retain the chance of influencing future policy, getting into office, and capturing the party machinery. The present Parliament was due to expire in November 1940 and in the normal course of events an election could be expected in 1939. At the very least the critics had to stay in the party's good graces until voting day; but in order to insure their political lives further they began to make overtures to the Labour Opposition. These moves, however, were not very impressive.

On 6 October the erratic Sir Stafford Cripps, soon to be expelled from the Labour party for promoting a popular front, urged Hugh Dalton to start talks with the Conservative rebels. Cripps suggested putting socialism aside for the present in favour of 'a programme to preserve our democratic liberties, to rebuild collective security, and for national control of our economic life'. He urged that such an appeal, issued by a small group of Labourites, Liberals, and such Conservatives as were willing to take their political lives in their hands, would produce a tremendous response in the country. Dalton was sceptical of Cripps's scheme but agreed that it was worth a try: 'To split the Tory Party would be real big politics.' When he suggested talks to co-ordinate their attacks on the Government, however, it was the dissident Conservatives who drew back:

> Macmillan sounded out Duff Cooper, who would not come [to the meeting] without Eden, and Eden would not come at all. Churchill was quite willing to come, but in view of the refusal of the others, we on our side thought it best to call a halt. Certainly the big Tory breakaway was off for the time being. And with Churchill himself, either alone or accompanied by Macmillan, it would always be easy to conspire.[10]

[10] Dalton, *Fateful Years*, pp. 201–3. Dalton pointed out to Macmillan that 'at some point it would really be necessary for Conservatives to be prepared to vote against the Government, not merely to abstain. Otherwise the buds of rebellion would never break.'

Despite this unpromising overture observers continued to speculate on the chances of a split in the Conservative party. 'At no time since the summer of 1931', observed the *Spectator*, 'has the immediate political outlook been so uncertain. The volume of discontent among the supporters of the Government is greater than it has ever been during its whole lifetime.'[11] The *New Statesman* predicted that if a split came it would be between 'the Chamberlainites, whose policy is that of international finance, and the Churchillites, whose imperialism is of the old-fashioned patriotic variety'. The key to the situation, the writer continued, lay with Anthony Eden,

> and I think he is playing not for a Tory split and a new Coalition, but for the leadership of the Conservative Party on a policy which he hopes will win Labour and Liberal support. He leaves the door open for possible combinations in the future, but he sticks chiefly to safe phrases about national unity. Make no mistake about it. Mr. Eden is very much a Conservative; social reform has crept into recent speeches as if by an afterthought, but really, I'm told, as the result of Lord Baldwin's reminder that national leadership is still the product of domestic as well as of foreign policy.[12]

In the same issue of the magazine G. D. H. Cole warned of the dangers involved in soliciting Conservative support and recommended that the Labour party impose strict conditions in the event of co-operation with them:

> Only when they have shown themselves ready, as a group, to advocate both an international order and a domestic policy broadly in line with those of the Labour Party, will there be any chance of considering their part in a possible Left bloc as a basis for an alternative Government. . . . But it would be insanity to break up the solidarity of the Labour Party in order to make a bid for their problematic support, at the risk of being led into an imperialistic war policy under their influence.[13]

These cool phrases were hardly encouraging to the dissident Conservatives, but they, for their part, were not enthusiastic about crossing the floor of the House of Commons. They might have been more inclined to favour such a course if a general election had been called, but failing such a perilous situation all

[11] 'News of the Week', 18 Nov. 1938.
[12] Critic, 'A London Diary', 19 Nov. 1938.
[13] 'Independent Progressive', *New Statesman*, 19 Nov. 1938.

they wanted was assurance from the Opposition that help would be available if it were needed. They certainly had no intention of becoming socialists. What they really wanted was to seize the Conservative party machine, but they were unable to agree on how this could best be done. Winston Churchill, perhaps because he considered that he had nothing to lose at this point, favoured a full-blooded revolt against the Government. Anthony Eden, who had more to lose, favoured more cautious tactics which would preserve his reputation as a statesman above the hurly-burly of party politics. The *Spectator* commented on his position: 'None of the other ex-Ministers on the Government side commands anything like the same volume of support. His constant refusal to indulge in recriminations is in itself a source of strength. He expresses no hostility towards his former colleagues, but the very fact that his speeches have to be delivered from a back bench is damaging.'[14] Most of the Conservative rebels associated with Eden and supported his moderate tactics because they realized that a general election could not be very far in the future. To antagonize the party leaders unnecessarily would be fatal. Writing to his wife after a meeting of the dissenters in November 1938 Harold Nicolson said: 'We decided that we should not advertise ourselves as a group or even call ourselves a group. We should merely meet together from time to time, exchange views, and organize ourselves for a revolt if needed. I feel happier about this. Eden and Amery are wise people, and Sidney Herbert is very experienced. Obviously they do not mean to do anything rash or violent.'[15]

Eden and his followers were also careful about their relations with Winston Churchill, whom they regarded as a political liability, 'more bitter than determined, and more out for a fight than for reform'.[16] On one occasion they met with him at Brendan Bracken's house and Churchill, assuming that they had come to follow him, immediately took charge of the meeting. He outlined grandiose plans for raising a campaign fund of one million pounds, two million pounds, to publicize the dissenters' views and he urged the critics to go back to their constituencies

[14] 'News of the Week', 18 Nov. 1938.

[15] Harold Nicolson to Victoria Sackville-West, 9 Nov. 1938. Nicolson, *Diaries and Letters*, pp. 377–8.

[16] Loc. cit.

and rouse the people. But this was not an appealing prospect to the members of the Eden Group, who were already in trouble with the party Whips and their constituency associations. After this abortive meeting they maintained only a loose connection with Churchill through Duncan Sandys and Robert Boothby.[17] Churchill, for his part, followed his lonely course, sustained only by his egocentric sense of destiny and the ever-faithful Brendan Bracken, 'Winston's jackal'.

After attacking the Government on Munich some members of the Eden group went to extraordinary lengths to prove their basic loyalty to their party leader. Lord Lloyd, for example, wrote to tell Neville Chamberlain 'how deeply I have felt differing from you over this crisis. . . . But on this tremendous issue I have felt deeply, and thought it my duty to speak as I have done. I hope it will not affect our personal relations, for I should mind that still more.'[18] And in November Leopold Amery and 227 other M.P.s signed a motion, obviously inspired by the Whips, assuring the Prime Minister of their 'unqualified support for his successful efforts to preserve peace and his determination to strengthen the defences and improve the standard of living of the Nation.'[19]

A debate in the House of Commons on 17 November revealed the depths of the division between the dissenters. Speaking to a Liberal proposal to create a Ministry of Supply Winston Churchill urged all those who were concerned about the condition of the country's defences to vote against the Government: 'If only 50 Members of the Conservative Party went into the Lobby to-night to vote for this Amendment, it would not affect the life of the Government, but it would make them act.'[20] Churchill had given the signal for revolt but only Bracken and Macmillan followed him. Neville Chamberlain made the vote one of confidence in the Government and the members of The Group followed him into the lobby. Duff Cooper explained the dilemma in which the dissenters found themselves after the application of a three-line whip:

[17] Private information.

[18] Lord Lloyd to Neville Chamberlain, 6 Oct. 1938. Quoted in Feiling, *Life of Neville Chamberlain*, p. 384.

[19] *Notices of Motions etc.*, 21 Nov. 1938.

[20] 341 H.C. Deb. 5s., col. 1129.

It is quite possible to be a more loyal supporter of the National Government's policy even than the right hon. Gentleman the Member for Epping (Mr. Churchill), to believe profoundly that they are a very good Government, to support their internal and foreign policy, and yet to think that a Ministry of Supply might possibly help them to carry out that policy. But if anyone evinces that opinion to-night . . . he has immediately committed a crime against the party, the Government and his constituents, and renders himself liable to all the pains and penalties that inevitably ensue.[21]

In the same speech Cooper also stated that he could not agree entirely with Churchill's indictment of the defence preparations of a Government from which he had so recently resigned as First Lord of the Admiralty. Churchill did not like the tone of these remarks, feeling that the Eden Group was attacking him, but his suspicions were allayed by a note from Cooper. In his reply, however, Churchill said:

It is a great mistake ever to take off points against one another. The only rule is: 'Help each other when you can, but never harm . . .' Although there was nothing in what you said to which I could possibly object, yet the fact that you went out of your way to answer me led several of my friends to wonder whether there was some purpose behind it; for instance, the desire to isolate me as much as possible from the other Conservatives who disagree with the Government.[22]

By the end of 1938, as a result of the vigorous activities of the Whips and local constituency Chairmen as well as Anthony Eden's reluctance to attack the Government, the threat of a split in the Conservative party was receding. 'Looking back on the last three months', the *Spectator* could not 'help being struck by the amazing solidarity of the Conservative Party'.[23] Indeed some of the Munich rebels were beginning to accept that settlement just before the next international crisis arose. Commander Bower, for example, wrote to the editor of *The Times* on 8 March saying that if only Chamberlain had adopted the same tactic after Munich as Baldwin after the Hoare–Laval agreement, openly admitting that the events had been a 'bitter humiliation' to him, he would have been spared much criticism not only from

[21] 341 H.C. Deb. 5s., col. 1177.

[22] Winston Churchill to Duff Cooper, 22 Nov. 1938. Quoted in Churchill, *The Gathering Storm*, p. 331.

[23] 'News of the Week', 30 Dec. 1938.

the Opposition but also from his own supporters. But Chamberlain, of course, did not believe, and had no intention of admitting, that he had made a mistake at Munich, much less that he had been humiliated by the German dictator. Nor was he prepared to re-admit the dissenters to the good graces of the party on the basis of such gestures as Bower's. Their political lives were really saved only by the renewal of the international crisis which gave greater credibility to their arguments and narrowed the gap between their policy and the Government's.

12. No Amnesty

Sir Henry Page Croft, a staunch imperialist and isolationist Conservative who had consistently supported Neville Chamberlain's conduct of foreign affairs, declared that Hitler's seizure of Prague on 15 March 1939 was the 'turning point of our times'.[1] At one stroke the German dictator had violated the pledge solemnly given at Munich and undermined the moral basis of his external claims by occupying non-German territory. This sudden action brought to fruition seeds of doubt that had been planted in some minds a year earlier at the time of the *Anschluss*; suspicions were confirmed; and even those who had previously accepted Hitler's assurances came to believe that his foreign policy had always been based on a master-plan for the domination of Europe.

The German seizure of Prague also produced a change in the relations between the Conservative rebels and their leaders, though not so much as might have been expected. As the National Government's foreign policy came closer to the critics' the persecution that had been going on since Munich was relaxed and there was a tendency to play down differences in favour of party solidarity to face the troubles ahead. The dissenters, however, continued to be dissatisfied with the Administration's policy and there were several bitter clashes before Chamberlain finally resigned. But in these disputes the critics could afford to attack more vigorously as the German violation of the Munich agreement seemed to prove that they had been right all along.

When the news of Hitler's latest move reached London it did not make much immediate impact on the Prime Minister. Rather than being embarrassed by the collapse of his agreement with the German dictator he blandly announced to the House that, as Czechoslovakia had 'become disintegrated', Britain was no longer bound by its guarantee to the rump state. He also stressed that he had no intention of being deflected from his course by this set-back:

[1] Brigadier-General The Lord Croft, *My Life of Strife* (London, 1948), p. 294.

Let us remember that the desire of all the peoples of the world still remains concentrated on the hopes of peace and a return to the atmosphere of understanding and good will which has been so often disturbed. . . . Though one may have to suffer checks and disappointments, from time to time, the object we have in mind is of too great significance to the happiness of mankind for us lightly to give it up or set it on one side.[2]

Only in the mildest terms did Chamberlain reprove the Germans for occcupying territory 'inhabited by people with whom they have no racial connection. These events . . . are bound to administer a shock to confidence, all the more regrettable because confidence was beginning to revive and to offer a prospect of concrete measures which would be of great benefit.'[2]

Unfortunately for the Prime Minister the House of Commons was in no mood for this kind of complacent acceptance. Opponents of the Administration were full of righteous indignation as all their misgivings about the Munich settlement were verified. David Grenfell, speaking for the Labour party, attacked Chamberlain's 'callous statement' of the Czech problem. Clearly the Prime Minister had not understood the significance of events in the last five or six years: 'We have been told that the Government are trying to find appeasement. All that we witness day after day is a steady disintegration of the European system and appeasement, instead of modifying or restricting that disintegration, only gives added impetus to it.' Grenfell characterized Chamberlain's faith in the Munich agreement as 'a simple belief, an unjustified belief, an unwarranted belief', but he vitiated his criticism of appeasement by claiming that the condition of Europe was

largely a question of land and of economic security . . . I am exceedingly anxious that we should make an effort to convince the world that we, who are deemed to be fortunate, as regards large geographical expansion, are not too selfish to sit around a common board and give and take in free exchange with others. This is the underlying issue in Europe and we can disarm the armed nations of Europe if we convince people that we have only peaceful intentions towards them.[3]

From behind the Government, too, there were protests about the Prime Minister's cavalier attitude towards the seizure of

[2] 15 Mar. 1939. 345 H.C. Deb. 5s., cols. 435–40.

[3] Ibid., cols. 441–9.

Prague. Winston Churchill, perhaps hoping for office if he did not embarrass his leader at this point, left the attack to Anthony Eden and his followers. As on innumerable occasions in the last year Eden dragged out his usual remedy for meeting the international crisis—a new national government which would include members of the Opposition and the back-bench supporters of the present Administration. 'I believe that in that way this House and this country could now make its greatest contribution to peace. Only by that way out of the present tragedy can we hope to gain anything. . . . There could be no greater encouragement to the peace-loving Powers of the world than the consolidation of the strength of this great country.'[4] His appeal was taken up by two other members of his group. Viscount Wolmer argued that 'we have passed from the state when it is legitimate or patriotic to try to make party capital out of our past disagreements'. He claimed that a close concentration of the country's political leaders would enable the House of Commons to 'give an answer to the dictator States which I believe would have resounding effects throughout the world'.[5] Richard Law made a similar appeal and pointed out that Hitler's latest move should not have come as a surprise:

Those events were immanent in 'Mein Kamf'; they were immanent in the whole policy of Herr Hitler . . . All that has happened has been that we have been driving along on a dark night along a difficult and tortuous road, and suddenly the headlights of our car have picked out a precipice at the edge of the road. The events of the last 48 hours have shown us quite unmistakably the danger in which we stand to-day, and they have shown us that the road to peace is not going to be an easy one.[6]

Commander Bower revived the argument of the dissenters at the time of Munich by calling for an association with the U.S.S.R. to stop Hitler, even though this might offend some Conservatives:

I am not prepared to regard Soviet Russia as a freedom-loving nation, but we cannot do without her now . . . I should like to ask why we have not had staff talks long ago . . . I know they have shot a lot of people but there are about 170,000,000 of them left. It seems to me that we must get some closer co-operation between the nations

[4] Ibid., cols. 461–2.
[5] Ibid., cols. 465–7.
[6] Ibid., col. 471.

who are prepared to stand up to the Fascist ideology, which is spreading rapidly, and that can only be done by much closer co-operation than we have had and a realisation that we are in an era of power politics.[7]

The only exception to this chorus of criticism came from A. A. Somerville, the ancient M.P. for Windsor, who rose to bolster the Prime Minister's statement in orthodox isolationist-imperialist terms: 'Let Herr Hitler expand as far as he can in South-East Europe; we shall still have our share of the trade. He will certainly create difficulties for himself, and opposition, and the more we oppose him the less difficult the opposition will be for him. Let us remember our Empire and develop it.'[8] In the context of the discussion it is hard to tell whether Somerville's speech strengthened or weakened Chamberlain's case.

The debate in the House of Commons on 15 March was a serious set-back for the Prime Minister. For the first time his opponents had been able to bring forth objective proof that his policy had been mistaken. The confidence of his critics reached a new height; their hand was suddenly strengthened; and dissent which had been receding since the turn of the year suddenly revived. Even those average back-benchers who knew and cared little about foreign affairs but were instinctively loyal to their party leader were impressed. Harold Nicolson, noticing that 'all the tadpoles are beginning to swim into the other camp', wrote in his diary on 17 March:

The feeling in the lobbies is that Chamberlain will either have to go or completely reverse his policy. Unless in his speech tonight [in Birmingham] he admits that he was wrong, they feel that resignation is the only alternative. . . . The Opposition refuse absolutely to serve under him. The idea is that Halifax should become Prime Minister and Eden Leader of the House.[9]

On the same day the *Spectator* commented:

Unless the Government can show very soon that they are fully alive to the German danger and are prepared to take the most drastic steps to meet it it does really seem that there will be a revolt of Government supporters . . . Sadly the electioneers are realizing that this latest exploit of Herr Hitler will convince the country, as nothing previously has done, of the value of the Munich agreement. Not only

[7] 15 Mar. 345 H.C. Deb. 5s., cols. 488–9.
[8] Ibid., col. 480.
[9] Nicolson, *Diaries and Letters*, p. 393.

is the policy of appeasement dead . . . but it must be hastily buried, and the least said about it in future the better.[10]

Even the Foreign Secretary, presumably alarmed by the threat to the Government, 'asserted himself and imposed his will on the Prime Minister'. Apparently it was this pressure from his old political friend which induced Chamberlain to amend a speech he was scheduled to make in Birmingham on the evening of 17 March. Halifax warned that if he did not take a firmer line with Hitler he could expect an insurrection in the Conservative party and in the House of Commons.[11]

The main body of Chamberlain's speech was certainly mild and conventional enough, consisting as it did of a long defence of the Munich Agreement and his efforts to save the peace. Only at the very end, in a section that had probably been added at the last moment, did he indicate that the Government intended to adopt a stiffer attitude towards Hitler: 'I am convinced that after Munich the great majority of the British people shared my hope, and ardently desired that the policy should be carried further. But to-day I share their disappointment, their indignation [cheers] that those hopes have been so wantonly shattered.'[12] Chamberlain had conceded little enough to his critics, but the alteration in his tone was sufficient to save his position in the party, the House of Commons, and the country. For the first time since becoming Prime Minister party opinion had forced him to modify a policy even if he had no intention of abandoning it.

After Prague there was plenty of evidence to show that the Government was not really hardening its heart towards the dictators. Hitler was allowed to occupy Memel on 22 March and on 7 April (Good Friday) Mussolini boldly annexed Albania.[13] Harold Macmillan, furious that the National Government's policy had not changed fundamentally, expostulated to Harold Nicolson that

[10] 'News of the Week', 17 Mar. 1939.

[11] Birkenhead, *Halifax*, p. 432.

[12] Reported in *The Times*, 18 Mar. 1939.

[13] Even after this outrage Winston Churchill remained optimistic about Italy: 'In spite of the bad faith with which we have been treated by the Italian Government, I am still not convinced that Italy has made up her mind, particularly the Italian nation, to be involved in a mortal struggle with Great Britain and France in the Mediterranean.' 13 Apr. 1939. 346 H.C. Deb. 5s., col. 15.

all we Edenites have been too soft and gentlemanlike. That we should have clamoured for Chamberlain's removal. That no man in history has made such persistent and bone-headed mistakes, and that we shall go on pretending that all is well. If Chamberlain says that black is white, the Tories applaud his brilliance. If a week later he says that black is after all black, they applaud his realism. Never has there been such servility.[14]

Perhaps the chief reason there was no revolt, apart from the usual reluctance of back-benchers to attack their leaders, was that after Prague the National Government adopted just enough of the critics' prescriptions—and their rhetoric—to avoid it. On 31 March Britain and France guaranteed Poland[15] and, following Mussolini's action, Greece and Rumania as well as negotiating an alliance with Turkey. Lord Halifax even made a pilgrimage to the League of Nations on 23 May—the day after Hitler and Mussolini concluded the 'Pact of Steel'. In his speech to the League assembly Halifax frankly admitted that Britain's latest guarantees had not been carried out through the League: 'That was in the circumstances impossible. But everything that the Government have done is in strict conformity with the spirit of the League of Nations.' The Foreign Secretary also blandly claimed that 'the Government hold no less strongly than they have ever done to the ideals of international collaboration of which the League was and is the symbol'.[16]

Now that Chamberlain had adopted the pose of 'deceived apostle of appeasement'—and was receiving new support in it—there was considerable justification for Winston Churchill's decision to publish a collection of his newspaper articles as a year earlier he had published some of his speeches. 'It is a gratification to me', he wrote in the preface, 'that His Majesty's Government have at length by leisurely progress along their

[14] Harold Nicolson, diary entry, 11 Apr. 1939. Nicolson, *Diaries and Letters*, p. 397.

[15] The interesting story of how Chamberlain proposed this guarantee as a result of an interview with the expelled Berlin correspondent of the *News Chronicle* (Ian Colvin) is related in Colvin, *Vansittart in Office*, pp. 298–311. Characteristically *The Times* tried to minimize the significance of this step: 'The new obligation which this country yesterday assumed does not bind Great Britain to defend every inch of the present frontiers of Poland. The key word in the declaration is not integrity but "independence". The independence of every negotiating State is what matters.' 'A Stand for Ordered Diplomacy', 1 Apr. 1939.

[16] Reported in *The Times*, 24 May 1939.

own paths of thought adopted in detail the policy and theme set forth. I cannot conceal my sorrow that they did not reach these conclusions earlier.' It was these contradictory emotions, he claimed, that led him 'with all diffidence' to present his story in a 'connected and permananent form.'[17] Like the volume of his speeches the book was well timed to capture the new public mood, bolster Churchill's claim to having been the only clear-sighted person in the years of general blindness, and increase his chance of office.

The mutations of official policy considerably increased the prestige of the dissident Conservatives. Loyal members of the party, hastening to echo the new orthodoxy that appeasement had failed—though it had been right to try it—and that the country must look for allies, found themselves using arguments which they had ridiculed a few weeks before when they had been put forth by the critics. It became respectable, perhaps even politic, to compliment those who had almost been run out of the party. Beverley Baxter, an ardent Chamberlainite and imperialist, found himself telling the House of Commons that it was urgent to get back to 'the League of Nations, or to a league of justice or a league of assistance'. And he reminded his fellow M.P.s that they should give 'great credit to the courage and magnanimity of the right hon. Gentleman for Epping (Mr. Churchill), who has fought for those ideals.'[18] The Whips, as was only to be expected, remained suspicious. One of them told J. R. J. Macnamara, who passed on the information to Harold Nicolson, that they respected

> Eden, Duff Cooper, Amery and the big bugs. But they are terribly rattled by the existence and secrecy of the group itself. They know that we meet, and what they do not like is that we do not attack them in the House. If we came out and attacked them in the open they would know where they stood. What they hate is this silent plotting . . . They start from the assumption that we wish to upset the present Government, to force them to take our leaders in, and that we juniors imagine that we shall get some pickings from the victory of our leaders . . . They take it for granted that a person who opposes his party is out for some sinister and egoistic short-cut.[19]

[17] *Step by Step.* The preface is dated 21 May 1939.

[18] 3 Apr. 1939. 345 H.C. Deb. 5s., col. 2544.

[19] Harold Nicolson, diary entry, 31 May 1939. Nicolson, *Diaries and Letters*, p. 402.

It is rather surprising that Chamberlain did not try to neutralize this discontent and strengthen the Government and party by bringing some of the critics into the Administration. The logic of modifying his policy indicated such a step and many observers advised the Prime Minister to take it. 'Is the Government to remain the only unchanged thing in a transformed Parliamentary scene?' asked the *Manchester Guardian*. If policy were the only test, 'nothing stands in the way of the instant admission to the Government of Mr. Churchill, Mr. Eden, and Mr. Duff Cooper'. The newspaper also maintained that Winston Churchill's appointment as Minister of Supply would command almost universal approval.[20] The Liberal M.P., Kingsley Griffith, pointed out that doubts as to whether the policy of appeasement was finished or not could easily be dispelled by changing some members of the cabinet: 'After all, when the policy changed from collective security to appeasement, there were resignations, there were reconstructions of the Government. Now that it is going back to collective security again, it would only be natural to expect that there would be another reconstruction in the other direction.'[21] The *Spectator* elaborated on this theme and urged the inclusion of some former critics to prove that Britain intended to resist any further aggression: 'The Prime Minister is not a symbol of vigour. Nor is his Cabinet. If it is to remain unchanged, the conclusion will be drawn, both at home and abroad, that a policy of drift has prevailed.'[22] On 28 March the Conservative back-benchers themselves tabled a motion in the House of Commons calling for 'a National Government . . . formed on the widest possible basis, and that such a Government should be entrusted with full power over the nation's industry, wealth and man-power, to enable this country to put forward its maximum military effort in the shortest possible time'. This motion, which stood in the name of Anthony Eden, was supported by forty M.P.s, including Winston Churchill, Leopold Amery, and Duff Cooper. The Whips, however, immediately countered it with an amendment declaring that the House of Commons 'affirms its complete confidence in the Prime Minister and deprecates any attempt at the present critical time to undermine the confidence

[20] *Manchester Guardian*, 5 Apr. 1939.
[21] 31 July 1939. 350 H.C. Deb. 5s., col. 2090.
[22] 'Britain's Rejoinder', 24 Mar. 1939.

of the House and the Country in the Prime Minister and the Government'. The Administration might be altering its policy slightly but it had no intention of being dictated to by the rank and file.

The campaign to broaden the National Government went on all through the fateful summer of 1939 but nothing came of it.[23] Part of the reason was the fear that including the dissenters could make the international situation even worse. The Whips assured the backbenchers that 'the mere appointment of Mr. Churchill to the Cabinet would bring a declaration of war, and that those who want Churchill in more truthfully desire Chamberlain out'. No doubt there was considerable truth in the last part of that assertion, but the Whips had no very difficult task as 'a very large body of Tories still distrust Mr. Churchill and dislike his friends'.[24] Neville Chamberlain confided in his diary: 'The nearer we get to war, the more [Churchill's] chances improve and *vice versa*. If there is any possibility of easing the tension and getting back to normal relations with the dictators, I wouldn't risk it by what would certainly be regarded by them as a challenge.'[25] Another important reason that the dissenters were not offered Government posts was that Chamberlain and most of his followers still resented those who had had such little regard for the party as to attack it at a vulnerable moment. The Prime Minister was undoubtedly not anxious to work with men who had attacked his policy and conduct of affairs so vigorously in recent months. Such men would be troublesome, disagreeable colleagues and their inclusion would constitute an admission that Chamberlain and his colleagues needed advice from outside their circle to redeem them from their past mistakes. An ideal opportunity to appoint Winston Churchill to the Cabinet came on 14 July, when a Ministry of Supply was finally established, but the post went to Leslie Burgin, the former Minister of Transport. On the eve of war the *Spectator* expressed its exasperation

[23] Winston Churchill recalled: 'Thousands of enormous posters were displayed for weeks on end on metropolitan hoardings, "Churchill Must Come Back". Scores of young volunteer men and women carried sandwich-board placards up and down before the House of Commons. I had nothing to do with such methods of agitation, but I should certainly have joined the Government had I been invited.' Churchill, *The Gathering Storm*, p. 358.

[24] 'News of the Week', *Spectator*, 14 July 1939.

[25] Feiling, *Life of Neville Chamberlain*, p. 406.

with the Prime Minister's conduct: 'His treatment of the Opposition, of Mr. Churchill, and Mr. Eden is a real disappointment to many of those who follow him. The long years of Mr. Baldwin's leadership taught people to expect a different attitude from a Prime Minister than that of party champion.'[26]

The main issue which continued to divide the dissenters from the Government after 15 March was the question of an agreement with the Soviet Union to help check Hitler's expansion. Without some kind of Russian support the British guarantees to Poland and Rumania were virtually worthless. But if the National Government realized this and was really seeking an association with the U.S.S.R. its negotiations were, in A. J. P. Taylor's trenchant phrase, 'the most incompetent transactions since Lord North lost the American colonies'.[27] More likely it was making overtures to Russia in the hope that these alone would impress Hitler and deter him from any further aggression. Neville Chamberlain admitted that he had

> the most profound distrust of Russia. I have no belief whatever in her ability to maintain an effective offensive, even if she wanted to. And I distrust her motives, which seem to me to have little connection with our ideas of liberty, and to be concerned only with getting every one else by the ears. Moreover, she is both hated and suspected by many of the smaller States, notably by Poland, Rumania and Finland.[28]

Although Chamberlain had flown to see Hitler three times he made no effort to go to Moscow. Neither did the Foreign Secretary, although he was invited.[29] Anthony Eden told Halifax that Stalin would expect at least the same consideration as Mussolini whom the Prime Minister and the Foreign Secretary had visited in January. Eden even offered to go to Russia himself as the British Government's representative, and Halifax, in his amiable way, seemed to like the idea, but when it was suggested to the Prime Minister he rejected it.[30] Eventually it was decided that William Strang, the head of the Central Department in the Foreign Office, should go to Moscow to assist the British Ambassador in his negotiations with the Kremlin.

26 'News of the Week', 11 Aug. 1939.
27 Taylor, *Origins of the Second World War* (London, 1961), p. 229.
28 Diary entry, 26 Mar. 1939. Feiling, *Life of Neville Chamberlain*, p. 403.
29 Birkenhead, *Halifax*, p. 440.
30 Eden, *The Reckoning*, p. 55.

The talks between the British, the French, and the Russians dragged on all summer until the Nazi-Soviet pact was suddenly announced on 23 August. The British Government, in strange but understandable contrast to its conduct towards Czechoslovakia, was unwilling to force Russian assistance on the guaranteed states. It was also unwilling to become irrevocably committed to Communist Russia against Nazi Germany and rejected the Soviet proposal of a 'Triple Alliance' of the two Western Democracies and the U.S.S.R. No doubt the Prime Minister and his colleagues had genuine fears lest Russia come into conflict with Germany and call on her new ally for assistance, but if they were really interested in stopping Hitler they had no alternative but to take this risk in the summer of 1939. And after all they had taken great risks in their dealings with Germany and Italy. Probably the chief reason that the talks were so protracted was that even at this date the British Government did not believe that war with Germany was inevitable or even a serious possibility and was hoping that talks with the Soviet Union would be sufficient to make Hitler more reasonable in his European ambitions.

Most of the Government's supporters, of course, shared their leaders' reluctance to become diplomatically bound to the U.S.S.R.[31] If anything the Cabinet was ahead of general opinion in the Conservative party, certainly not behind it. Victor Raikes expressed his colleagues' fears of the dangers inherent in an Anglo-Soviet alliance if Hitler decided to launch an attack on the west:

> Then Russia would see, what time after time her speakers at Moscow Conferences have said they wanted to see—the great countries in Europe falling out. Then Russia would come into her own, and you would have given Russia the best chance of doing it . . . You are playing into a trap if you put Russia in such a position that she is to be the final judge of what she does and at the same time losing all your old friends.[32]

Even at this late date it was quite clear that Conservatives, both

[31] Apparently they did not take the diplomatic guarantees too seriously either. Commander Bower told Harold Nicolson of a conversation he had heard on the bench behind him: 'I suppose we *shall* be able to get out of the ghastly guarantee business?' 'Oh, of course. Thank God we have Neville.' Nicolson, diary entry, 2 May 1939. Nicolson, *Diaries and Letters*, p. 401.

[32] 19 May 1939. 347 H.C. Deb. 5s., cols. 1853–4.

inside the Government and behind it, were more afraid of Communism than Nazism and believed that Russia presented a greater threat to British interests than Germany.

Opponents of the National Government were appalled at the dilatory and half-hearted approach to the Soviet Union at this critical moment in international affairs. Lloyd George, who had recovered from his admiration of Hitler by this time, asked the Cabinet in a characteristically colourful and angry speech how it intended to implement its pledges to Poland and Rumania without some kind of arrangement with the U.S.S.R. 'For months', he charged, 'we have been staring this powerful gift horse in the mouth'—'And seen its false teeth' shouted a Conservative M.P. He accused the Administration, which had eagerly entered negotiations with Hitler and Mussolini, of 'political snobbery' in its dealings with the Russian Communists and warned that the situation was too desperate for such fastidiousness:

> To say simply that she must come in with a guarantee here and must send her troops there—that is not a full and wholehearted alliance. Why do we not make up our mind and make it up without loss of time, that we shall come to the same terms with Russia as we do with France? If you do that, then I should say—though it is a dangerous thing to predict in a world like this—that the chances against war would go up. If they are fifty-fifty now, I should put it at ten to one against war.[33]

To most members of the Opposition it was obvious that the Cabinet was not sincere in its talks with Russia and had no intention of stopping Hitler when he made his next demand.

Supporters of the Government were also uneasy about the way in which these negotiations were being conducted. Immediately after the Polish guarantee Winston Churchill began to press the Administration on this matter. At first he did so in the hope that the Cabinet's attitude towards the U.S.S.R. was 'well conceived'. Declaring that he was in 'the most complete agreement with the Prime Minister' Churchill simply encouraged him along the road that he seemed to be taking of his own accord: 'Having begun to create a Grand Alliance against aggression, we cannot afford to fail . . . It has become a matter of life and death.' And he expressed his confidence that the 'natural forces' would soon produce an agreement:

[33] 19 May 1939. 347 H.C. Deb. 5s., cols. 1815–20.

Why should we expect Soviet Russia to be willing to work with us? Certainly we have no special claim on her good will, nor she on ours. But Soviet Russia is profoundly affected by the German Nazi ambitions . . . No one can say that there is not a solid identity of interest between the Western democracies and Soviet Russia and we must do nothing to obstruct the natural play of the identity of interest.[34]

Later on, when it was clear that the Administration was dragging its feet in the Russian negotiations, Churchill's tone became more truculent. By 19 May he was no longer encouraging the Prime Minister but attacking him. Churchill professed himself unable to understand the 'refinements of diplomacy and delay' that were preventing the British Government from accepting the Russian offer of a triple alliance: 'What is wrong with this simple proposal? It is said: "Can you trust the Russian Soviet Government?" I suppose in Moscow they say: "Can we trust Chamberlain?" I hope that we may say that the answer to both questions is in the affirmative. I earnestly hope so.' Once more he pointed out that there was an identity of interests between Britain and the U.S.S.R. to keep Hitler out of Eastern Europe and he had no difficulty in showing that 'none of these States in Eastern Europe can maintain themselves for, say, a year's war unless they have behind them the massive, solid backing of a friendly Russia joined to the combination of the Western Powers'. He urged the Government to 'get some of these brutal truths into their head. Without an effective Eastern front, there can be no satisfactory defence of our interests in the West, and without Russia there can be no effective Eastern front.'[35]

Anthony Eden's line of attack was much the same as Churchill's, but as usual he was more temperate. Examining the Government's assurances that it was not influenced by ideological antipathy in its dealings with the U.S.S.R. he reminded the House of Commons that 'in the conduct of foreign affairs it is really not our business what political colour a Government has, nor even how it conducts its affairs at home, although it is desperately our business how it conducts itself abroad'.[36] And he professed to see no reason why 'on any part of the earth's

[34] 3 Apr. 1939. 345 H.C. Deb. 5s., cols. 2497–2502.
[35] 347 H.C. Deb. 5s., cols. 1840–9.
[36] 3 Apr. 1939. 345 H.C. Deb. 5s., col. 2513.

surface, the relations of this country and the Soviet Government should come into conflict. If there is one country that has surely got plenty to do at home, that country is Russia.' He also agreed with Churchill that there was little danger but much to be gained for all Europe by a full tripartite alliance between Britan, France, and the Soviet Union:

Then, if any other nations of Europe were victims of aggression and called for help, we should make it clear that we should be prepared, all three of us, to give that help at once and to the fullest extent of our resources. That is the instrument which I conceive, and I really cannot understand why an arrangement of that kind should be thought to run contrary to the peace front.[37]

On one occasion when the critics were castigating the Government for its hesitations and dilatory approach to the U.S.S.R. about a dozen Conservative M.P.s signified their hostility by abstaining from voting with the Administration. But in spite of their objections to the way in which the Prime Minister and his associates were going about their task the dissenters expected an agreement with Russia eventually. Their chief argument in the spring and summer of 1939 was that time was valuable, but no one expected the talks to end with the announcement of the Nazi–Soviet pact. As Duff Cooper, one of the critics, wrote after the negotiations had collapsed: 'It appeared to those of us who, like myself, had no access to special sources of information, that if the Government with the Diplomatic and Secret Services at their disposal were complacent there could be little cause for alarm for the private citizen.'[38]

Certainly when Parliament rose for the summer early in August more politicians were concerned about the general election which was expected that autumn than about the possibility that the Anglo-Russian talks would collapse. Anthony Eden, who had gone to join the Territorial Army in camp, aired the problem of what The Group should do in the event of a Parliamentary dissolution:

Ought we to form a group of our own? Would we stand as Independent Conservatives? Would we seek to create a new party? What should our relations be with Winston?

[37] 3 Apr. 1939. 345 H.C. Deb. 5s., col. 2513.
[38] Duff Cooper, *The Second World War: First Phase* (London, 1939), p. 334.

These seem to me to be some of the questions which will require urgent thought in the next few weeks. In any event we shall have to have a clear statement of our own views in respect of the past and our intentions for the future.

So far we have done virtually no propaganda and have allowed charges to be made against us which we have made no attempt to refute. I am not saying that this was wrong in the past but the time has now definitely come, I think, when we should consider a reply.[39]

On the same day (12 August) Eden also wrote to J. P. L. Thomas asking him to collect material from the Cabinet Ministers' optimistic speeches which he considered dangerously deceptive.[40] These were hardly impressive steps with a general election, not to mention a possible international crisis, looming on the horizon. It is hard to see how the members of Eden's group could have had much confidence in a leader who had abandoned the political battle-front for summer camp and who, instead of sending instructions merely addressed vague queries to them from afar; but no doubt they were no more eager to launch a major offensive against the Government than Eden. A month earlier Harold Nicolson had written resignedly in his diary: 'Anthony does not wish to defy the Tory Party and is in fact missing every boat with exquisite elegance. We drift and pass the rudder into other hands. I am much depressed.'[41] It is hard to tell what the outcome would have been if the political courage of the dissident Conservatives had been put to the test of a general election, but as it turned out they were saved from that fate by the news from Moscow on 23 August: the Soviet Government had accepted a non-aggression pact with Germany and in England everyone's thoughts turned to war.[42]

A month before the war began Neville Chamberlain dealt a severe blow to the chances of party and national solidarity in the face of international troubles. On 2 August he proposed that Parliament adjourn for the summer from 4 August to 3 October. This customary motion provoked a storm of protest in the House

[39] Anthony Eden to Richard Law and Lord Cranborne, 12 Aug. 1939. Eden, *The Reckoning*, pp. 57–8.

[40] Ibid., p. 57.

[41] 18 July 1939. Nicolson, *Diaries and Letters*, p. 406.

[42] It is rather surprising that the memoirs of this period contain little on the Nazi–Soviet pact, and when the House of Commons met a couple of days after the announcement the members were too preoccupied with the dangers ahead to indulge in recriminations.

of Commons as members recalled the fateful negotiation with Hitler that had taken place during the previous year's summer recess. The Labour party asked that the House meet again on 21 August, making no secret of its distrust of the Prime Minister when he was free from parliamentary control. Arthur Greenwood, speaking for the Labour party, argued that the international situation required

> vigilance on the part of the British House of Commons. Apart from the feeling of apprehension with regard to the immediate weeks which lie ahead of us, there is a suspicion that, once the House rises, the Government may take the wrong turning. I want to put it quite bluntly. A considerable number of Members of this House, not confined to my colleagues on these benches, do not trust the Government. That is the root of the matter to-day. Because of that feeling of distrust we have thought it right to ask for an earlier meeting of this House than the Government propose.[43]

Greenwood's charge that the Government's own followers also distrusted their leaders was soon confirmed. Winston Churchill led off by pointing to the importance which other countries attached to the House of Commons as a 'most formidable expression of the British national will and an instrument of that will in resistance to aggression'. It was his opinion that if the House were sitting it would strengthen the Government's hand in 'the danger months of Europe when the harvests have been gathered, and when the powers of evil are at their strongest'. In the present situation he considered it unfitting for the Cabinet to tell Members of Parliament:

> 'Begone! Run off and play. Take your gas masks with you. Do not worry about public affairs.' Leave them to the gifted and experienced Ministers who, after all, so far as our defences are concerned, landed us where we landed in September of last year, and who, after all—I make allowances for the many difficulties—have brought us in foreign policy at this moment to the point where we have guaranteed Poland and Rumania, after having lost Czecho-Slovakia and not having gained Russia.

And he advised the Prime Minister not to imperil the fundamental agreement on foreign policy by pushing through the motion for adjournment on party lines: 'We are not going to get through these troubles on the basis of party loyalty and calling

[43] 2 Aug. 1939. 350 H.C. Deb. 5s., cols. 2427–8.

everyone who differs unpatriotic. If that atmosphere were created I am sure that it would be absolutely swept away by the wind from the country.' Instead he urged Chamberlain to concede this small point in the interests of national unity:

What does national unity mean? It surely means that reasonable sacrifice of party opinions, personal opinion and party interest should be made to contribute to the national security. Here is an opportunity for my right hon. Friend to take a quite important step to put himself in a better relation with those forces in the country who lie outside the ranks of his numerous and faithful adherents.[44]

Harold Nicolson hoped Anthony Eden would take a strong line towards the Government's conduct in this matter, but Eden advised his followers to 'toe the line'.[45] In spite of this advice Churchill was supported by Leopold Amery and several of the younger M.P.s. Richard Law complained of the

rumours in the Press and whispers in the Lobby that anyone who wants in any way to limit the discretion of my right hon. Friend the Prime Minister in any regard to this matter of the summoning of Parliament is, by that very fact, plotting against the Prime Minister and trying to humiliate, embarrass and hamper him in his activities . . . I think it is monstrous to cast that kind of aspersion on Members of this House in that kind of way.[46]

Harold Nicolson rejected Eden's advice when Churchill decided to vote against the Government: 'I cannot let the old lion enter the lobby alone. But apart from this I do feel very deeply that the House ought not to adjourn for the whole of two months. I regard it as a violation of constitutional principle and an act of disrespect to the House.'[47]

The arguments against the long recess did not carry any weight with the Prime Minister or rather they provoked him to make the vote one of confidence in his Administration. Adressing himself primarily to his own followers he said:

It does not matter whether you mistrust the Government because you mistrust their good faith or because you mistrust their judgement; the question is whether you trust the Government or distrust

[44] Ibid., cols. 2438–44.

[45] Harold Nicolson to Victoria Sackville-West, 2 Aug. 1939. Nicolson, *Diaries and Letters*, p. 407.

[46] 2 Aug. 1939. 350 H.C. Deb. 5s., col. 2468.

[47] Harold Nicolson to Victoria Sackville-West, loc. cit.

the Government. If you distrust them, and show it by your vote, very well; it is a vote of no confidence in the Government and no confidence in the Prime Minister in particular.[48]

The announcement produced an angry outburst from Ronald Cartland, the Prime Minister's political neighbour in Birmingham. Chamberlain's decision, he declared, would make it difficult for M.P.s to dispel the notion that he was trying to become a dictator. By accepting the Labour party's amendment he could instead have shown his 'tremendous faith in this democratic institution' and made 'a great gesture in the interests of national unity. It is much more important . . . to get the whole country behind you than make jeering, pettifogging party speeches which divide the nation. . . . I frankly say that I despair when I listen to speeches like that to which I have listened this afternoon.' In the same speech Cartland told the House: 'We are in a situation that within a month we may be going to fight, and we may be going to die.' At this point another Birmingham M.P., Sir Patrick Hannon, laughed, provoking Cartland to add: 'It is all very well for hon. Gentlemen to say "Oh". There are thousands of young men at the moment in training in camps, and giving up their holidays, and the least that we can do here, if we are not going to meet together from time to time and keep Parliament in session, is to show that we have immense faith in this democratic institution.'[49] Cartland was to be killed in the retreat from Dunkirk; Sir Patrick Hannon, who became a rear gunner, a few years later.

Some Government back-benchers were so incensed by Cartland's attack that twenty of them demanded that the Whips take 'severe measures' against him, protesting that 'it is not right that they should be expected to share even the nominal association with Mr. Cartland of belonging to the same party'. But for once the Prime Minister was not out for blood, either Cartland's or that of the other dissenters who had abstained from the division.[50] Perhaps he realized his tactical mistake; perhaps he did not want to promote discord in the party with a general election

[48] 2 Aug. 1939. 350 H.C. Deb. 5s., col. 2484.

[49] Ibid., cols. 2494–5.

[50] Those who abstained were: Winston Churchill, Leopold Amery, Sir Derrick Gunston, Richard Law, Harold Macmillan, Duncan Sandys, and Vyvyan Adams. *The Times*, 4 Aug. 1939; *Manchester Guardian*, 5 Aug. 1939.

in the offing; or perhaps he was preoccupied with international affairs. But as it turned out Parliament had to be recalled on 24 August to pass emergency legislation to deal with the situation produced by the Nazi–Soviet pact. The House reassembled, in Anthony Eden's words, 'not in a mood of demonstration, still less of recrimination, but rather in a mood of sober resolution'.[51] For the moment at least the bitterness of three weeks before was forgotten in the light of more serious matters. It was soon revived.

[51] Aug. 1939. 351 H.C. Deb. 5s., col. 23.

13. Cads Like the Apostles

THE spectre of Conservative revolt, which had haunted the National Government practically every year since 1931, became a reality early in the Second World War. During the first six months of the so-called 'phoney war', in which there was little actual fighting, the Administration was fairly safe; but as the strategic set-backs, defeats, and losses began to mount in the spring of 1940 even those who had steadfastly supported Chamberlain's foreign policy came to feel that the military emergency demanded someone who was more dynamic and who could inspire more confidence than 'the coroner', as Brendan Bracken always called the Prime Minister. Party discipline and party loyalty, which had protected the Cabinet from any serious threat of rebellion in peace time, were simply unequal to a situation in which national survival was at stake. As in the First World War a man who had previously been regarded as a threat to the political establishment and the smooth workings of government emerged as the leader of an effective political coalition and very shortly as the national saviour.

As soon as war was declared Chamberlain broadened his Government by including Winston Churchill and Anthony Eden, the former as First Lord of the Admiralty—the post he had occupied twenty-five years earlier at the beinning of the First World War—with a seat in the War Cabinet, the latter as Secretary of State for the Dominions. Churchill accepted the offer with alacrity, which is hardly surprising considering that he had been trying to get back into office by every conceivable means since the day he had left it in 1929. Eden was more reluctant to serve under Chamberlain once more until Churchill told him in blunt terms that he had 'no right to go on soldiering . . . my place was in the Government. We could effect much more there together.'[1]

The Prime Minister's invitation to Churchill was a shrewd political move. Not only could the Government now share the prestige of a man who had built up a popular reputation for

[1] Eden, *The Reckoning*, p. 62.

infallibility in defence and foreign policy matters, but also the leading critic became the Administration's most formidable champion—at least in public—from the moment he took office. In his first speech to the House of Commons in his new position Churchill appealed to all members to follow his example and forget old quarrels in the face of present dangers.

In this solemn hour [he said] it is a consolation to recall and to dwell upon our repeated efforts for peace. All have been ill-starred, but all have been faithful and sincere. . . . This moral conviction alone affords that ever-fresh resilience which renews the strength and energy of people in long, doubtful and dark days. Outside, the storms of war may blow and the lands may be lashed with the fury of its gales, but in our hearts this Sunday morning there is peace. Our hands may be active but our consciences are at rest.[2]

Chamberlain must have listened to this defence of his foreign policy from his new-found ally with considerable satisfaction; he must have congratulated himself on his cleverness in making the appointment; and he must have reflected that if Churchill, in his erratic way, made a bad mistake he could be pushed out of the Cabinet in disgrace as an administrator and discredited as a critic.

If the Prime Minister calculated that the inclusion of Churchill and Eden would stop the criticism from the back benches, however, he was greatly mistaken. Their leaders may have gone but the dissenters were still there, keeping their hatred warm, watching the conduct of war and waiting for an opportunity to sweep away the old gang of Chamberlain, Simon, Hoare, and Halifax. In the meantime they identified with Churchill and Eden rather than with the Prime Minister and his principal pre-war colleagues, assigning the credit for success to the former and the blame for failure to the latter. This discrimination may have been unfair but its inspiration was understandable. Indeed from the very beginning the dissenters were suspicious of the Prime Minister's motives in taking Churchill and Eden into the Cabinet. Well-informed friends told Brigadier-General Spears that 'Winston had been given a Department to prevent his exercising too great an influence over his colleagues. It was certainly true that had he not had his

[2] 3 Sept. 1939. 351 H.C. Deb. 5s., cols. 294–5.

hands full he would have been running the war, and overshadowing the Prime Minister in a matter of days.'[3]

It was not long before the back-benchers were criticizing the Government for conducting the war in the same half-hearted fashion that had characterized their efforts in foreign policy and rearmament. The *National Review*, observing that the 'tired old men who have weighed upon the country like lead' were still in the Government, concluded that they were not likely to lead the country to rapid victory. As an example: 'Our Air Force made four trips over Germany, in the first week of war, to drop—*leaflets*. The revulsion of feeling against this inane proceeding has not prevented it from being repeated. The leaflets were welcome in Germany where the shortage of paper is very severe. It is probable that the suggestion that we should make a paper war came from a German source.'[4] Leopold Amery encountered the same turn of mind when he suggested to Kinsley Wood, the Secretary of State for Air, that incendiary bombs be dropped on the Black Forest, which was full of munitions and other stores. Wood was appalled: 'Are you aware that it is private property? . . . Why you will be asking me to bomb Essen next!'[5] Perhaps the former appeasers were correct in their argument that bombing Germany would provoke a massive retaliation against France and Britain which they were not prepared to meet; but a vigorous offensive might have enabled the two democracies to get in an important first blow or at least convince Hitler that they really intended to fight.

After Eden went to the Dominions Office the members of his group continued to meet under the leadership of Leopold Amery. Every Wednesday they dined together and discussed the war situation in the Carleton Restaurant.[6] And although they were concerned about the direction of the war, and particularly the fact that British forces seldom took the initiative in their encounters with the enemy, they voiced their misgivings in private rather than in public so that they would not undermine the national solidarity. In 1940 other groups were formed in response to the deteriorating military situation. Early in the year

[3] Major-General Sir Edward Spears, *Assignment to Catastrophe*, vol. i: *Prelude to Dunkirk, July 1939–May 1940* (New York, 1954), p. 27.

[4] 'Episodes of the Month', Oct. 1939.

[5] Quoted in Spears, *Assignment to Catastrophe*, i. 32.

[6] Amery, *Unforgiving Years*, p. 339.

an All-Party Action group was formed with Clement Davies as chairman and Robert Boothby as one of the secretaries.[7] And at the beginning of April a Watchdog Committee began to meet under the leadership of the venerable Marquis of Salisbury, whose political career had begun forty years before when his father was Prime Minister. Its most active members were Leopold Amery, Lord Robert Cecil, Lord Hailsham, Lord Horne, Lord Lloyd, Harold Macmillan, General Spears, Lord Swinton, Lord Trenchard, Lord Wolmer, and Paul Emrys-Evans. Useful ideas which were brought out in their discussions were conveyed directly to the Minister concerned by Lord Salisbury, whose position in the party gave him a prescriptive right to see any member of the Cabinet.[8] The activities of these groups are not very clear and in the circumstances perhaps they could do little but discuss the issues and press the Ministers informally. But their very existence testified to the amount of criticism and hostility towards the Government which existed among its followers. No doubt these groups had much to do with mobilizing Conservative M.P.s to vote against their leaders in May.

In the spring of 1940, as the Administration's inadequacies became glaringly obvious, the back-benchers demanded a new National Government and a smaller, more efficient War Cabinet. Following the Finnish fiasco, in which the British Government had first promised aid to Finland in its struggle against the U.S.S.R. and then did nothing until the Finns made terms with the Russians, Richard Law broke the customary discrete silence to denounce the Cabinet in the House of Commons:

In the last few years I and every hon. Member have witnessed one or other prominent members of the Government—the Prime Minister or the Chancellor of the Exchequer [Sir John Simon] or the Lord Privy Seal [Sir Samuel Hoare]—come down to the House and stand at that Box in the midst of some defeat or other, and explain that there was nothing that could possibly have been done. That has happened time after time.... I am convinced that the country to-day is not getting the leadership, drive, determination and decision that it deserves. That is a matter, not of personalities, but of organisation.

[7] Loc. cit. Davies was a National Liberal M.P. who later became leader of the Liberal party.

[8] Lord Salisbury to Lord Robert Cecil, 20 Mar., 31 Mar., 1 May 1940. British Museum, Add. MS. 51086.

I hope and pray that the War Cabinet will be reorganised before it is too late.[9]

Whether the Government realized it or not Law's outburst was an omen of the anger that was building up over the conduct of the war.

The next failure, in Norway, was more serious. When British troops were forced to withdraw from that country because the Germans had seized the airfields Richard Law expressed his criticism of the Government in public once more. Addressing his constituents he said that

it was becoming increasingly obvious that there was something wrong with the political direction of the war. . . . If Mr. Chamberlain was the right man to lead a united nation then let him lead it. If he was not, then let the right man be found. The important thing was that all the qualities of leadership in the nation should be harnessed to the national effort.[10]

By a strange irony on the same day (3 May) Sir John Simon was telling his followers:

We have the situation in hand, and the Government are well prepared, at the first moment that it is right to do so, to explain the whole situation frankly and fully to the British people, to whom they are responsible. You may dismiss from your minds the idea that this is going to be material for some exciting political controversy or combat.[11]

But Simon was wrong: the day had finally dawned when the National Government faced a crisis which it could not deal with on party lines, with party loyalty and party discipline.

From the moment that the two-day debate on Norway started on 7 May it was obvious that the House of Commons had found an opportunity to vent its anger and frustration on the Prime Minister and his closest allies. Strictly speaking the brunt of the attack should have been borne by the Minister most directly concerned with the failure in Norway, Winston Churchill, the First Lord of the Admiralty and Chairman of the Military Co-ordination Committee. Indeed Churchill told the House that he accepted 'complete responsibility for everything that has been

[9] 19 Mar. 1940. 358 H.C. Deb. 5s., cols. 1879–81.

[10] Reported in *The Times*, 4 May 1940.

[11] Address to the Liberal National Organization in Caxton Hall, 3 May 1940. Reported in *The Times*, 4 May 1940.

done by the Admiralty', but Lloyd George warned his old friend not to let himself be 'converted into an air-raid shelter to keep splinters from hiting his colleagues'.[12] Lloyd George's remark was apt, for the debate was not so much over the specific failure in Norway as over the whole conduct of the war and the political responsibility for it. One after another the leading Conservative back-benchers rose to denounce the Prime Minister and his principal pre-war associates in more categorical and bitter terms than those which had been used in the Munich debate. The attack was led by Sir Roger Keyes, a First World War hero, who appeared in the House of Commons for the first time in his uniform as Admiral of the Fleet, 'because I wish to speak for some officers and men of the fighting, sea-going Navy who are very unhappy'. Keyes charged that it was not their fault that

> the German warships and transports which forced their way into Norwegian ports by treachery were not followed in and destroyed as they were at Narvik. It is not the fault of those for whom I speak that the enemy have been left in undisputed possession of vulnerable ports and aerodromes for nearly a month, have been given time to pour in reinforcements by sea and air . . . If they had been more courageously and offensively employed they might have done much to prevent these unhappy happenings and much to influence unfriendly neutrals.

An old political and personal friend of Churchill's, Keyes argued that the solution to the situation lay in giving more power to the First Lord of the Admiralty: 'I am longing to see proper use made of his great abilities. I cannot believe it will be done under the existing system. The war cannot be won by committees, and those responsible for its prosecution must have full power to act, without the delays of conferences.'[13] The effect of Keyes's speech was even greater than Sir Sidney Herbert's in the Munich debate, because he was speaking for the whole House, not just the Conservative party. Everyone recognized his authority in naval matters, but more than that they knew that 'here was no scheming politician, no seeker after office, no captious critic and, although his principles were Conservative, no party hack. The loyalest of men, he could no longer offer his loyalty to the Prime Minister.'[14]

[12] 8 May 1940. 360 H.C. Deb. 5s., col. 1283.
[13] 7 May 1940. Ibid., cols. 1125–9.
[14] Cooper, *Old Men Forget*, p. 278.

Although Keyes had addressed himself primarily to the military aspect of the war, the tone of his speech and the response which it met encouraged others to go further in attacking the Administration. Leopold Amery, who spoke shortly after Keyes, told the House that 'there are no loyalties to-day except to the common cause' and he warned his fellow M.Ps: 'The whole of Parliament has a grave responsibility at this moment; for, after all, it is Parliament itself that is on trial in this war. If we lose this war, it is not this or that ephemeral Government but Parliament as an institution that will be condemned, for good and all.' And he poured scorn on the Prime Minister's explanation for the failure in Norway: 'Making a case and winning a war are not the same thing. Wars are won, not by explanations after the event but by foresight, by clear decision and by swift action.' His remedy was 'a supreme war directorate of a handful of men free from administrative routine, free to frame policy among themselves, and with the task of supervising, inspiring, and impelling a group of departments clearly allocated to each one of them.' This War Cabinet should be based on a new National Government representing 'all the elements of real political power in this country, whether in this House or not'. Amery also took the opportunity to denounce the present National Government, which he had disliked ever since its inception:

> In recent years the normal weakness of our political life has been accentuated by a coalition based upon no clear political principles . . . Surely for the Government of the last ten years to have bred a band of warrior statesmen would have been little short of a miracle. We have waited for eight months, and the miracle has not come to pass. Can we afford to wait any longer?

He concluded by telling the House: 'Somehow or other we must get into this Government men who can match our enemies in fighting spirit, in daring, in resolution, and in thirst for victory.' And as a parting thrust he addressed to the front bench Oliver Cromwell's words to the Long Parliament: 'You have sat too long here for any good you have been doing. Depart, I say, and let us have done with you. In the name of God, go.'[15]

The Labour party was quick to see the potentialities of this split in the ministerial ranks and on the following day it announced its intention of calling for a division on the motion

[15] 360 H.C. Deb. 5s., cols. 1140–50.

for adjournment which was the technical basis of the debate. Neville Chamberlain immediately retorted by calling on his 'friends' to support him. But this appeal to party loyalty, far from stopping the attacks simply increased them. Duff Cooper told the House that he resented the Prime Minister's appeal 'because I felt it would only be with the deepest reluctance and regret that I should vote against a Government led by him'. Nevertheless 'in time of war I feel that the issue is too urgent, I feel that this is not a time when any man has a right to wash his hands like Pontius Pilate, and take neither one side nor the other. On this occasion, with the deepest reluctance, I shall be obliged to signify the lack of confidence I feel in the present Administration by going into the Lobby against him.' Although the debate was to be concluded by Winston Churchill—'and those who so often trembled before his sword will be only too glad to shrink behind his buckler'—Cooper urged his colleagues 'not to allow the charm of his eloquence and the power of his personality to carry them away to-night, and not to allow him to persuade them that all is well, that they can go away happily for a somewhat increased Whitsun holiday, because if they do so, they will be untrue and unrepresentative of the mood of their constituents and unworthy to represent their fellow countrymen.'[16]

Commander Bower, just back from active service, also objected to Chamberlain's appeal to close ranks at this critical moment:

> Of course he has a multitude of friends in this House, and I count myself among them. He has spoken for me in my constituency and he has been more than kind to me, especially when I was a young and inexperienced Member of this House. But what has that to do with it? . . . To-day our loyalty is not to a man or to a party, or even to a country. It is a loyalty to all those things which two thousand years of Christian civilisation have built up and which we cannot possibly let go.

Warming to his theme Bower charged that the fatal weakness in the British war effort lay in the fact that the Government had not abandoned its peacetime mentality and adjusted to war: 'When you are fighting for your life against a ruthless opponent you cannot be governed by Queensbury rules. This Government would rather lose the war under Queensbury rules than do

[16] Ibid., cols. 1300–8.

anything unbecoming to an absolutely perfect gentleman. That kind of thing will not do.' Calling for a more aggressive attitude Bower used an illustration which he hoped would appeal to the present leaders:

Some years ago I went into a church and I heard a sermon which was rather striking. After declaiming that the church was decadent and that Christianity was too respectable, the preacher made the somewhat surprising statement, 'What we want are some more cads like the Apostles.' There is a good deal of substance in that; we want a few more cads in this Government.[17]

When Winston Churchill rose to close the debate he spent most of his time answering specific questions about the Norwegian campaign. Towards the end of his speech he came to the matter of the Opposition's vote of censure and here he trod warily. He was careful not to deny the right to challenge the Ministry but he maintained that this was not the proper time or place:

The question of the dismissal of a Government has always been open to the House of Commons, and no Minister would condescend to hold office unless he had the confidence and support of the House. But if the Government are to be dismissed from office, and that is the claim which has been made without scruple, then I think that in time of war at least there should be a solemn Resolution put down on the Paper and full notice be given of the Debate.

Turning to the resentment against Chamberlain's appeal to his friends Churchill, no doubt recalling his own efforts to rouse the back-benchers, said half-ruefully: 'He certainly had a good many when things were going well. I think it would be most ungenerous and unworthy of the British character, and the Conservative party, to turn in a moment of difficulty without all the processes of grave Debate which should be taken.' This shrewd defence of his colleagues did Churchill no harm. While his speech could be seen as a loyal and vigorous defence of the Government it also contained plenty of hints to its opponents to bring up the matter again. And his concluding exhortation for national unity and solidarity demonstrated his own claims to bring it about: 'Let pre-war feuds die; let personal quarrels be forgotten, and let us keep our hatreds for the common enemy. Let party interests be ignored, let all our energies be harnessed, let the whole ability

[17] 360 H.C. Deb. 5s., cols. 1326–8.

and forces of the nation be hurled into the struggle, and let all the strong horses be pulling on the collar.'[18]

All in all Churchill's speech probably had no effect on the way members voted. But the Prime Minister's concern about the division led him to send his Parliamentary Private Secretary, Lord Dunglass (now Sir Alec Douglas-Home) running around the back benches promising a reconstruction of the Government, and possibly the sacrifice of Simon and Hoare, if the M.P.s would support their leaders once more. Apparently this had some effect[19] but Paul Emry-Evans, speaking for the leading opponents, told him that it was too late, even though Lord Salisbury had urged the members of his Watching Committee that morning not to vote against the Government.[20] When the vote was taken 33 of the National Government's supporters voted against it while another 65 were absent. Among those listed as absent were many Conservatives who were in the House but who deliberately abstained from the division.[21] In addition another 30 M.P.s voted with the party on the understanding that there would be changes in the Government.[22] Those who went into the Opposition lobby were a mixed group of old rebels such as Robert Boothby, Harold Macmillan, and General Spears, active-service officers such as Commander Bower, and Quintin Hogg (who had been elected as a supporter of the Prime Minister shortly after Munich), and even such formerly staunch supporters of Chamberlain as Lady Astor.

Although the Government was not defeated its customary majority of 250 was reduced to 81, revealing that many of Chamberlain's 'friends' had not heeded his call. As soon as the figures were announced the House broke out into a great demonstration, Colonel Wedgwod and Harold Macmillan began to sing 'Rule Britannia' while other M.P.s shouted 'Go, go, go, go' as the Prime Minister stalked out to ponder his next move.[23]

Immediately after the vote Hugh Dalton told R. A. Butler, the Under-Secretary at the Foreign Office, that the Labour party

[18] Ibid., cols. 1361–2.

[19] Leopold Amery, diary entry, 8 May 1940. L. S. Amery Papers.

[20] Harold Nicolson, diary entry, 8 May 1940. Harold Nicolson, *Diaries and Letters 1939–45* (London, 1967), pp. 77–9.

[21] *The Times*, 9 May 1940.

[22] Laurence Thompson, *1940: Year of Legend Year of History* (London, 1966), p. 81.

[23] Harold Nicholson, diary entry, 8 May 1940. Nicholson, op. cit., p. 79.

would join the Administration only if Chamberlain, Simon, and Hoare left it. He also said that his party would prefer Lord Halifax as Prime Minister with Winston Churchill running the military side of the war as Defence Minister.[24] But according to his biographer the very thought of becoming Prime Minister gave Halifax

> a feeling of physical sickness in the pit of his stomach. . . . He had no illusions whatever as to his suitability for the rôle which a Prime Minister would have to play at this desperate moment in history. He was acutely conscious that his great gifts were in many ways the exact opposite of those required in the fighting leader of a forlorn cause, and that he was lacking in the drive and ruthlessness which the situation demanded. He knew that Churchill was pre-eminent in both, and to Halifax it seemed that the whole of that turbulent life might almost have been a preparation for this moment of destiny.[25]

If these were Halifax's thoughts they were not shared by many others. Some people thought that Lloyd George, the hero of the First World War, should be called upon to lead the country to victory once more.[26] Lord Beaverbrook and some Labour M.P.s thought that Leopold Amery, the man who had done so much to turn out the Government, was the best man for the task.[27] Chamberlain himself had no intention of resigning but was rather considering what concessions would be necessary to win over those who had voted against him. Hardly anyone, it seems, thought of Churchill as Prime Minister at this moment.

On the day after the vote about 60 Conservative back-benchers met and decided not to join, or even support, an Administration which did not include the Liberal and Labour parties. Leopold Amery was elected chairman of the group and Robert Boothby secretary. They also drafted a formal statement of their views which found its way into the newspapers:

> 1. That it was necessary to form a genuine National Government representative of all the three main political parties;
>
> 2. that the Prime Minister, whoever he might be, should choose his colleagues on merit, and not on the recommendation of any party manager;

[24] Dalton, *Fateful Years*, p. 307; Birkenhead, *Halifax*, p. 453.
[25] Birkenhead, *Halifax*, p. 453.
[26] Harold Nicolson, op. cit., pp. 74–5.
[27] Leopold Amery, diary entry, 9 May 1940. L. S. Amery Papers.

3. that the fullest support should be given to any man who could form such a Government, and no support to any man who could not.[28]

Shortly afterwards Amery learned that Sir Horace Wilson had advised the Prime Minister to decapitate the Conservative opposition by taking him into the cabinet.[29] Amery had no intention of accepting such an offer.

Chamberlain, seeing the handwriting on the wall, then tried to get Halifax to accept the prime ministership. Halifax, however, put

all the arguments I could think of against myself, laying considerable emphasis on the difficult position of a Prime Minister unable to make contact with the centre of gravity in the House of Commons. . . . I told him again, as I had told him the day before, that if the Labour people said they would only serve under me I should tell them that I was not prepared to do it, and see whether a definite attitude would make them budge. If it failed we should all, no doubt, have to boil our broth again.[30]

At 4.30 Chamberlain met again with Halifax, Churchill, and Captain David Margesson, the Chief Whip. He told them it was essential to find out if the leaders of the Labour party would serve under him or under someone else before they departed for their annual conference at Bournemouth the following day. Margesson pointed out that unity was essential but that it could no longer be attained under Chamberlain. The key to the situation thus lay with the other two ministers and Margesson refrained from expressing a preference.[31] No doubt he hoped to continue serving under whoever became leader. Halifax, his stomach still aching, finally broke the silence to say:

I thought for the reasons given the P.M. must probably go, but that I had no doubt at all in my own mind that for me to take it would create a quite impossible position. Quite apart from Winston's qualities as compared with my own at this particular juncture, what would in fact be my position? Winston would be running Defence, and in this connection one could not but remember how rapidly the position had become impossible between Asquith and Lloyd George, and I should have no access to the House of Commons.

[28] *The Times*, 10 May 1940; Dalton, *Fateful Years*, p. 308; Harold Nicolson, diary entry, 9 May 1940. Nicolson, op. cit., p. 81.

[29] Leopold Amery, diary entry, 9 May 1940. L. S. Amery Papers.

[30] Lord Halifax, diary entry. Birkenhead, *Halifax*, p. 454.

[31] Loc. cit.

After Halifax had finished his disquisition on the perils of office, Churchill, 'with suitable expressions of regard and humility, said he could not but feel the force of what I had said, and the P.M. reluctantly, and Winston evidently with much less reluctance, finished by accepting my view'.[32]

Two hours later this group was joined by Clement Attlee and Arthur Greenwood, the Labour party representatives. Apparently they were not informed of the earlier discussion as Chamberlain blandly asked if they were prepared to join his Government. Clement Davies, who got the story from the Labour leaders, told Amery that Chamberlain's request

> completely flabbergasted Attlee but Greenwood took up the running and explained that the Prime Minister was entirely mistaken and that there was not the slightest prospect of the Opposition joining a government under him; they not only disliked him but regarded him as something evil. Meanwhile Winston delivered himself of an eloquent eulogy of the Prime Minister's efficiency in the despatch of business and personal charm to work with to which Greenwood replied that that was perhaps true but irrelevant to the main issue.[33]

The discussion finally ended with Attlee and Greenwood saying that they could not commit themselves until they consulted their party executive at the conference the following day and they undertook to telephone the decision to the Prime Minister.[34]

Early the next day (10 May) German troops and bombers struck west against France and the Low Countries. Chamberlain hoped that this latest crisis would keep him in office. While the Labour leaders were in the train for Bournemouth he spread the idea that this was no time to change or even reconstruct the Government. Unfortunately for him Clement Davies heard of this, telephoned to Greenwood on his arrival in Bournemouth, secured his denial that the Labour party would agree to this, and issued it to the press.[35] At their meeting the Labour party decided that the military situation called for Churchill as Prime Minister.[36] Lord Salisbury's group also insisted that Churchill become Prime Minister before the day was out, though some of them

[32] Lord Halifax, diary entry. Birkenhead, *Halifax*, pp. 454–5.

[33] Leopold Amery, diary entry, 9 May 1940. L. S. Amery Papers.

[34] Neville Chamberlain to Ida Chamberlain, 11 May 1940. Quoted in Macleod, *Neville Chamberlain*, p. 292.

[35] Leopold Amery, diary entry, 10 May 1940. L. S. Amery Papers.

[36] Dalton, *Fateful Years*, p. 312.

were prepared to accept a temporary triumvirate of Chamberlain, Churchill, and Halifax for the immediate emergency.[37] Chamberlain received the news from the Labour party during a Cabinet meeting. Sir Kingsley Wood, hitherto the Prime Minister's Sancho Panza,[38] told him that he would have to go.[39] He resigned that evening and the King called Winston Churchill to form a new administration.

During the next few days Churchill put together what he claimed was 'the most broad-based Government that Britain has ever known. It extends from Lord Lloyd of Dolobran to Miss Ellen Wilkinson.'[40] It was also remarkable for those who were included and those excluded. At first Churchill intended to keep Chamberlain as Chancellor of the Exchequer and Leader of the House of Commons and he was only dissuaded from this by the strong objections of Attlee and Greenwood and the intervention of Lord Salisbury.[41] The Labour leaders finally agreed to let Chamberlain stay as Lord President of the Council in order to prevent his followers attacking the new Government. However, they insisted Sir Samuel Hoare be removed and that Sir John Simon be sent to the Woolsack where he would not be able to cause any trouble.[42] Churchill issued an invitation to Lloyd George to join the Cabinet provided that Chamberlain, who disliked the old warrior intensely, did not object. Lloyd George, whose low opinion of Chamberlain went back to the First World War, replied with some bitterness that he had no interest in joining any administration in which Chamberlain was 'so indispensable to you that you cannot invite to your counsels the man who had the greatest and the most successful experience in the conduct of the last War, without first of all obtaining his doubtful consent'.[43]

The invitation to Lloyd George illustrates the precariousness of Churchill's position. Even though he was Prime Minister he was, like Lloyd George in the First World War, a national leader

[37] Harold Nicolson, diary entry, 10 May 1940. Nicolson, op. cit., pp. 82–3.
[38] Taylor, *Origins of the Second World War*, p. 474.
[39] Gilbert and Gott, *The Appeasers*, p. 351.
[40] Quoted in Dalton, *Fateful Years*, p. 320.
[41] Leopold Amery, diary entry, 11 May 1940. L. S. Amery Papers.
[42] Dalton, *Fateful Years*, pp. 313–15.
[43] David Lloyd George to Winston Churchill, 29 May 1940. Lloyd George Papers, G/4/5/47.

without a party. If he were to avoid Lloyd George's fate he had to keep on good terms with Chamberlain, who was still the leader of the party with an overwhelming majority, and with the other prominent Conservatives. As soon as he received the seals of office he wrote to Chamberlain: 'I am under no illusions about what lies ahead, and of the long dangerous defile through which we must march for many months. With your help and counsel, and with the support of the great party of which you are the leader, I trust that I shall succeed.'[44] And to Lord Halifax he wrote: 'Now that I have taken up this task, I write to thank you for the chivalry and kindness with which you have treated me. The task I have assumed is one of sombre and dire consequences. . . . However, with your help and Neville's I do not shrink from the ordeal.'[45] Churchill was also careful not to outrage Conservative opinion by sweeping out those who had been most closely associated with appeasement and filling the Government with those who had criticized defence and foreign policy before and after the outbreak of war. When Leopold Amery called on Churchill to press his considerable claims for a major defence or economics portfolio on 10 May the new Prime Minister talked vaguely about the Ministry of Supply. Three days later Amery reluctantly accepted the India Office. There was a certain poetic justice in this as Amery had opposed Churchill on India for years but his disappointment at not being in the War Cabinet was understandable, especially considering all he had done to bring down Chamberlain and the fact that the obedient arch-mediocrity Sir Kingsley Wood had been appointed Chancellor of the Exchequer.[46]

Churchill's precautions were by no mean superfluous. When the new Government entered the House of Commons for the first time Chamberlain drew a greater cheer than Churchill.[47] The *Spectator* complained:

Mr. Chamberlain himself has set a fine example of sacrifice and restraint. Unfortunately the same cannot be said of some of his followers in the House of Commons . . . No doubt it was fitting and

[44] Winston Churchill to Neville Chamberlain, 10 May 1940. Quoted in Feiling, *Life of Neville Chamberlain*, p. 442.

[45] Winston Churchill to Lord Halifax, 10 May 1940. Quoted in Birkenhead, *Halifax*, pp. 455–6.

[46] Leopold Amery, *Unforgiving Years*, pp. 373–5.

[47] Harold Nicolson, diary entry, 13 May 1940. Nicolson, op. cit, p. 85.

proper that when Mr. Chamberlain took his seat on Monday he should be accorded an ovation from the back benches. But we felt that the demonstrators might at least have had the fairness to receive the new Prime Minister with equal enthusiasm.[48]

The significance of this reception was not lost on Churchill, who warned the Liberal and Labour members of the War Cabinet on 6 June to refrain from heresy hunts against members of the previous Administration, particularly Chamberlain and Sir Kingsley Wood.[49] Not until 9 October, when Churchill succeeded the dying Neville Chamberlain as Conservative leader and finally achieved his ambition of controlling the party machine did he really become master in his own house. But by that time the Battle of Britain was over and Churchill was the national, indeed world hero. Looking back everyone realized, some of them painfully, that the essential change, the change in spirit, had occurred on 10 May. The belligerent had taken over from the appeaser at last.

[48] 'News of the Week', 17 May 1940.
[49] Birkenhead, *Halifax*, p. 458.

Bibliography

A. PRIVATE PAPERS

L. S. Amery Diary, 1939–1940 (in the possession of the Rt. Hon. Julian Amery, M.P.).

Sir Austen Chamberlain Papers (Birmingham University Library).

Viscount Cecil of Chelwood Papers (British Museum).

Lloyd George Papers (Beaverbrook Library).

B. GOVERNMENT DOCUMENTS AND REFERENCE WORKS

Cabinet Minutes (Cab. 23) and Cabinet Documents (Cab. 24) (Public Record Office).

Notices of Motions, Questions, and Orders of the Day.

Parliamentary Debates. Official Report. Fifth Series.

Dod's Parliamentary Companion.

Butler, David, and Freeman, Jennie. *British political facts 1900–1960* (New York, 1963).

C. THE PRESS

The Times newspaper, which supported the National Government almost unswervingly, is important not only for its editorials but also for its reports of speeches in the country by leading M.P.s. The *Manchester Guardian*, an influential Liberal newspaper, was generally hostile to the Administration, but its well-informed comments on parliamentary affairs and foreign policy are important for an understanding of this period. The editorials in the *Observer* and the *Sunday Times*, two Conservative papers, shed valuable light on the problem of appeasement. Articles from the *Daily Telegraph* (Conservative) and the *Daily Herald* (Labour) were also used.

The periodical which best reflected the views of moderate, progressive Conservatives was the *Spectator*, a weekly publication. Right-wing Conservative views were expressed by the following monthly magazines: the *English Review*, the *National Review* (which incorporated the *English Review* after July 1937), and the *Saturday Review* which was controlled by the wealthy and eccentric Lady Houston, a fervent nationalist and an admirer of Hitler and Mussolini, from 1933 to her death on 29 December 1936. It ceased publication at the end of 1937. *The Economist*, a weekly Liberal publication, had many incisive comments on politics and foreign affairs; so did the *New Statesman and Nation*, another weekly which generally supported the Labour party. Collective security was championed by two small journals: *Headway* (the League of Nations Union's publication) and the *New Commonwealth* published by the little-known peace society of the same name.

D. MEMOIRS, BIOGRAPHIES, AND PUBLISHED PAPERS

Neither of the Conservative leaders in this period wrote an autobiography. Stanley Baldwin was ill-served by G. M. Young's slim and unsympathetic biography, *Stanley Baldwin* (London, 1952). A corrective to this book was written by Baldwin's son, A. W. Baldwin, *My father: the true story* (London, 1956). More recently Keith Middlemas and John Barnes have produced a massive biography, *Baldwin* (London, 1969), which is in the best 'life and times' tradition: long on detail and rather short on analysis. The standard biography of Neville Chamberlain is Keith Feiling, *The life of Neville Chamberlain* (London, 1946), which contains extracts from his diaries and letters. More passages are reproduced in Iain Macleod, *Neville Chamberlain* (London, 1961).

Of the other Cabinet Ministers Sir Samuel Hoare was the only one who undertook the thankless task of defending appeasement in his memoirs: Viscount Templewood, *Nine troubled years* (London, 1954). Sir John Simon's vague recollections, *Retrospect* (London, 1952), are virtually worthless. So is Lord Halifax's thin autobiography, *Fulness of days* (London, 1957). An admiring account of Halifax was written early in the Second World War by Alan Campbell-Johnson, *Viscount Halifax: a biography* (London, 1941). This has been superseded by the Earl of Birkenhead, *Halifax: the life of Lord Halifax* (London, 1965). Birkenhead was a friend of Halifax's and made good use of the papers to which he was given access. R. J. Minney, *The private papers of Hore-Belisha* (London, 1960), contains letters and diary entries of the Secretary of State for War, most of them of course having to do with defence matters. Viscount Samuel's *Memoirs* (London, 1945) contain little of interest. R. F. V. Heuston, *Lives of the Lord Chancellors 1885–1940* (Oxford, 1964), contains many interesting extracts from the papers of the Lord Chancellors in this period (Viscount Sankey, Viscount Hailsham, Lord Maugham, and Viscount Caldecote, formerly Sir Thomas Inskip).

Of the Conservative critics Winston Churchill's memoirs and other published works are of prime importance. Half *The gathering storm* (Boston, 1948) deals with the period before he became Prime Minister. This account was published while Churchill was the head of the Conservative party and Leader of the Opposition; and in its pages he stands out as the one man who properly grasped the situation in the 1930s. Churchill also published two volumes of his speeches in this period, *Arms and the Covenant* (London, 1938) and *Blood, sweat, and tears* (New York, 1941). His newspaper articles from 1936 to 1939 were compiled in *Step by step* (London, 1939). Kenneth Young, *Churchill and Beaverbrook: a study in friendship and Politics* (London, 1966), contains very little on this period, but it reveals clearly that Beaverbrook was not much interested in a political has-been whose views were often the opposite of his own. The best complete biography of Churchill so far is Virginia Cowles, *Winston Churchill: the era and the man* (New York, 1956).

Anthony Eden's prolix memoirs, *Facing the dictators* and *The reckoning* (London, 1962 and 1965), contain some contemporary material but more *ex-post-facto* moralizing. Alan Campbell-Johnson, *Sir Anthony*

Eden (London, 1955), is a laudatory biography; Randolph S. Churchill, *The rise and fall of Sir Anthony Eden* (London, 1959), very critical. The third volume of Leopold Amery's political memoirs, *The unforgiving years 1929–1940* (London, 1955), represents him as a more determined opponent of the National Government than he was in fact. Sir Charles Petrie, *The life and letters of the Right Hon. Sir Austen Chamberlain* (2 vols., London, 1939 and 1940), contains little on this period. For the years after 1935, when he was elected to Parliament, Harold Nicolson's published diaries and letters provide valuable, relatively detached comment, *Diaries and letters 1930–1939* and *Diaries and letters 1939–1945* (ed. Nigel Nicolson, London, 1966 and 1967). His articles in the *Spectator* were also published as *Marginal comment: January 6–August 4, 1939* (London, 1939). In 1936 Nicolson also published an odd pamphlet to justify his position as a National Labour M.P., *Politics in the train* (London, 1936). Duff Cooper reproduced some pages of his diary in *Old men forget* (London, 1953) and an edited version of his newspaper articles appeared as *The Second World War: the first phase* (London, 1939). Harold Macmillan's *Winds of change 1914–1939* and *The blast of war 1939–1945* contain no new information about his activities in the 1930s. Nor do Emrys Hughes's *Macmillan: portrait of a politician* (London, 1962) and Anthony Sampson's *Macmillan: a study in ambiguity* (London, 1967). Robert Boothby, *I fight to live* (London, 1947), contains a lively account of the 1930s. A few thoughts on the period also appear in Lord Boothby, *My yesterday your tomorrow* (London, 1962). Earl Winterton wrote two useless volumes on his half-century in Parliament, *Orders of the day* (London, 1953) and *Fifty tumultuous years* (London, 1955). His official biography is no better, Alan Houghton Brodrick, *Near to greatness: a life of the sixth Earl of Winterton* (London, 1965). Barbara Cartland, *Ronald Cartland* (London, 1941), is an engaging biography of one of the young dissenters who was killed early in the Second World War. Sir Edward Spears, *Assignment to catastrophe*. vol. i: *Prelude to Dunkirk, July 1939–May 1940* (New York, 1954), contains valuable information on the political situation after the outbreak of war. Cecil Aspinall-Oglander, *Roger Keyes: being the biography of Admiral of the Fleet Lord Keyes of Zeebrugge and Dover* (London, 1951), has a few pages on his activities in the 1930s. The autocratic Sir Robert Vansittart was surprisingly guarded in his remarks in his memoirs, which stop in 1935, Lord Vansittart, *The mist procession* (London, 1958). Some of his papers are reproduced in Ian Colvin, *Vansittart in office: an historical survey of the origins of the Second World War based on the papers of Sir Robert Vansittart* (London, 1965), but most of the book is taken up with the author's own activities in that period.

The following books also contained useful material:

ANGELL, NORMAN, *After all: the autobiography of Norman Angel* (London, 1951).

ATHOLL, DUCHESS OF, *Working partnership* (London, 1958).

ATTLEE, C. R., *As it happened* (New York, 1954).

BIRKENHEAD, EARL OF, *The Prof. in two worlds: the official life of Professor F. A. Lindemann, Viscount Cherwell* (London, 1961).

BRABAZON OF TARA, LORD, *The Brabazon story* (London, 1956).

BUTLER, J. R. M., *Lord Lothian (Philip Kerr) 1882–1940* (London, 1960).

CHANNON, SIR HENRY, *Chips: the diaries of Sir Henry Channon*, edited by Robert Rhodes James (London, 1967).

CITRINE, LORD, *Men and work: an autobiography* (London, 1964).

CROFT, BRIGADIER-GENERAL LORD, *My life of strife* (London, 1948).

DALTON, HUGH, *The fateful years: memoirs 1931–1945* (London, 1957).

—— *Hitler's war* (London, 1940).

GOLLIN, A. M., *Proconsul in politics: a study of Lord Milner in opposition and in power* (London, 1964).

HANCOCK, W. K., *Smuts: the sanguine years 1870–1919* (Cambridge, 1962).

HENDERSON, RT. HON. SIR NEVILE, *Failure of a mission: Berlin 1937–1939* (London, 1940).

JAMES, ROBERT RHODES, *Memoirs of a Conservative: J. C. C. Davidson's memoirs and papers 1910–37* (London, 1969).

JONES, THOMAS, *A diary with letters 1931–1950* (London, 1954).

—— *Lloyd George* (London, 1951).

MASSEY, VINCENT, *What's past is prologue* (Toronto, 1963).

MACNAMARA, MAJOR J. R. J., *The whistle blows* (London, 1938).

NICOLSON, HAROLD, *King George the Fifth: his life and reign* (London, 1952).

OWEN, FRANK, *Tempestuous journey: Lloyd George, his life and times* (London, 1954).

PERCY, EUSTACE (Percy of Newcastle), *Some memories* (London, 1958).

SMITH, JANET ADAM, *John Buchan* (London, 1965).

'Watchman' [VYVYAN ADAMS], *Right Honourable Gentlemen* (London, 1939).

WEDGWOOD, C. V., *The last of the radicals: Josiah Wedgwood, M.P.* (London, 1951).

WEDGWOOD, RT. HON. JOSIAH C., *Memoirs of a fighting life* (London, 1951).

WHEELER-BENNETT, J. W., *King George VI, his life and reign* (London, 1958).

WRENCH, JOHN EVELYN, *Geoffrey Dawson and our times* (London, 1955).

E. SECONDARY WORKS

BASSETT, R., *Democracy and foreign policy: a case history: the Sino-Japanese dispute, 1931–33* (London, 1952).

—— *Nineteen Thirty-One: political crisis* (London, 1958).

BRAND, C. F., *The British Labour party, a short history* (Stanford, 1964).

BROOK-SHEPERD, GORDON, *Anschluss: the rape of Austria* (London, 1963).

CARR, E. H., *Britain: a study of foreign policy from the Versailles Treaty to the outbreak of war* (London, 1939).

—— *The Twenty Years' Crisis 1919–1939* (London, 1939).

CHURCHILL, WINSTON S., *Great contemporaries* (London, 1937).

Ciano's diplomatic papers, edited by Malcolm Muggeridge (London, 1948).

'CONNELL, JOHN' [J. H. ROBERTSON], *The 'Office': a study of British foreign policy and its makers 1919–1951* (London, 1958).

CRAIG, GORDON A., and GILBERT, FELIX, eds., *The diplomats 1919–1939* (Princeton, 1953).

CROSS, COLIN, *The fascists in Britain* (London, 1961).

EUBANK, KEITH, *Munich* (Norman, Oklahoma, 1963).

FOOT, M. R. D., *British foreign policy since 1898* (London, 1956).

GATHORNE-HARDY, C. M., *A short history of international affairs, 1920–1939*, 4th edn. (Oxford, 1950).

GEORGE, MARGARET, *The warped vision: British foreign policy 1933–1939* (Pittsburgh, 1965).

Germany—What next? (London, 1938).

GILBERT, MARTIN, *The roots of appeasement* (London, 1966).

—— and GOTT, RICHARD, *The appeasers* (London, 1963).

GRIGG, SIR EDWARD, *Britain looks at Germany* (London, 1938).

HAXEY, SIMON, *England's money lords: Tory M.P.* (New York, 1939).

The history of 'The Times': the 150th anniversary and beyond 1912–1948 (London, 1952).

HYAMS, EDWARD, *The New Statesman: the history of the first fifty years, 1913–1963* (London, 1963).

JORDAN, W. M., *Great Britain, France, and the German problem 1918–1939: a study of Anglo-French relations in the making and maintenance of the Versailles settlement* (London, 1943).

KENNEDY, JOHN F., *Why England slept* (London, [1940] 1962).

KLEINE-AHLBRANDT, W. LAIRD, *The policy of simmering: a study of British policy during the Spanish Civil War 1936–1939* (The Hague, 1962).

LAMMERS, DONALD L., *Explaining Munich: the search for motive in British policy* (Stanford, 1966).

LIDDELL HART, B. H., *Memoirs* (2 vols., London, 1965).

LIVINGSTONE, DAME ADELAIDE, *The Peace Ballot: the official history* (London, 1935).

MCKENZIE, R. T., *British political parties: the distribution of power within the Conservative and Labour parties*, 2nd edn. (London, [1955] 1963).

MEDLICOTT, W. N., *British foreign policy since Versailles* (London, 1940).

MIDDLEMAS, ROBERT KEITH, *The Clydesiders: a left wing struggle for parliamentary power* (London, 1965).

MOWAT, C. L., *Britain between the wars* (Chicago, 1955).

NAMIER, L. B., *Diplomatic prelude 1938–1939* (London, 1948).

—— *Europe in decay: a study in disintegration 1936–1940* (London, 1950).

NAYLOR, JOHN F., *Labour's international policy: the Labour party in the 1930s* (London, 1969).

PUZZO, DANTE, A., *Spain and the Great Powers 1936–1941* (New York, 1962).

RAYMOND, JOHN A., ed., *The Baldwin age* (London, 1960).

REYNOLDS, P. A., *British foreign policy in the inter-war years* (London, 1954).

ROBBINS, KEITH, *Munich 1938* (London, 1968).

ROCK, WILLIAM R., *Appeasement on trial: British foreign policy and its critics, 1938–1939* (Hamden, Conn., 1966).

ROWSE, A. L., *All Souls and appeasement: a contribution to contemporary History* (London, 1961).

SETON-WATSON, R. W., *Britain and the dictators: a survey of post-war British policy* (Cambridge, 1938).

SMITH, SARA R., *The Manchurian crisis 1931–1932: a tragedy in international relations* (New York, 1948).

SPIER, EUGEN, *Focus: a footnote to the history of the thirties* (London, 1963).

TAYLOR, A. J. P., *English history 1914–1945* (Oxford, 1965).

—— *The origins of the Second World War* (London, 1961).

—— *The trouble makers: dissent over foreign policy 1792–1939* (London, 1957).

THOMPSON, LAURENCE, *1940: year of legend, year of history* (London, 1966).

WALTERS, F. P., *A history of the League of Nations* (London, [1952] 1960).

WATKINS, K. W., *Britain divided: the effects of the Spanish Civil War on British political opinion* (London, 1963).

WHEELER-BENNETT, JOHN W., *Munich: prologue to tragedy* (London, 1948).

WILLIAMS, LORD FRANCIS, *A pattern of rulers* (London, 1965).

WINDRICH, ELAINE, *British Labour's foreign policy* (Stanford, 1952).

WOLFERS, ARNOLD, *Britain and France between the wars: conflicting strategies of peace since Versailles* (New York, 1940).

F. ARTICLES

AMERY, L. S., 'The Problem of the Cession of Mandated Territories in Relation to the World Situation', *International Affairs*, xvi (1937).

KENNEY, MARION L., 'The Role of the House of Commons in British Foreign Policy During the 1937–8 Session', in Norton Downs, ed., *Essays in Honor of Conyers Read* (Chicago, 1953).

LAW, RICHARD, 'The Individual and the Community', in Ernest Barker, ed., *The Character of England* (Oxford, 1947).

PORTER, HARRY W., 'Churchill and the Empire', *South Atlantic Quarterly*, li (1952).

POTTER, MARGUERITE, 'What Sealed Baldwin's Lips?', *The Historian*, xxvii (1964).

POWERS, RICHARD HOWARD, 'Winston Churchill's Parliamentary Commentary on British Foreign Policy, 1935–1938', *Journal of Modern History*, xxvi (1954).

STEWART, HERBERT L., 'The "Imperialism" of Winston Churchill', *Public Affairs*, xiii.

Index